Vocabulary Workshop

Level B

Jerome Shostak

Senior Series Consultant

Alex Cameron, Ph.D.
Department of English
University of Dayton
Dayton, Ohio

Series Consultants

Sylvia A. Rendón, Ph.D.
Coord., Secondary Language Arts
  and Reading
Cypress-Fairbanks I.S.D.
Houston, Texas

Mel H. Farberman
Supervisor of Instruction
Brooklyn High Schools
New York City Board of Education
Brooklyn, New York

John Heath, Ph.D.
Department of Classics
Santa Clara University
Santa Clara, California

Sadlier-Oxford
A Division of William H. Sadlier,

Reviewers

The publisher wishes to thank for their comments and suggestions the following teachers and administrators, who read portions of the series prior to publication.

Photo Credits

Steve Brown: 163. *Corbis/*Bettmann: 41, 97, 123; Alfred Russell: 57; Bill Varie: 71; Raymond Gehman: 83; Steve Kaufman: 104; *Reuters NewMedia Inc.*: 130; Dallas & John Heaton: 149; *The Farmers' Museum Inc., Cooperstown, New York:* 64. *Index Stock/*Matthew Borkoski:116. Adam Jones: 27. *Major League Baseball:* 170. *Mid-America Museum:* 137. NASA: 90; 182. *National Portrait Gallery, Smithsonian Institution/*Art Resource, NY: 156. *Stone:* John Lund: 34

PREFACE

For over five decades, VOCABULARY WORKSHOP has proven a highly successful tool for guiding systematic vocabulary growth. It has also been a valuable help to students preparing for the vocabulary-related parts of standardized tests. In this, the latest edition of the series, many new features have been added to make VOCABULARY WORKSHOP even more effective in increasing vocabulary and improving vocabulary skills.

The **Definitions** sections in the fifteen Units, for example, have been expanded to include synonyms and antonyms and for each taught word an illustrative sentence for each part of speech.

In the **Synonyms** and **Antonyms** sections, exercise items are now presented in the form of phrases, the better to familiarize you with the range of contexts and distinctions of usage for the Unit words.

New to this edition is **Vocabulary in Context**, an exercise that appears at the end of each Unit and in the Reviews. In this exercise, you will read an expository passage containing a selection of Unit words. In addition to furnishing you with further examples of how and in what contexts Unit words are used, this exercise will also provide you with practice with vocabulary questions in standardized-test formats.

In the five Reviews, you will find two important new features, in addition to Analogies, Two-Word Completions, and other exercises designed to help you prepare for standardized tests. One of these new features, **Building with Classical Roots**, will acquaint you with Latin and Greek roots from which many English words stem and will provide you with a strategy that may help you find the meaning of an unknown or unfamiliar word.

Another new feature, **Writer's Challenge**, is designed to do just that—challenge you to improve your writing skills by applying what you have learned about meanings and proper usage of selected Unit words.

Finally, another new feature has been introduced in the four Cumulative Reviews. **Enriching Your Vocabulary** is meant to broaden and enhance your knowledge and understanding of the relationships, history, and origins of the words that make up our rich and dynamic language.

In this Level of VOCABULARY WORKSHOP, you will study three hundred key words, and you will be introduced to hundreds of other words in the form of synonyms, antonyms, and other relatives. Mastery of these words will make you a better reader, a better writer and speaker, and better prepared for the vocabulary parts of standardized tests.

CONTENTS

Pronunciation Key 6
The Vocabulary of Vocabulary 7
   Denotation and Connotation 7
   Literal and Figurative Usage 7
   Synonyms and Antonyms 8
Vocabulary Strategy: Using Context 9
Vocabulary Strategy: Word Structure 11
Working with Analogies 13
Vocabulary and Writing 17
Diagnostic Test 18
Unit One 21
Unit Two 28
Unit Three 35
Review Units One–Three
   Analogies 42
   Word Associations 43
   Vocabulary in Context 44
   Choosing the Right Meaning 45
   Antonyms 45
   Word Families 46
   Two-Word Completions 47
   Building with Classical Roots 48
   Writer's Challenge 50
Unit Four 51
Unit Five 58
Unit Six 65
Review Units Four–Six
   Analogies 72
   Word Associations 73
   Vocabulary in Context 74
   Choosing the Right Meaning 75
   Antonyms 75
   Word Families 76
   Two-Word Completions 77
   Building with Classical Roots 78
   Writer's Challenge 80
Cumulative Review I (Units One–Six)
   Analogies 81
   Choosing the Right Meaning 81
   Two-Word Completions 82
   Enriching Your Vocabulary 83
Unit Seven 84
Unit Eight 91
Unit Nine 98
Review Units Seven–Nine
   Analogies 105
   Word Associations 106
   Vocabulary in Context 107

Choosing the Right Meaning 108
Antonyms 108
Word Families 109
Two-Word Completions 110
Building with Classical Roots 111
Writer's Challenge 113
Cumulative Review II (Units One–Nine)
Analogies 114
Choosing the Right Meaning 114
Two-Word Completions 115
Enriching Your Vocabulary 116
Unit Ten 117
Unit Eleven 124
Unit Twelve 131
Review Units Ten–Twelve
Analogies 138
Word Associations 139
Vocabulary in Context 140
Choosing the Right Meaning 141
Antonyms 141
Word Families 142
Two-Word Completions 143
Building with Classical Roots 144
Writer's Challenge 146
Cumulative Review III (Units One–Twelve)
Analogies 147
Choosing the Right Meaning 147
Two-Word Completions 148
Enriching Your Vocabulary 149
Unit Thirteen 150
Unit Fourteen 157
Unit Fifteen 164
Review Units Thirteen–Fifteen
Analogies 171
Word Associations 172
Vocabulary in Context 173
Choosing the Right Meaning 174
Antonyms 174
Word Families 175
Two-Word Completions 176
Building with Classical Roots 177
Writer's Challenge 179
Cumulative Review IV (Units One–Fifteen)
Analogies 180
Choosing the Right Meaning 180
Two-Word Completions 181
Enriching Your Vocabulary 182
Final Mastery Test 183
Index 190

PRONUNCIATION KEY

The pronunciation is indicated for every basic word introduced in this book. The symbols used for this purpose, as listed below, are similar to those appearing in most standard dictionaries of recent vintage. The author has consulted a large number of dictionaries for this purpose but has relied primarily on *Webster's Third New International Dictionary* and *The Random House Dictionary of the English Language (Unabridged)*.

There are, of course, many English words for which two (or more) pronunciations are commonly accepted. In virtually all cases where such words occur in this book, the author has sought to make things easier for the student by giving just one pronunciation. The only significant exception occurs when the pronunciation changes in accordance with a shift in the part of speech. Thus we would indicate that *project* in the verb form is pronounced prə jekt', and in the noun form, präj' ekt.

It is believed that these relatively simple pronunciation guides will be readily usable by the student. It should be emphasized, however, that the *best* way to learn the pronunciation of a word is to listen to and imitate an educated speaker.

Vowels						
ā	lake	e	str*e*ss	ü	l*oo*t, n*ew*
a	m*a*t	ī	kn*i*fe	u̇	f*oo*t, p*u*ll
â	c*a*re	i	s*i*t	ə	r*u*g, brok*e*n
ä	b*a*rk, b*o*ttle	ō	fl*ow*	ər	b*ir*d, bett*er*
au̇	d*ou*bt	ô	*a*ll, c*o*rd		
ē	b*ea*t, word*y*	oi	*oi*l		

Consonants						
ch	*ch*ild, lec*t*ure	s	*c*ellar	wh	*wh*at
g	*g*ive	sh	*sh*un	y	*y*earn
j	*g*entle, bri*dg*e	th	*th*ank	z	i*s*
ŋ	si*ng*	t̶h̶	*th*ose	zh	mea*s*ure

All other consonants are sounded as in the alphabet.

Stress	The accent mark *follows* the syllable receiving the major stress: en rich'

Abbreviations					
adj.	adjective	*n.*	noun	*prep.*	preposition
adv.	adverb	*part.*	participle	*v.*	verb
int.	interjection	*pl.*	plural		

THE VOCABULARY OF VOCABULARY

There are some interesting and useful words that are employed to describe and identify words. The exercises that follow will help you to check and strengthen your knowledge of this "vocabulary of vocabulary."

Denotation and Connotation

The **denotation** of a word is its specific dictionary meaning. Here are a few examples:

Word	Denotation
eminent	distinguished or noteworthy
cumbersome	hard to handle or manage
remember	call to mind

The **connotation** of a word is its **tone**—that is, the emotions or associations it normally arouses in people using, hearing, or reading it. Depending on what these feelings are, the connotation of a word may be *favorable* (*positive*) or *unfavorable* (*negative, pejorative*). A word that does not normally arouse strong feelings of any kind has a *neutral* connotation. Here are some examples of words with different connotations:

Word	Connotation
eminent	favorable
cumbersome	unfavorable
remember	neutral

Exercises *In the space provided, label the connotation of each of the following words* **F** *for "favorable,"* **U** *for "unfavorable," or* **N** *for "neutral."*

_____ **1.** unfit   _____ **3.** effective   _____ **5.** festive

_____ **2.** absurd   _____ **4.** ration   _____ **6.** sinister

Literal and Figurative Usage

When a word is used in a **literal** sense, it is being employed in its strict (or primary) dictionary meaning in a situation (or context) that "makes sense" from a purely logical or realistic point of view. For example:

Yesterday I read an old tale about a knight who slew a *fire-breathing* dragon.

In this sentence, *fire-breathing* is employed literally. The dragon is pictured as breathing real fire.

Sometimes words are used in a symbolic or nonliteral way in situations that do not "make sense" from a purely logical or realistic point of view. We call this nonliteral application of a word a **figurative** or **metaphorical** usage. For example:

Suddenly my boss rushed into my office *breathing fire*.

In this sentence *breathing fire* is not being used in a literal sense. That is, the boss was not actually breathing fire out of his nostrils. Rather, the expression is intended to convey graphically that the boss was very angry.

Exercises *In the space provided, write **L** for "literal" or **F** for "figurative" next to each of the following sentences to show how the italicized expression is being used.*

_____ **1.** The carpenter *pried* the nails out of the wall.

_____ **2.** The police officer tried to *pry* information from the accused.

_____ **3.** She walked *at a snail's pace* through the mall.

Synonyms

A **synonym** is a word that has *the same* or *almost the same* meaning as another word. Here are some examples:

eat—consume
hurt—injure
big—large

clash—conflict
fire—discharge
slim—slender

Exercises *In each of the following groups, circle the word that is most nearly the **synonym** of the word in **boldface** type.*

1. resign	**2. origin**	**3. prevent**	**4. confirm**
a. quit	a. model	a. roar	a. destroy
b. restore	b. field	b. mumble	b. prove
c. remove	c. beginning	c. sing	c. amaze
d. install	d. ending	d. stop	d. hate

Antonyms

An **antonym** is a word that means *the opposite* of or *almost the opposite* of another word. Here are some examples:

enter—leave
wild—tame
buy—sell

happy—sad
leader—follower
war—peace

Exercises *In each of the following groups, circle the word that is most nearly the **antonym** of the word in **boldface** type.*

1. consent	**2. denounce**	**3. variety**	**4. hardship**
a. guarantee	a. recall	a. sameness	a. scholarship
b. arrange	b. ignore	b.scarcity	b. strength
c. remove	c. praise	c. speed	c. distance
d. refuse	d. forget	d. annoyance	d. ease

VOCABULARY STRATEGY: USING CONTEXT

How do you go about finding the meaning of an unknown or unfamiliar word that you come across in your reading? You might look the word up in a dictionary, of course, provided one is at hand. But there are two other useful strategies that you might employ to find the meaning of a word that you do not know at all or that is used in a way that you do not recognize. One strategy is to analyze the **structure** or parts of the word. (See pages 15 and 16 for more on this strategy.) The other strategy is to try to figure out the meaning of the word by reference to context.

When we speak of the **context** of a word, we mean the words that are near to or modify that word. By studying the context, we may find **clues** that lead us to its meaning. We might find a clue in the immediate sentence or phrase in which the word appears (and sometimes in adjoining sentences or phrases, too); or we might find a clue in the topic or subject matter of the passage in which the word appears; or we might even find a clue in other parts of a page itself. (Photographs, illustrations, charts, graphs, captions, and headings are some examples of such features.)

One way to use context as a strategy is to ask yourself what you know already about the topic or subject matter in question. By applying what you have learned before about deserts, for example, you would probably be able to figure out that the word *arid* in the phrase "the arid climate of the desert" means "dry."

The **Vocabulary in Context** exercises that appear in the Units and Reviews and the **Choosing the Right Meaning** exercises that appear in the Reviews and Cumulative Reviews both provide practice in using subject matter or topic to determine the meaning of given words.

When you do the various word-omission exercises in this book, look for **context clues** built into the sentence or passage to guide you to the correct answer. Three types of context clues appear in the exercises in this book.

A **restatement clue** consists of a *synonym* for, or a *definition* of, the missing word. For example:

"I'm willing to <u>tell</u> what I know about the matter," the reporter said, "but I can't _____ my sources."
a. conceal   b. defend   c. find   (d. reveal)

In this sentence, *tell* is a synonym of the missing word, *reveal*, and acts as a restatement clue for it.

A **contrast clue** consists of an *antonym* for, or a phrase that means the *opposite* of, the missing word. For example:

"I'm trying to <u>help</u> you, <u>not</u> (**assist,** (hinder))you!" she exclaimed in annoyance.

In this sentence, *help* is an antonym of the missing word, *hinder*. This is confirmed by the presence of the word *not*. *Help* thus functions as a contrast clue for *hinder*.

An **inference clue** implies but does not directly state the meaning of the missing word or words. For example:

A utility infielder has to be a very _____ player because he is a veritable jack-of-all-trades on the _____ diamond.

a. veteran . . . football
b. versatile . . . baseball
c. experienced . . . hockey
d. energetic . . . golf

In this sentence, there are several inference clues: (a) the term *jack-of-all-trades* suggests the word *versatile* because a jack-of-all-trades is by definition versatile; the word *utility* in the term *utility infielder* suggests the same thing; (b) the words *infielder* and *diamond* suggest *baseball* because they are terms employed regularly in that sport. Accordingly, all these words are inference clues because they suggest or imply, but do not directly state, the missing word or words.

Exercises   *Use context clues to choose the word or words that complete each of the following sentences or sets of sentences.*

1. I threw out all my old notes, but made certain not to _____ the new ones.

a. understand
b. overrate
c. keep
d. discard

2. The search crew _____ through all the evidence, and their hard work was rewarded with _____ for all of them.

a. sifted . . . promotions
b. rushed . . . grief
c. wandered . . . sentences
d. jumped . . . policies

3. I am looking not for temporary solutions but for a (**permanent, gallant**) settlement.

VOCABULARY STRATEGY: WORD STRUCTURE

One important way to build your vocabulary is to learn the meaning of word parts that make up many English words. These word parts consist of **prefixes**, **suffixes**, and **roots**, or **bases**. A useful strategy for determining the meaning of an unknown word is to "take apart" the word and think about the parts. For example, when you look at the word parts in the word *invisible,* you find the prefix *in-* ("not") + the root *-vis-* ("see") + the suffix *-ible* ("capable of"). From knowing the meanings of the parts of this word, you can figure out that *invisible* means "not capable of being seen."

Following is a list of common prefixes. Knowing the meaning of a prefix can help you determine the meaning of a word in which the prefix appears.

Prefix	Meaning	Sample Words
bi-	two	bicycle, biannual
com-, con-	together, with	compatriot, contact
de-, dis-	lower, opposite	devalue, disloyal
fore-, pre-	before, ahead of time	forewarn, preplan
il-, im-, in-, ir, non-, un-	not	illegal, impossible, inactive, irregular, nonsense, unable
in-, im-	in, into	inhale, import
mid-	middle	midway, midday, midterm
mis-	wrongly, badly	mistake, misbehave
re-	again, back	redo, repay
sub-	under, less than	submarine, subzero
super-	above, greater than	superimpose, superstar
tri-	three	triangle

Following is a list of common suffixes. Knowing the meaning and grammatical function of a suffix can help you determine the meaning of a word.

Noun Suffix	Meaning	Sample Nouns
-acy, -ance, -ence, -hood, -ity, -ment, -ness, -ship	state, quality, or condition of, act or process of	adequacy, attendance, persistence, neighborhood, activity, judgment, brightness, friendship
-ant, -eer, -ent, -er, -ian, -ier, -ist, -or	one who does or makes something	contestant, auctioneer, resident, banker, comedian, financier, dentist, doctor
-ation, -ition, -ion	act or result of	organization, imposition, election

Verb Suffix	Meaning	Sample Verbs
-ate	to become, produce, or treat	validate, salivate, chlorinate
-en	to make, cause to be	weaken, shorten, lengthen
-fy, -ify, -ize	to cause, make	liquefy, glorify, legalize

Adjective Suffix	Meaning	Sample Adjectives
-able, -ible	able, capable of	believable, incredible
-al, -ic,	relating to, characteristic of	natural, romantic
-ful, -ive, -ous	full of, given to, marked by	beautiful, protective, poisonous
-ish, -like	like, resembling	foolish, childlike
-less	lacking, without	careless

A **base** or **root** is the main part of a word to which prefixes and suffixes may be added. Many roots come to English from Latin, such as *-socio-,* meaning "society," or from Greek, such as *-logy-,* meaning "the study of." Knowing Greek and Latin roots can help you determine the meaning of a word such as *sociology,* which means "the study of society."

In the **Building with Classical Roots** sections of this book you will learn more about some of these Latin and Greek roots and about English words that derive from them. The lists that follow may help you figure out the meaning of new or unfamiliar words that you encounter in your reading.

Greek Root	Meaning	Sample Word
-astr-, -aster-, -astro-	star	astral, asteroid, astronaut
-auto-	self	autograph
-bio-	life	biography
-chron-, chrono-	time	chronic, chronological
-cosm-, -cosmo-	universe, order	microcosm, cosmopolitan
-cryph-, -crypt-	hidden, secret	apocryphal, cryptographer
-dem-, -demo-	people	epidemic, democracy
-dia-	through, across, between	diameter
-dog-, -dox-	opinion, teaching	dogmatic, orthodox
-gen-	race, kind, origin, birth	generation
-gnos-	know	diagnostic
-graph-, -graphy-, -gram-	write	graphite, autobiography, telegram
-log-, -logue-	speech, word, reasoning	logic, dialogue
-lys-	break down	analysis
-metr-, -meter-	measure	metric, kilometer
-micro-	small	microchip
-morph-	form, shape	amorphous
-naut-	sailor	cosmonaut
-phon-, -phone-, -phono-	sound, voice	phonics, telephone, phonograph
-pol-, -polis-	city, state	police, metropolis
-scop-, -scope-	watch, look at	microscope, telescope
-tele-	far off, distant	television
-the-	put or place	parentheses

Latin Root	Meaning	Sample Word
-cap-, -capt-, -cept-, -cip-	take	capitulate, captive, concept, recipient
-cede-, -ceed-, -ceas-, -cess-	happen, yield, go	precede, proceed, decease, cessation
-cred-	believe	incredible
-dic-, -dict-	speak, say, tell	indicate, diction
-duc-, -duct-, -duit-	lead, conduct, draw	educate, conduct, conduit
-fac-, -fact-, -fect-, -fic-, -fy-	make	faculty, artifact, defect, beneficial, clarify
-ject-	throw	eject
-mis-, -miss-, -mit-, -mitt-	send	promise, missile, transmit, intermittent
-note-, -not-	know, recognize	denote, notion
-pel-, -puls-	drive	expel, compulsive
-pend-, -pens-	hang, weight, set aside	pendulum, pension
-pon-, -pos-	put, place	component, position
-port-	carry	portable
-rupt-	break	bankrupt
-scrib-, -scribe-, -script-	write	scribble, describe, inscription
-spec-, -spic-	look, see	spectator, conspicuous
-tac-, -tag-, -tang-, -teg-	touch	contact, contagious, tangible, integral
-tain-, -ten-, -tin-	hold, keep	contain, tenure, retinue
-temp-	time	tempo, temporary
-ven-, -vent-	come	intervene, convention
-vers-, -vert-	turn	reverse, invert
-voc-, -vok-	call	vocal, invoke

WORKING WITH ANALOGIES

Today practically every standardized examination involving vocabulary, especially the SAT I, employs the **analogy** as a testing device. For that reason, it is an excellent idea to learn how to read, understand, and solve such verbal puzzles.

What Is an Analogy?

An analogy is a kind of equation using words rather than numbers or mathematical symbols and quantities. Normally, an analogy contains two pairs of words linked by a word or symbol that stands for an equal sign (=). A complete analogy compares the two pairs of words and makes a statement about them. It asserts that the logical relationship between the members of the first pair of words is *the same as* the logical relationship between the members of the second pair of words. This is the only statement a valid analogy ever makes.

Here is an example of a complete analogy. It is presented in two different formats.

Format 1
maple is to tree as rose is to flower

Format 2
maple : tree :: rose : flower

Reading and Interpreting Analogies

As our sample indicates, analogies are customarily presented in formats that need some deciphering in order to be read and understood correctly. There are a number of these formats, but you need concern yourself with only the two shown.

Format 1: Let's begin with the format that uses all words:

maple is to tree as rose is to flower

Because this is the simplest format to read and understand, it is the one used in the student texts of VOCABULARY WORKSHOP. It is to be read exactly as printed. Allowing for the fact that the word pairs change from analogy to analogy, this is how to read every analogy, no matter what the format is.

Now you know how to read an analogy. Still, it is not clear exactly what the somewhat cryptic statement "maple is to tree as rose is to flower" means. To discover this, you must understand what the two linking expressions *as* and *is to* signify.

- The word *as* links the two word pairs in the complete analogy. It stands for an equal sign (=) and means "is the same as."

- The expression *is to* links the two members of each word pair, so it appears twice in a complete analogy. In our sample, *is to* links *maple* and *tree* (the two words in the first pair) and also *rose* and *flower* (the two words in the second word pair). Accordingly, the expression *is to* means "has the same logical relationship to" the two words it links.

Putting all this information together, we can say that our sample analogy means:

> The logical relationship between a *maple* and a *tree* is *the same as* (=) the logical relationship between a *rose* and a *flower*.

Now you know what our sample analogy means. This is what every analogy means, allowing for the fact that the word pairs will vary from one analogy to another.

Format 2: Our second format uses symbols, rather than words, to link its four members.

> maple : tree :: rose : flower

This is the format used on the SAT I and in the *TEST PREP Blackline Masters* that accompany each Level of VOCABULARY WORKSHOP. In this format, a single colon (:) replaces the expression *is to*, and a double colon (::) replaces the word *as*. Otherwise, format 2 is the same as format 1; that is, it is read in exactly the same way ("maple is to tree as rose is to flower"), and it means exactly the same thing ("the logical relationship between a *maple* and a *tree* is the same as the logical relationship between a *rose* and a *flower*").

Completing Analogies

So far we've looked at complete analogies. However, standardized examinations do not provide the test taker with a complete analogy. Instead, the test taker is given the first, or key, pair of words and then asked to *complete* the analogy by selecting the second pair from a given group of four or five choices, usually lettered *a* through *d* or *e*.

Here's how our sample analogy would look on such a test:

1. maple is to tree as
a. acorn is to oak
b. hen is to rooster
c. rose is to flower
d. shrub is to lilac

or

1. maple : tree ::
a. acorn : oak
b. hen : rooster
c. rose : flower
d. shrub : lilac

It is up to the test taker to complete the analogy correctly.

Here's how to do that in just four easy steps!

Step 1: *Look at the two words in the key (given) pair, and determine the logical relationship between them.*

In our sample analogy, *maple* and *tree* form the key (given) pair of words. They indicate the key (given) relationship. Think about these two words for a moment. What is the relationship of a maple to a tree? Well, a maple is a particular kind, or type, of tree.

Step 2: *Make up a short sentence stating the relationship that you have discovered for the first pair of words.*

For our model analogy, we can use this sentence: "A maple is a particular kind (type) of tree."

Step 3: *Extend the sentence you have written to cover the rest of the analogy, even though you haven't completed it yet.*

The easiest way to do this is to repeat the key relationship after the words *just as*, leaving blanks for the two words you don't yet have. The sentence will now read something like this:

A maple is a kind (type) of tree, just as a ? is a kind of ? .

Step 4: *Look at each of the lettered pairs of words from which you are to choose your answer. Determine which lettered pair illustrates the same relationship as the key pair.*

The easiest and most effective way to carry out step 4 is to substitute each pair of words into the blanks in the sentence you made up to see which sentence makes sense. Only one will.

Doing this for our sample analogy, we get:

a. A maple is a kind of tree, just as an acorn is a kind of oak.
b. A maple is a kind of tree, just as a hen is a kind of rooster.
c. A maple is a kind of tree, just as a rose is a kind of flower.
d. A maple is a kind of tree, just as a shrub is a kind of lilac.

Look at these sentences. Only *one* of them makes any sense. Choice *a* is clearly wrong because an acorn is *not* a kind of oak. Choice *b* is also wrong because a hen is *not* a kind of rooster. Similarly, choice *d* is incorrect because a shrub is *not* a kind of lilac, though a *lilac* is a kind of shrub. In other words, the two words are in the wrong order. That leaves us with choice *c*, which says that a rose is a kind of flower. Well, that makes sense; a rose is indeed a kind of flower. So, choice *c* must be the pair of words that completes the analogy correctly.

Determining the Key Relationship

Clearly, determining the nature of the key relationship is the most important and the most difficult part of completing an analogy. Since there are literally thousands of key relationships possible, you cannot simply memorize a list of them. The table on page 16, however, outlines some of the most common key relationships. Study the table carefully.

Table of Key Relationships

Complete Analogy	Key Relationship
big is to **large** as **little** is to **small**	**Big** means the same thing as **large**, just as **little** means the same thing as **small**.
tall is to **short** as **thin** is to **fat**	**Tall** means the opposite of **short**, just as **thin** means the opposite of **fat**.
brave is to **favorable** as **cowardly** is to **unfavorable**	The tone of **brave** is **favorable**, just as the tone of **cowardly** is **unfavorable**.
busybody is to **nosy** as **klutz** is to **clumsy**	A **busybody** is by definition someone who is **nosy**, just as a **klutz** is by definition someone who is **clumsy**.
cowardly is to **courage** as **awkward** is to **grace**	Someone who is **cowardly** lacks **courage**, just as someone who is **awkward** lacks **grace**.
visible is to **see** as **audible** is to **hear**	If something is **visible**, you can by definition **see** it, just as if something is **audible**, you can by definition **hear** it.
invisible is to **see** as **inaudible** is to **hear**	If something is **invisible**, you cannot **see** it, just as if something is **inaudible**, you cannot **hear** it.
frigid is to **cold** as **blistering** is to **hot**	**Frigid** is the extreme of **cold**, just as **blistering** is the extreme of **hot**.
chef is to **cooking** as **tailor** is to **clothing**	A **chef** is concerned with **cooking**, just as a **tailor** is concerned with **clothing**.
liar is to **truthful** as **bigot** is to **fair-minded**	A **liar** is by definition not likely to be **truthful**, just as a **bigot** is by definition not likely to be **fair-minded**.
starvation is to **emaciation** as **overindulgence** is to **corpulence**	**Starvation** will cause **emaciation**, just as **overindulgence** will cause **corpulence**.
practice is to **proficient** as **study** is to **knowledgeable**	**Practice** will make a person **proficient**, just as **study** will make a person **knowledgeable**.
eyes are to **see** as **ears** are to **hear**	You use your **eyes** to **see** with, just as you use your **ears** to **hear** with.
sloppy is to **appearance** as **rude** is to **manner**	The word **sloppy** can refer to one's **appearance**, just as the word **rude** can refer to one's **manner**.
learned is to **knowledge** as **wealthy** is to **money**	Someone who is **learned** has a great deal of **knowledge**, just as someone who is **wealthy** has a great deal of **money**.

Exercises In each of the following, circle the item that best completes the analogy. Then explain the key relationship involved.

1. amiable is to **favorable** as
a. rude is to favorable
b. friendly is to unfavorable
c. contented is to unfavorable
d. happy is to favorable

2. popcorn is to **food** as
a. dinner is to chicken
b. song is to ring
c. tea is to drink
d. snack is to lunch

3. soaked is to **damp** as
a. blinding is to bright
b. arid is to moist
c. dark is to light
d. wet is to dry

4. extinguish is to **light** as
a. cook is to heat
b. destroy is to create
c. burn is to scorch
d. construct is to build

VOCABULARY AND WRITING

When you study vocabulary, you make yourself not only a better reader but also a better writer. The greater the number of words at your disposal, the better you will be able to express your thoughts. Good writers are always adding new words to their personal vocabularies, the pool of words that they understand *and* know how to use properly. They use these words both when they write and when they revise.

There are several factors to consider when choosing words and setting the tone of your writing. First, your choice of words should suit your purpose and your audience. If you are writing an essay for your social studies teacher, you will probably want to choose words that are formal in tone and precise in meaning. If you are writing a letter to a friend, however, you will probably choose words that are more informal in tone and freer in meaning. Your **audience** is the person or people who will be reading what you write, and your **purpose** is the reason why you are writing. Your purpose, for example, might be to explain; or it might be to describe, inform, or entertain.

Almost any kind of writing—whether a school essay, a story, or a letter to a friend—can be improved by careful attention to vocabulary. Sometimes you will find, for example, that one word can be used to replace a phrase of five or six words. This is not to say that a shorter sentence is always better. However, readers usually prefer and appreciate **economy** of expression. They grow impatient with sentences that plod along with vague, unnecessary words rather than race along with fewer, carefully chosen ones. Writing can also be improved by attention to **diction** (word choice). Many writers use words that might make sense in terms of *general* meaning but that are not precise enough to convey *nuances* of meaning. In the **Writer's Challenge** sections of this book, you will have an opportunity to make word choices that will more clearly and precisely convey the meaning you intend.

Exercises   *Read the following sentences, paying special attention to the words and phrases underlined. From the words in the box, find better choices for the underlined words and phrases.*

1. Do you feel afraid about going to the dentist?

enjoy	dread	postpone	endorse

2. The sign on that street corner says to forsake the right of way.

endure	go around	yield	seize

3. The teacher tried to get the dizzy students to settle down.

boring	giddy	sad	proud

4. The sea was unaffected by disturbances on that moonlit night.

projecting	choppy	serene	stormy

5. We all muttered discontentedly when we found out the game had been cancelled.

bragged	slurred	pestered	grumbled

DIAGNOSTIC TEST

This test contains a sampling of the words that are to be found in the exercises in this Level of VOCABULARY WORKSHOP. It will give you an idea of the types of words to be studied and their level of difficulty. When you have completed all the units, the Final Mastery Test at the end of this book will assess what you have learned. By comparing your results on the Final Mastery Test with your results on the Diagnostic Test below, you will be able to judge your progress.

 **Synonyms**
*In each of the following groups, circle the word or phrase that **most nearly** expresses the meaning of the word in **boldface** type in the given phrase.*

1. an **abnormal** situation
  a. typical   b. terrible   c. funny   d. unusual

2. **lubricate** the car
  a. start   b. oil   c. stop   d. repair

3. set **ultimate** goals
  a. temporary   b. hasty   c. sincere   d. final

4. an act of **vengeance**
  a. mercy   b. revenge   c. daring   d. fate

5. **proficient** workers
  a. inexperienced   b. awkward   c. slow   d. skillful

6. become a **fugitive**
  a. criminal   b. runaway   c. jailer   d. victim

7. without **prior** planning
  a. earlier   b. intelligent   c. necessary   d. careful

8. **insinuate** that I eat too much
  a. claim   b. deny   c. admit   d. imply

9. accused of **homicide**
  a. killing   b. lying   c. stealing   d. cheating

10. **prominent** members of our community
  a. shady   b. wealthy   c. leading   d. foreign

11. bring down their **wrath**
  a. troubles   b. rage   c. self-esteem   d. temperature

12. **reluctant** assistants
  a. experienced   b. awkward   c. unwilling   d. paid

13. a **legitimate** government
  a. lawful   b. foreign   c. new   d. tyrannical

14. a **legible** report
  a. detailed   b. recent   c. readable   d. thorough

15. **sagacious** remarks
  a. nasty   b. humorous   c. kind   d. wise

16. live a **humdrum** life
   a. exciting   b. poor   c. unusual   d. dull

17. a highly **disputatious** person
   a. likable   b. annoying   c. logical   d. argumentative

18. be ever **vigilant**
   a. careless   b. carefree   c. merciless   d. alert

19. procure assistance
   a. seek   b. offer   c. reject   d. obtain

20. indulge the children
   a. coddle   b. discipline   c. mistreat   d. feed

21. miscellaneous objects
   a. worthless   b. expensive   c. various   d. similar

22. inflict pain
   a. deal out   b. cure   c. study   d. fear

23. vicious animals
   a. gentle   b. trained   c. savage   d. useful

24. flourish their swords
   a. hold   b. seize   c. destroy   d. wave

25. a **sodden** pile of leaves
   a. little   b. wet   c. huge   d. messy

26. in a **melancholy** mood
   a. typical   b. angry   c. strange   d. sad

27. interrogate the witness
   a. question   b. believe   c. punish   d. listen to

28. nothing more than a **hoax**
   a. fraud   b. nobody   c. thief   d. problem

29. loom on the horizon
   a. see   b. notice   c. discover   d. appear

30. a **customary** procedure
   a. wrong   b. profitable   c. clever   d. usual

Antonyms

*In each of the following groups, circle the word or expression that is most nearly opposite in meaning to the word in **boldface** type in the given phrase.*

31. very **hardy** plants
   a. unusual   b. beautiful   c. fragile   d. expensive

32. a **cluttered** room
   a. spacious   b. tidy   c. carpeted   d. messy

33. a major **catastrophe**
   a. war   b. problem   c. disaster   d. triumph

34. prudent in her use of money
   a. foolish   b. stingy   c. thoughtful   d. wise

35. a **fruitless** effort
   a. costly   b. hurried   c. successful   d. halfhearted

36. **vital** to our well-being
   a. important   b. sympathetic   c. unnecessary   d. accustomed

37. very **lax** about discipline
   a. unconcerned b. happy   c. strict   d. forgetful

38. voiced **trivial** objections to the plan
   a. silly   b. significant   c. several   d. separate

39. a truly **hospitable** welcome
   a. warm   b. unexpected   c. cold   d. fitting

40. a **hilarious** movie
   a. long   b. sad   c. profitable   d. foreign

41. feel very **lethargic** today
   a. energetic   b. gloomy   c. tired   d. confident

42. **ignite** a fire
   a. extinguish b. feed   c. ignore   d. report

43. an unexpected **surplus** of wheat
   a. harvest   b. demand   c. use   d. lack

44. a **graphic** account
   a. partial   b. vivid   c. long-winded   d. colorless

45. a **grim** forecast
   a. detailed   b. rosy   c. gloomy   d. recent

46. **despondent** about his grades
   a. overjoyed   b. careful   c. unhappy   d. concerned

47. **hostile** actions
   a. sensitive   b. friendly   c. cheerful   d. unusual

48. a **lavish** gift
   a. costly   b. unusual   c. beautiful   d. skimpy

49. **gigantic** tomatoes
   a. ripe   b. tiny   c. poisonous   d. expensive

50. a **clarification** of the issue
   a. discussion b. avoidance   c. confusion   d. explanation

Definitions

Note carefully the spelling, pronunciation, part(s) of speech, and definition(s) of each of the following words. Then write the word in the blank space(s) in the illustrative sentence(s) following. Finally, study the lists of synonyms and antonyms given at the end of each entry.

1. adjacent
(ə jās′ ənt)

(*adj.*) near, next to, adjoining

Boston and its _____ suburbs were severely flooded after three days of heavy rain.

SYNONYMS: alongside, nearby, neighboring
ANTONYMS: faraway, distant, remote

2. alight
(ə līt′)

(*v.*) to get down from, step down from; to come down from the air, land; (*adj.*) lighted up

The passengers hurried to _____ from the airplane.

The sky was _____ with a red glow as the fire raged in the distance.

SYNONYMS: (*v.*) dismount, descend, land, touch down
ANTONYMS: (*v.*) mount, ascend, board, take off

3. barren
(bar′ ən)

(*adj.*) not productive, bare

In contrast to the rich land we left behind, the plains appeared to be a _____ landscape.

SYNONYMS: unproductive, sterile, desolate, arid
ANTONYMS: fertile, productive, fruitful

4. disrupt
(dis rəpt′)

(*v.*) to break up, disturb

Even the loud demonstration on the street below was not enough to _____ the meeting.

SYNONYMS: upset, displace, disorder
ANTONYMS: organize, arrange

5. dynasty
(dī′ nə stē)

(*n.*) a powerful family or group of rulers that maintains its position or power for some time

The Han _____ of China was in power for about 400 years.

SYNONYMS: ruling house, regime

6. foretaste
(fôr′ tāst)

(*n.*) an advance indication, sample, or warning

The eye-opening first scene of the new play gave the audience a _____ of things to come.

SYNONYMS: preview, anticipation

7. germinate
(jər' mə nāt)

(v.) to begin to grow, come into being

After he interrogated the suspect, suspicion began to
_____ in the inspector's mind.

SYNONYMS: sprout, shoot up, grow, burgeon
ANTONYMS: wither, die, stagnate, shrivel up

8. humdrum
(həm' drəm)

(adj.) ordinary, dull, routine, without variation

All household tasks are _____,
according to my brother, who never helps with them.

SYNONYMS: monotonous, uneventful, prosaic, boring
ANTONYMS: lively, exciting, thrilling, exhilarating

9. hurtle
(hər' təl)

(v.) to rush violently, dash headlong; to fling or hurl forcefully

After separating from its booster rocket, the capsule began
to _____ through space.

SYNONYMS: speed, fly, race, catapult, fling
ANTONYMS: crawl, creep

10. insinuate
(in sin' yü āt)

(v.) to suggest or hint slyly; to edge into something indirectly

The attorney attempted to _____ that
the witness's testimony was false.

SYNONYMS: imply, intimate
ANTONYMS: barge in, broadcast

11. interminable
(in tər' mə nə bəl)

(adj.) endless, so long as to seem endless

We had an _____ wait in the hot,
crowded train station.

SYNONYMS: never-ending, ceaseless
ANTONYMS: brief, short, fleeting

12. interrogate
(in ter' ə gāt)

(v.) to ask questions, examine by questioning

Two detectives helped the young, inexperienced officer to
_____ the suspect.

SYNONYMS: question, query

13. recompense
(rek' əm pens)

(v.) to pay back; to give a reward; (n.) a payment for loss,
service, or injury

My grandparents were happy to
_____ the little girl who found their
lost puppy.

As _____, the landlord offered all
tenants a month free of rent.

SYNONYMS: (v.) repay; (n.) compensation

14. renovate
(ren′ ə vāt)

(*v.*) to repair, restore to good condition, make new again

The young couple brought in an architect and a contractor to help them _____ the old house.

SYNONYMS: repair, fix up, recondition

15. résumé
(rez′ ə mā)

(*n.*) a brief summary; a short written account of one's education, working experience, or qualifications for a job

The job applicant gave a copy of her

_____ to the person in charge of the employment agency.

SYNONYMS: synopsis, job history

16. sullen
(səl′ ən)

(*adj.*) silent or brooding because of ill humor, anger, or resentment; slow moving, sluggish

The _____ student sat down in the back of the classroom.

SYNONYMS: grumpy, surly, peevish, morose
ANTONYMS: cheerful, blithe, sociable, vivacious

17. trickle
(trik′ əl)

(*v.*) to flow or fall by drops or in a small stream; (*n.*) a small, irregular quantity of anything

The water began to _____ from the rusty old pipe.

The runoff, which is quite heavy in the spring, dwindles to a

_____ by late summer.

SYNONYMS: (*v.*) dribble, drizzle, drip; (*n.*) small amount
ANTONYMS: (*v.*) gush, pour, flood; (*n.*) deluge

18. trivial
(triv′ ē əl)

(*adj.*) not important, minor; ordinary, commonplace

The general left all _____ details to subordinates.

SYNONYMS: insignificant, petty, trifling
ANTONYMS: important, weighty, momentous

19. truce
(trüs)

(*n.*) a pause in fighting, temporary peace

After tense negotiations, the warring nations reluctantly agreed to a five-day _____.

SYNONYMS: cease-fire, armistice
ANTONYMS: war, warfare, fighting

20. vicious
(vish′ əs)

(*adj.*) evil, bad; spiteful; having bad habits or an ugly disposition; painfully severe or extreme

The _____ rumor was damaging to their friendship.

SYNONYMS: wicked, malicious, savage
ANTONYMS: good, kind, kindly, mild, harmless

**Completing
the Sentence**

*From the words for this unit, choose the one that best
completes each of the following sentences. Write the
word in the space provided.*

1. Many people who lead rather _____ lives get a great thrill from
watching the exciting adventures of TV and movie superheroes.

2. The "coming attractions" shown before the main feature gave us a distinct
_____ of what the next film would be like.

3. Although they lived in a house _____ to ours, we never really got to
know them well.

4. The judge said to the lawyer, "You have a right to _____ the
witness, but there is no need to bully her."

5. I never would have thought that so bitter and long-lasting a quarrel could result from
such a(n) _____ and unimportant cause.

6. We need large sums of money to keep our school system going, but we are getting
only a(n) _____ of funds from the state.

7. When I applied for the job, I left a(n) _____ of my previous work
experience with the personnel office.

8. Though they didn't say so in so many words, they did _____ that I
was responsible for the accident.

9. Although the building is old and needs repair, we are convinced that we can
_____ it without spending a lot of money.

10. After the big party, cleaning up, which was supposed to take "just a few minutes,"
proved to be an almost _____ job.

11. After the warring nations had agreed to a(n) _____, they faced the
far more difficult task of working out a real peace.

12. She was so happy and grateful that I felt more than _____ for all
that I had tried to do to help her.

13. Though my dog Rover is huge and fierce-looking, children are fond of him because
he doesn't have a(n) _____ disposition.

14. As the drought continued without a letup, the once fertile farmlands of the region
slowly became _____ "dust bowls."

15. The suspect's only reaction to the detective's question was a wry smile and
_____ silence.

16. In only a few days, the seeds that I had planted in the fertile soil of the garden began
to _____ and take root.

17. During the exciting chase, the police cars _____ through the town.

18. In the 11th century, a foreign warlord invaded the country and set up a(n) _____ that ruled for more than 250 years.

19. As we sat at the side of the lake, we enjoyed watching the wild geese swoop down and _____ on the surface of the water.

20. Our carefully laid plans were completely _____ by a sudden and totally unexpected turn of events.

Synonyms

*Choose the word from this unit that is **the same** or **most nearly the same** in meaning as the **boldface** word or expression in the given phrase. Write the word on the line provided.*

1. given the day off as **compensation** _____

2. chased by the **savage** dog _____

3. decided to **fix up** the old theater _____

4. **question** the guilty-looking man _____

5. sit through a seemingly **never-ending** play _____

6. attempt to **touch down** on the ground _____

7. **imply** that it was the teacher's fault _____

8. sent a **job history** to the company _____

9. sign a binding **armistice** to end the fighting _____

10. got a **preview** of what was in store _____

11. **race** through space at an amazing speed _____

12. is a **petty** matter not worth pursuing _____

13. watch water **drip** from the tap _____

14. begun during the time of the old **regime** _____

15. started to **sprout** overnight _____

Antonyms

*Choose the word from this unit that is **most nearly opposite** in meaning to the **boldface** word or expression in the given phrase. Write the word on the line provided.*

16. acres of **fertile** soil _____

17. was known as a **cheerful** patient _____

18. had a **lively** existence _____

19. walked to the **remote** building _____

20. would **organize** the meeting _____

 **Choosing the Right Word** *Circle the **boldface** word that more satisfactorily completes each of the following sentences.*

1. He said that he was going to ask only "a few casual questions," but I soon saw that he wanted to (**recompense, interrogate**) me thoroughly.

2. When we are having fun, time rushes by, but even five minutes in the dentist's waiting room may seem (**adjacent, interminable**).

3. The administration had no major scandals, but it was also (**barren, sullen**) of outstanding accomplishments.

4. With flattery and clever half-truths, the newcomers (**insinuated, renovated**) themselves into the inner circle of the organization.

5. The principal asked the students not to hang around in front of the houses and other buildings (**adjacent to, alighting**) the school.

6. "The program the usher handed you contains a brief (**résumé, dynasty**) of the action of the opera you are about to see," I replied.

7. As he grew old, the torrent of beautiful music that he had produced for so many years was reduced to a mere (**foretaste, trickle**).

8. Even the most (**humdrum, vicious**) work can be interesting if you regard it as a challenge to do the very best you can.

9. The flight attendant asked the passengers to make sure that they had all their personal belongings before (**disrupting, alighting**) from the aircraft.

10. Regardless of who started this silly quarrel, isn't it time for us to declare a (**dynasty, truce**) and work together for the best interests of the school?

11. Planted in the fertile soil of her imagination, the seed of a great idea soon (**germinated, disrupted**) into a workable proposal.

12. I am angry not because she criticized me but because she made remarks that were untrue and (**trivial, vicious**).

13. What we want to do is (**recompense, renovate**) the old house without harming its charm and beauty.

14. Only twenty yards from the finish line, the horse stumbled and (**hurtled, insinuated**) its rider to the ground.

15. For three generations their family has formed one of the leading automotive (**truces, dynasties**) of this country.

16. When I saw a big "A" on my term paper in English, I felt that I had been fully (**germinated, recompensed**) for all my hours of hard work.

17. Our team spirit is so high that there is never a (**sullen, trivial**) reaction from players who aren't chosen to start a game.

18. Are we going to allow minor disagreements to (**disrupt, recompense**) the club that we have worked so hard to organize?

19. The way to be successful at a job is to carry out all instructions carefully, even though you think some of them are (**trivial, sullen**) or silly.

20. If the sights we've seen today are a true (**recompense, foretaste**) of what lies ahead, we're in for some real treats.

Vocabulary in Context

*Read the following passage, in which some of the words you have studied in this unit appear in **boldface** type. Then complete each statement given below the passage by circling the letter of the item that is **the same** or **almost the same** in meaning as the highlighted word.*

Underground Majesty

(Line)

The hill country midway between Nashville and Louisville along Interstate 65 looks like much of the land in rural America. Its landforms are typical of vistas you will see in Tennessee, Kentucky, and the surrounding states. Yet there is nothing **humdrum** about what lurks beneath those ridges, bluffs, and streams. For
(5)   underneath the old-growth forest of black oak, beech, sugar maple, tulip poplar, and hickory lies the world's longest cave system, Mammoth Cave, with its seemingly **interminable** number of underground passageways and rooms.

Prehistoric hunters were the first to discover, explore, and use Mammoth Cave for shelter. Later, Native Americans
(10)   also lived in the cave. About 200 years ago, American settlers came to this region. Unlike Native Americans, these settlers considered the caves to be of **trivial** importance. During the
(15)   War of 1812, however, the cave's resources became valuable: saltpeter, used in making gunpowder, was mined there. After the war, with the help of explorer-guides, the cave
(20)   gained national attention as a tourist attraction.

Park rangers with visitors to Mammoth Cave

Nowadays, visitors can get a **foretaste** of the cave's history and uses within a few hundred yards of its historic entrance. There they will come to the
(25)   Rotunda, a huge chamber that features the remains of the saltpeter mine that was in full operation during the War of 1812.

Today, Mammoth Cave is both a national park and a World Heritage Site. To accommodate its many visitors, hotels and restaurants have been built **adjacent to** the cave's Historic Entrance. As a safety precaution, many miles of its
(30)   passageways have handrails that are lit with electric lights. Yet even with these improvements, the cave remains a dangerous place. In fact, all visitors must tour the cave accompanied by a park ranger.

---

1. The meaning of **humdrum** (line 4) is
  a. morose   c. exciting
  b. ordinary   d. disruptive

2. Interminable (line 7) most nearly means
  a. brief   c. internal
  b. fruitful   d. endless

3. Trivial (line 14) is best defined as
  a. minor   c. weighty
  b. important   d. extended

4. The meaning of **foretaste** (line 23) is
  a. payment   c. indication
  b. review   d. gulp

5. Adjacent to (line 28) most nearly means
  a. near   c. distant
  b. similar   d. remote

Definitions

Note carefully the spelling, pronunciation, part(s) of speech, and definition(s) of each of the following words. Then write the word in the blank space(s) in the illustrative sentence(s) following. Finally, study the lists of synonyms and antonyms given at the end of each entry.

1. available
(ə vā′ lə bəl)

(*adj.*) ready for use, at hand

Bean sprouts and bean curd are

_____ in the Chinese market on Main Street.

SYNONYMS: obtainable, on hand
ANTONYMS: unobtainable, not to be had

2. cater
(kā′ tər)

(*v.*) to satisfy the needs of, try to make things easy and pleasant; to supply food and service

Our grandmother cared for the twins all summer, but she refused to _____ to their every whim.

SYNONYMS: pamper, indulge, gratify, provide
ANTONYMS: frustrate, deny, refuse

3. customary
(kəs′ tə mer ē)

(*adj.*) usual, expected, routine

The _____ tip given to a waiter for service is 15 percent of the bill.

SYNONYMS: regular, normal, traditional
ANTONYMS: strange, odd, unusual, untraditional

4. dissuade
(dis wād′)

(*v.*) to persuade not to do something

Despite offering big raises and bonuses, the boss was unable to _____ workers from quitting.

SYNONYMS: discourage, talk out of
ANTONYMS: persuade, talk into

5. entrepreneur
(än trə prə nər′)

(*n.*) a person who starts up and takes on the risk of a business

In the first year of business, an _____ often assumes losses for the sake of future profits.

SYNONYMS: businessperson, impresario

6. firebrand
(fī′ ər brand)

(*n.*) a piece of burning wood; a troublemaker; an extremely energetic or emotional person

A rash young _____, the new editor of the newspaper strove to expose corruption in the mayor's office.

SYNONYMS: hothead, agitator, rabble-rouser
ANTONYMS: peacemaker, pacifier, conciliator

7. hazard
(haz′ ərd)

(*n.*) risk, peril; (*v.*) to expose to danger or harm; to gamble

Snow tires can help eliminate the

_____ of driving on icy roads.

When asked to predict when the long drought would end, the meteorologist would not _____ a guess.

SYNONYMS: (*n.*) danger; (*v.*) venture

8. homicide
(hom′ ə sīd)

(*n.*) the killing of one person by another

It did not take the jury very long to find the drifter guilty of

_____ .

SYNONYMS: manslaughter, murder

9. indifference
(in dif′ rəns)

(*n.*) a lack of interest or concern

The outcome of the rugby match between the two teams is a matter of complete _____ to me.

SYNONYMS: apathy, unconcern
ANTONYMS: interest, concern, enthusiasm

10. indignant
(in dig′ nənt)

(*adj.*) filled with resentment or anger over something unjust, unworthy, or mean

Angered by the editorial in the newspaper, my mother wrote an _____ letter to the editor.

SYNONYMS: offended, resentful, outraged, exasperated
ANTONYMS: pleased, delighted, overjoyed, elated

11. indispensable
(in di spen′ sə bəl)

(*adj.*) absolutely necessary, not to be neglected

Oxygen is a gas that is _____ to life processes.

SYNONYMS: essential, crucial, vital
ANTONYMS: unnecessary, nonessential

12. lubricate
(lü′ brə kāt)

(*v.*) to apply oil or grease; to make smooth, slippery, or easier to use

The workers had to _____ the equipment regularly so that production would not suffer.

SYNONYMS: oil, grease

13. mutual
(myü′ chü əl)

(*adj.*) shared, felt, or shown equally by two or more

During the course of the summer, the adoring couple formed a _____ admiration society.

SYNONYMS: two-sided, joint, shared, reciprocal
ANTONYMS: one-sided, unilateral

14. pelt
(pelt)

(v.) to throw a stream of things; to strike successively; to hurry

The children resisted the urge to

_____ the cars with snowballs.

SYNONYMS: bombard, shower, pepper

15. plague
(plāg)

(n.) an easily spread disease causing a large number of deaths; a widespread evil; (v.) to annoy or bother

In the 14th century, a _____ spread by infected rats wiped out about one fourth of the population of Europe.

Mosquitoes will _____ the campers if they forget to wear insect repellent on the hike.

SYNONYMS: (n.) epidemic, pestilence; (v.) pester, vex
ANTONYMS: (n.) boon, blessing

16. poised
(poizd)

(adj., part.) balanced, suspended; calm, controlled; ready for action

The captain and other members of the crew were

_____ for takeoff.

SYNONYMS: (adj.) collected, self-confident, ready
ANTONYMS: (adj.) nervous, tense

17. regime
(rā zhēm′)

(n.) a government in power; a form or system of rule or management; a period of rule

The present _____ in that country came to power through democratic elections.

SYNONYMS: administration, rule

18. retard
(ri tärd′)

(v.) to make slow, delay, hold back

Nothing will _____ economic progress more than a new tax on imports.

SYNONYMS: slow down, restrain, impede
ANTONYMS: hasten, speed up

19. transparent
(trans par′ ənt)

(adj.) allowing light to pass through; easily recognized or understood; easily seen through or detected

The students could see the other class through the

_____ glass door.

SYNONYMS: clear, translucent, obvious
ANTONYMS: frosted, sooty, smoky, unclear, indistinct

20. unscathed
(ən skathd′)

(adj.) wholly unharmed, not injured

Remarkably, the captain and the entire crew emerged from the wreck _____.

SYNONYMS: unhurt, sound, intact, unimpaired
ANTONYMS: injured, damaged, harmed, hurt

Completing the Sentence

From the words for this unit, choose the one that best completes each of the following sentences. Write the word in the space provided.

1. Having spent many years as political opponents, the two senators have developed a(n) _____ respect for each other.

2. Though they have done nothing to hasten passage of the bill, they haven't tried to _____ the process either.

3. It takes a special kind of bravery to face the _____ of life in the jungle.

4. Until it was almost too late, the hunters did not see the leopard crouching in a tree, _____ to leap on them.

5. When the wounded shopkeeper died, the charges against the person who had been arrested were raised from robbery to _____ .

6. Eventually, the army toppled the country's democratic _____ and set up a military dictatorship in its place.

7. It took the authorities quite some time to put down the riot that a few rash _____ had managed to start.

8. Although we arrived at the stadium only a few minutes before the game, we found that many good seats were still _____ .

9. Angry at the call, the crowd began to _____ the referee with all kinds of refuse.

10. Since the seat covers in the car were _____ , we could see the attractive pattern of the upholstery underneath.

11. Most of the homeowners in this area have tried in vain to overcome the _____ of crabgrass that threatens to overrun their lawns.

12. At the front desk, a(n) _____ guest was angrily complaining about the shabby treatment he had received from the staff of the hotel.

13. Though the habit of taking a siesta in the afternoon may seem strange to a foreigner, it is quite _____ in this part of the world.

14. With the emergence of market economies in Eastern Europe have come hordes of _____ seeking business opportunities there.

15. No one has ever been able to explain to my satisfaction how Indian holy men can walk _____ across beds of hot coals.

16. Mother prepares wholesome, tasty meals, but she says she is not going to _____ to the special tastes of six different children.

17. A sense of humor is _____ if you are to cope with all the strains and difficulties of everyday life.

18. Only a really hard-hearted person could show such _____ to the plight of the homeless who wander our streets.

19. The guidance counselor tried to _____ me from taking the job because she thought the work would be too pressured for me.

20. When we _____ the engine of a car, we try to cut down the friction at every point.

Synonyms

*Choose the word from this unit that is **the same** or **most nearly the same** in meaning as the **boldface** word or expression in the given phrase. Write the word on the line provided.*

1. met the new **impresario** of sports entertainment _____

2. is **vital** to the good of the community _____

3. found guilty of **murder** _____

4. entered into a **joint** agreement _____

5. began to **bombard** the windshield with hailstones _____

6. had a very **obvious** allegiance to the interest group _____

7. is considered a **rabble-rouser** by colleagues _____

8. a law that would **vex** the firm for years to come _____

9. was needed to **grease** the bicycle chain _____

10. hired to **provide** the wedding supper _____

11. is a **danger** to motorists and pedestrians _____

12. thrived under the new **administration** _____

13. uses any excuse **at hand** _____

14. wants to **discourage** her from taking the job _____

15. is **ready** to serve on the jury _____

Antonyms

*Choose the word from this unit that is **most nearly opposite** in meaning to the **boldface** word or expression in the given phrase. Write the word on the line provided.*

16. was **overjoyed** when the candidate lost _____

17. was **harmed** in the explosion _____

18. became a matter of **concern** to the coach _____

19. would **hasten** his recovery _____

20. used **unusual** healing methods _____

Choosing the Right Word

Circle the **boldface** word that more satisfactorily completes each of the following sentences.

1. The aid that we have (**indignantly, mutually**) given each other during the years has enabled both of us to overcome many problems.

2. All during that nightmarish period, I found myself (**plagued, dissuaded**) by doubts and fears about the future.

3. It seems that only last year she was an awkward child, but now she is a charming and (**poised, unscathed**) young woman.

4. When the new (**hazard, regime**) took power, it canceled or reversed most of the policies of its predecessor.

5. Innocent or guilty, no one involved in a major political scandal ever comes away from it entirely (**dissuaded, unscathed**).

6. The public's (**indifference, hazard**) to government may be measured in the number of citizens who do not bother to vote.

7. The judge explained to the jury that killing someone in self-defense may be considered justifiable, or noncriminal, (**homicide, plague**).

8. When my 8-year-old sister started up a chain of lemonade stands, I knew we had a budding (**entrepreneur, firebrand**) in the family.

9. Unfortunately, nothing any of us said could (**dissuade, cater**) Ned from his plan to quit his job.

10. Your excuse for missing practice was so (**transparent, indispensable**) that even a child would have seen right through it.

11. You cannot ignore me for months on end and then take it for granted that I will be (**available, customary**) whenever you want me.

12. Southern (**firebrands, hazards**) agitating for a complete break with the Union helped speed the coming of the Civil War.

13. A little courtesy can do much to (**dissuade, lubricate**) the machinery of our everyday social life.

14. Do you agree with the criticism that many television programs shamelessly (**cater, retard**) to the lowest tastes?

15. When the salesclerk replied rudely to my polite inquiry about the price of the garment, I became a bit (**transparent, indignant**).

16. Since I am a creature of habit, I find that I can't do anything in the morning without first having my (**customary, mutual**) cup of coffee.

17. In Shakespeare's day, an actor who displeased the audience might find himself (**poised, pelted**) with a barrage of rotten vegetables.

18. On our long camping trip, we learned that we could get along without many things that we had considered (**indispensable, indifferent**).

19. Though I have no means of knowing for sure where they happen to be, may I (**hazard, lubricate**) the guess that they're in the gym?

20. Modern medicine has found that antibiotics are a very effective means of (**catering, retarding**) or arresting the spread of some diseases.

Read the following passage, in which some of the words you have studied in this unit appear in **boldface** type. Then complete each statement given below the passage by circling the letter of the item that is **the same** or **almost the same** in meaning as the highlighted word.

Life on the Range

(Line)

Although cowboys have been portrayed as romantic figures in American folklore and film, in reality their life on the trail was anything but romantic. From about 1865 to 1890, cowboys drove approximately 10 million head of cattle from ranches in southern Texas to faraway northern locations. Where the herds went changed during the period. At first, the drives supplied cattle to forts, mining towns, and (5) reservations. Later, with the coming of the railroad, the destinations were railroad towns in Kansas or Nebraska, where the cattle were sold for beef to Eastern buyers. Regardless of the destination, the trip was dangerous and exhausting. In addition to stampedes, cowboys encountered many other **hazards** on the drive.

Along with dangers, almost anything (10) could **retard** the long journey. If the raging rivers they had to cross didn't slow the cowboys down, then the weather would. Cowboys were routinely **pelted** by hail and **plagued** by dust storms. They were also (15) often sickened by the food that was **available** to them.

The majority of the cowboys who drove cattle were Texans. Some were ex-Confederate soldiers. Others were former (20) slaves. Most were young. All were small. Their size made it easier for the horses to carry them over long distances. Cowboys also had something else in common. All worked long hours for very low pay, for up to four months at a time before resting or returning home. Only teamwork got them (25) through the ordeal. Cowboys soon learned that cattle could be managed most effectively in herds of about 2,500 head, with eight to twelve cowboys for each herd. Cattle drivers worked together to herd, round up, watch, and brand the cattle. This teamwork was **indispensable** to the success of any cattle drive.

Herd of longhorn cattle on the move

---

1. Hazards (line 9) most nearly means
   a. epidemics   c. agitators
   b. perils   d. challenges

2. The meaning of **retard** (line 11) is
   a. slow down   c. speed up
   b. grease   d. calm

3. Pelted (line 14) most nearly means
   a. offended   c. scalded
   b. pampered   d. showered

4. Plagued (line 15) is best defined as
   a. discouraged   c. pestered
   b. unhurt   d. oiled

5. The meaning of **available** (line 17) is
   a. usual   c. crucial
   b. obtainable   d. intact

6. Indispensable (line 29) most nearly means
   a. unnecessary   c. essential
   b. useless   d. useful

Definitions

Note carefully the spelling, pronunciation, part(s) of speech, and definition(s) of each of the following words. Then write the word in the blank space(s) in the illustrative sentence(s) following. Finally, study the lists of synonyms and antonyms given at the end of each entry.

1. animated
(an' ə māt id)

(adj.) full of life, lively, alive; *(part.)* moved to action

After the game the sportscaster found the winning team to be in an _____ mood.

SYNONYMS: *(adj.)* energetic, vigorous
ANTONYMS: *(adj.)* dull, lifeless, dead, flat

2. brood
(brüd)

(n.) a family of young animals, especially birds; any group having the same nature and origin; *(v.)* to think over in a worried, unhappy way

The mother bird fed her _____.

The pioneers did not _____ over the hardships they suffered on the long journey.

SYNONYMS: *(v.)* ponder, meditate, worry, agonize

3. culminate
(kəl' mə nāt)

(v.) to reach a high point of development; to end, climax

The President's military advisors hoped the overseas action would not _____ in disaster.

SYNONYMS: conclude, terminate
ANTONYMS: begin, initiate, kick off, commence

4. downright
(daùn' rīt)

(adv.) thoroughly; *(adj.)* absolute, complete; frank, blunt

Our neighbor, who chopped down our tree and destroyed our fence, is just _____ mean.

The actor felt like a _____ fool when he forgot his lines.

SYNONYMS: *(adj.)* total, out-and-out, unqualified

5. drone
(drōn)

(n.) a loafer, idler; a buzzing or humming sound; a remote-control device; a male bee; *(v.)* to make a buzzing sound; to speak in a dull tone of voice

The steady _____ of the engine put us all to sleep.

The speaker _____ on and on, ignoring the fact that much of the audience had left.

SYNONYMS: *(n.)* bum, do-nothing; *(v.)* hum, buzz, purr
ANTONYMS: *(n.)* hard worker, workaholic

6. goad
(gōd)

(v.) to drive or urge on; *(n.)* something used to drive or urge on

The sergeant had to _____ the reluctant soldiers into action.

The cowhand used a _____ to prod the sluggish cattle.

SYNONYMS: (v.) prod, spur on, incite
ANTONYMS: (v.) curb, check, restrain

7. indulge
(in dəlj′)

(v.) to give in to a wish or desire, give oneself up to

Sometimes the members of a losing team will _____ in self-pity.

SYNONYMS: oblige, humor, coddle, pamper
ANTONYMS: deny, refuse

8. ingredient
(in grē′ dē ənt)

(n.) one of the materials in a mixture, recipe, or formula

Before adding the _____ to the mixture, I first had to put it through a food processor.

SYNONYMS: element, component, constituent, factor

9. literate
(lit′ ə rət)

(adj.) able to read and write; showing an excellent educational background; having knowledge or training

Compared with others in the colonial settlement, she was a highly _____ young woman.

SYNONYMS: educated, trained
ANTONYMS: unlettered, unschooled, ignorant

10. loom
(lüm)

(v.) to come into view; to appear in exaggerated form; (n.) a machine for weaving

The climbers were awestruck to see the peak _____ up before them.

The antique _____, once used to make cloth, was on display in the crafts museum.

SYNONYMS: (v.) emerge, surface, hover, tower

11. luster
(ləs′ tər)

(n.) the quality of giving off light, brightness, glitter, brilliance

The polished gold dome atop the state capitol shone with a starry _____.

SYNONYMS: gloss, sheen, shine
ANTONYMS: tarnish, dullness

12. miscellaneous
(mis ə lā′ nē əs)

(adj.) mixed, of different kinds

A collection of _____ items was gathering dust in the attic.

SYNONYMS: varied, assorted, motley
ANTONYMS: identical, uniform, homogeneous

13. oration
(ô rā′ shən)

(n.) a public speech for a formal occasion

Cicero's _____ in the Roman Senate are still studied by speakers today.

SYNONYMS: address, harangue

14. peevish
(pē' vish)

(adj.) cross, complaining, irritable; contrary

Although the members of the tour group were usually in good humor, hunger made them

_____.

SYNONYMS: crabby, cranky, testy, stubborn
ANTONYMS: agreeable, amiable, even-tempered, pleasant

15. seethe
(sēth)

(v.) to boil or foam; to be excited or disturbed

Mother would _____ with rage each time she learned that a dog had been mistreated.

SYNONYMS: churn, simmer, stew

16. singe
(sinj)

(v.) to burn slightly; *(n.)* a burn at the ends or edges

Getting too close to the flame of the campfire caused the camper to _____ his eyelashes.

A _____ from a cigar ash had destroyed the last word in the document.

SYNONYMS: *(v.)* scorch, char, sear
ANTONYMS: *(v.)* incinerate

17. unique
(yü nēk')

(adj.) one of a kind; unequaled; unusual; found only in a given class, place, or situation

Most people would agree that finding an elephant in one's bathtub would constitute a _____ situation.

SYNONYMS: unparalleled, distinctive, singular
ANTONYMS: ordinary, commonplace, run-of-the-mill

18. upright
(əp' rīt)

(adj.) vertical, straight; good, honest; *(adv.)* in a vertical position

The senator showed her _____ character by voting for bills she believed to be morally right.

The patient was finally standing

_____.

SYNONYMS: *(adj.)* perpendicular, virtuous
ANTONYMS: *(adj.)* horizontal, prone, dishonest, corrupt

19. verify
(ver' ə fī)

(v.) to establish the truth or accuracy of, confirm

The reporter hurried to _____ the source of the controversial statement.

SYNONYMS: prove, validate, substantiate
ANTONYMS: disprove, refute, discredit

20. yearn
(yərn)

(v.) to have a strong and earnest desire

Who wouldn't _____ to see old friends again?

SYNONYMS: crave, long for, want

From the words for this unit, choose the one that best completes each of the following sentences. Write the word in the space provided.

1. The resentment of the American colonists against the harsh policies of the British government _____ in armed rebellion.

2. The Fourth of July _____ will be delivered in City Square by the mayor.

3. Only one half of the population of that underdeveloped nation is

_____ .

4. The dull conversation became much more _____ when it turned to a subject in which we were all interested.

5. The sunlight shining on her beautiful, copper-colored hair gave it an almost metallic

_____ .

6. The man was the prime suspect in the crime until two eyewitnesses came forward to _____ his alibi.

7. Those books which do not fit logically under any of the subjects indicated will be placed in a group labeled "_____ ."

8. When storm clouds _____ on the horizon, we hurried to find shelter.

9. We put supports around the tree that had been partially uprooted by the storm, and it was soon standing _____ again.

10. Like some storm-tossed sea, her inventive brain _____ with all kinds of new and imaginative answers to old problems and questions.

11. Like the traffic guard at a school crossing, the mother hen directed her large _____ across the yard toward a torn sack of feed.

12. Indian elephant keepers usually use a short wooden _____ to control and direct the movements of their huge charges.

13. The first mark of a good cook is the ability to choose the best possible _____ for the dishes he or she will prepare.

14. When I saw how handsome my father looked in his brand-new jacket, I _____ for one exactly like it.

15. I don't know which is worse—parents who are too strict with their children or parents who _____ them too much.

16. I believe in being careful, but Dan is _____ miserly when it comes to spending money.

17. I'm normally fairly even-tempered, but I can become _____ and irritable when I'm tired or frustrated.

18. Larry has the _____ distinction of being the only student in our school ever to win varsity letters in four sports.

19. "You're just supposed to _____ the meat," I shouted at him in dismay, "not burn it to a crisp!"

20. How pleasant it is for us city dwellers to smell the new-mown hay and listen to the _____ of bees in the clover patch!

Synonyms

*Choose the word from this unit that is **the same** or **most nearly the same** in meaning as the **boldface** word or expression in the given phrase. Write the word on the line provided.*

1. is the key **element** in the stew _____

2. despite the danger that seemed to **appear** ahead _____

3. started to **sear** the fringe of the tablecloth _____

4. found a mile-high **assorted** collection of magazines _____

5. will **pamper** her willful son _____

6. **trained** in that computer language _____

7. was a **total** disaster from any perspective _____

8. had a **singular** opportunity to excel _____

9. caused the player's stomach to **churn** with excitement _____

10. gave a wonderful **address** worthy of a standing ovation _____

11. began to **agonize** over her loss _____

12. became **crabby** when chores were assigned _____

13. would **desire** to be in Paris in the spring _____

14. lost some of its **brilliance** with each performance _____

15. attempted to **incite** the others into acting _____

Antonyms

*Choose the word from this unit that is **most nearly opposite** in meaning to the **boldface** word or expression in the given phrase. Write the word on the line provided.*

16. would **begin** in his being elected senator _____

17. had a deserved reputation as a **workaholic** _____

18. overheard a very **dull** discussion _____

19. unable to **refute** her story _____

20. was on stage in an almost **horizontal** position _____

Choosing the Right Word

*Circle the **boldface** word that more satisfactorily completes each of the following sentences.*

1. Probably no (**oration, luster**) in American history is so well known and loved as Lincoln's address on the battlefield of Gettysburg.

2. In his many years in Congress, he has been (**animated, culminated**) mainly by a strong desire to help the underdogs in our society.

3. Though the colonies long (**seethed, singed**) with resentment at the British, the cauldron of their discontent did not boil over into rebellion until 1776.

4. Modern scientists often try to (**loom, verify**) their ideas and theories by conducting extensive experiments in their laboratories.

5. The last thing I heard before falling asleep was the (**goad, drone**) of their voices as they continued their endless discussion of politics.

6. Each year the professional football season (**culminates, broods**) in the Super Bowl.

7. An important (**ingredient, oration**) of what is commonly called luck is the willingness to take chances when an opportunity appears.

8. Even those who do not like New York must admit that it is a truly (**unique, literate**) city, quite unlike any other in the world.

9. The man was not just "a little careless" in handling the club's funds; he was (**downright, upright**) dishonest!

10. Instead of (**droning, brooding**) about the misfortunes that have befallen you, why don't you go out and do something to correct the situation?

11. It's all right for us to disagree, but let's argue about the facts only, without (**indulging, yearning**) in name-calling.

12. I have my doubts about people who spend too much time telling the world how noble and (**upright, downright**) they are.

13. This magazine is published not for a mass circulation but for a very small audience of highly (**peevish, literate**) people.

14. The (**luster, loom**) of her reputation as a friend of humanity has grown brighter with the years.

15. "If you choose to play with fire," I warned them, "you run the risk of (**animating, singeing**) your fingers."

16. Glenn has such a store of (**miscellaneous, upright**) information in his head that we have nicknamed him "The Encyclopedia"!

17. The American people must take action right now to deal with the problem of pollution that (**looms, seethes**) so large on our horizons.

18. Neither threats nor force will (**indulge, goad**) me into doing something that in my heart I know is wrong.

19. You may make friends very easily, but if you continue to be so (**peevish, upright**), you aren't going to keep them for long.

20. By Friday afternoon, all of us were (**indulging, yearning**) for the weekend.

Vocabulary in Context

*Read the following passage, in which some of the words you have studied in this unit appear in **boldface** type. Then complete each statement given below the passage by circling the letter of the item that is **the same** or **almost the same** in meaning as the highlighted word.*

The Art of Speaking Out

(Line)

    In the period between the American Revolution and the Civil War, Americans—**literate** and unschooled alike—were fascinated with public speaking. People from all walks of life eagerly attended debates and lectures on the political and social issues of the day. Great speakers like Daniel Webster and Edward Everett
(5) engaged the passions of enthusiastic audiences, captivating listeners with their rhythmic and repetitive speech patterns.

    The style of **oration** during that era was both personal and interactive. Prominent minister Henry Ward Beecher ignored his notes and spoke from the heart, as did the
(10) suffragist Lucretia Mott. Henry Clay stood close to his audience, while the abolitionist William Lloyd Garrison encouraged audience involvement.

    The best-known debates of the period
(15) were probably the seven **animated** encounters between Abraham Lincoln and Stephen A. Douglas. At the time, Lincoln was not known outside of Illinois, while Douglas was a national political figure.
(20) Their debates drew thousands of listeners, who regularly interrupted the speakers with cheers, groans, and questions. Such

Lincoln speaking at a Lincoln-Douglas debate

audience participation proved to be a key **ingredient** of the debates, as reporters recorded everything said, including audience reactions and remarks.
(25) In the fashion of the time, the Lincoln-Douglas debates followed a preset format. One man spoke first, for an hour, attacking his opponent, who often **seethed** with anger while awaiting his turn. The second responded for an hour and a half, both defending himself and returning the fire. Then the first spoke again for another hour. The audience hung on every word as the two speakers applied their best
(30) arguments, for the stakes were enormous—no less than the future of slavery in the United States and the preservation of the Union.

---

1. The meaning of **literate** (line 2) is
  a. ignorant   c. educated
  b. unlettered   d. messy

2. Oration (line 7) is best defined as
  a. eating   c. celebration
  b. listening   d. speech

3. Animated (line 15) most nearly means
  a. lively   c. zoological
  b. dull   d. lifeless

4. The meaning of **ingredient** (line 23) is
  a. spice   c. mixture
  b. component   d. addition

5. Seethed (line 26) most nearly means
  a. warmed   c. twitched
  b. boiled   d. worried

Analogies

In each of the following, circle the item that best completes the comparison.

1. hurtle is to **fast** as
a. plod is to slow
b. trudge is to fast
c. scamper is to slow
d. creep is to fast

2. bee is to **drone** as
a. fly is to screech
b. ant is to hum
c. cricket is to chirp
d. beetle is to hoot

3. goad is to **elephant** as
a. crop is to horse
b. spur is to boot
c. collar is to neck
d. key is to lock

4. gambler is to **hazard** as
a. banker is to waste
b. spendthrift is to sell
b. thief is to invest
d. miser is to stockpile

5. loom is to **weaver** as
a. role is to actor
b. press is to printer
c. horse is to rider
d. article is to writer

6. murderer is to **homicide** as
a. thief is to robbery
b. villain is to cheating
c. burglar is to forgery
d. liar is to smuggling

7. trickle is to **little** as
a. gush is to much
b. deluge is to little
c. drizzle is to much
d. flood is to little

8. luster is to **shine** as
a. tarnish is to gleam
b. foretaste is to twinkle
c. glamour is to seethe
d. splendor is to dazzle

9. singe is to **fire** as
a. toast is to coffee
b. evaporate is to milk
c. broil is to juice
d. dampen is to water

10. lubricate is to **oil** as
a. start is to brake
b. polish is to wax
c. stop is to gas
d. drive is to engine

11. interminable is to **end** as
a. unique is to parallel
b. indispensable is to use
c. adjacent is to vicinity
d. miscellaneous is to variety

12. illiterate is to **read** as
a. noisy is to hear
b. blind is to see
c. deaf is to write
d. laugh is to grin

13. mutual is to **two** as
a. adjacent is to three
b. literate is to five
c. unique is to one
d. barren is to four

14. unscathed is to **injury** as
a. literate is to knowledge
b. wise is to intelligence
c. penniless is to wealth
d. celebrated is to position

15. firebrand is to **kindle** as
a. spoilsport is to yearn
b. pickpocket is to insinuate
c. peacemaker is to extinguish
d. showoff is to hide

16. indifferent is to **interest** as
a. poised is to control
b. sullen is to silence
c. humdrum is to excitement
d. upright is to honesty

17. poised is to **favorable** as
a. animated is to unfavorable
b. vicious is to favorable
c. peevish is to unfavorable
d. sullen is to favorable

18. indignant is to **anger** as
a. vicious is to boredom
b. sullen is to resentment
c. indifferent is to concern
d. poised is to fear

Word Associations

In each of the following groups, circle the word that is best defined or suggested by the given phrase.

1. to discourage from doing something
a. disrupt   b. germinate   c. recompense   d. dissuade

2. the basic element in a recipe
a. drone   b. foretaste   c. ingredient   d. indifference

3. a totally desolate wasteland
a. unique   b. barren   c. sullen   d. transparent

4. to bombard with snowballs
a. retard   b. goad   c. pelt   d. alight

5. to drive someone into a rage
a. goad   b. indulge   c. hurtle   d. plague

6. charged with the crime of murder
a. indifference   b. homicide   c. hazard   d. regime

7. to restore the building to its original condition
a. disrupt   b. renovate   c. culminate   d. cater

8. one who assumes the risk of a business
a. regime   b. dynasty   c. entrepreneur   d. firebrand

9. to burn one's eyebrows slightly
a. pelt   b. alight   c. seethe   d. singe

10. a routine procedure
a. indispensable   b. customary   c. available   d. mutual

11. tasks that are monotonous and dull
a. indignant   b. sullen   c. barren   d. humdrum

12. to declare a binding cease-fire
a. foretaste   b. firebrand   c. truce   d. oration

13. to worry over a loss or an illness
a. insinuate   b. brood   c. germinate   d. indulge

14. essential equipment
a. interminable   b. indispensable   c. trivial   d. customary

15. the honest citizens of the community
a. upright   b. downright   c. animated   d. literate

16. hurt by their unconcern
a. homicide   b. regime   c. hazard   d. indifference

17. to grease the axle of a car
a. retard   b. indulge   c. seethe   d. lubricate

18. to question a witness thoroughly
a. interrogate   b. insinuate   c. verify   d. yearn

19. to dismount from a horse
a. disrupt   b. alight   c. hurtle   d. dissuade

20. a sample of what is to come
a. foretaste   b. brood   c. dynasty   d. loom

Vocabulary in Context

*Read the following passage, in which some of the words you have studied in Units 1–3 appear in **boldface** type. Then complete each statement given below the passage by circling the item that is **the same** or **almost the same** in meaning as the highlighted word.*

(Line)

Help Wanted: Llama

For thousands of years, the llama has been a working animal. In fact, in the **barren**, rugged highlands of Peru, this **unique** animal has for
(5) centuries proved to be a reliable beast of burden, carrying heavy packs to lowland markets. Then, about one hundred years ago, the llama was brought to the United
(10) States. In this country, however, the llama has added to its **résumé** by gaining some unusual work experience, so strange in fact that here its "odd job" has all but
(15) replaced its **customary** use as a pack animal.

Because of its tendency to work hard, eat cheaply, go many miles without water, and get along well with
(20) people and other animals, the llama has proved to be a match for many other working animals. Yet it is not just in **trivial** matters, such as carrying golf bags (although llamas
(25) do serve as caddies) or in maintaining hiking trails (they do work for the National Park Service), that llamas have distinguished themselves in this country. In fact, in
(30) the United States the llama's true calling seems to be in "predator protection," acting as a kind of fantastic "sheepdog."

Interestingly, llamas make good
(35) "guard dogs" for the following reasons: They are quick studies, learning in a few days what it might take a dog a year to master. Also, llamas and sheep get along famously.
(40) Most importantly, llamas have a natural distaste for coyotes, the sheep's main predator, and they don't get frazzled in the face of danger. When brazen predators approach
(45) the herd, llamas aggressively chase away the intruders.

So serious is this problem that in the United States **vicious** predators have killed hundreds of millions of
(50) dollars worth of sheep in the past few years. Although efforts have been under way to destroy the coyotes, the thinking now is to focus on protecting the sheep. It would seem that the
(55) best way to do that is to "hire" a llama. In fact, when interviewed in an Iowa study, half the llama-owning sheep farmers reported sheep losses down to zero since getting a llama,
(60) which just goes to show that there's nothing like having a good guard dog, especially when it's a llama.

---

1. The meaning of **barren** (line 3) is
  a. fertile   c. fruitful
  b. arid   d. productive

2. Unique (line 4) most nearly means
  a. upright   c. singular
  b. peevish   d. crucial

3. Résumé (line 11) is best defined as
  a. job history   c. story
  b. administration d. regime

4. Customary (line 15) most nearly means
  a. untraditional c. energetic
  b. weighty   d. regular

5. Trivial (line 23) is best defined as
  a. significant   c. important
  b. singular   d. trifling

6. The meaning of **vicious** (line 48) is
  a. harmless   c. distinctive
  b. savage   d. hotheaded

Choosing the Right Meaning

Read each sentence carefully. Then circle the item that best completes the statement below the sentence.

At the height of the Cuban missile crisis, in October 1962, the world seemed poised on the brink of full-scale nuclear war. (2)

1. The word **poised** in line 2 is best defined as

a. calm b. suspended c. controlled d. collected

The boss's downright manner does not sit well with some; but I, for one, find his frankness downright refreshing. (2)

2. In line 1 the word **downright** is used to mean

a. blunt b. absolute c. complete d. unqualified

Although the vicious headaches called *migraines* have been known to medicine for centuries, their cause is still unknown. (2)

3. The word **vicious** in line 1 most nearly means

a. spiteful b. malicious c. evil d. severe

The fact that many species—including the kangaroo and platypus—are unique to Australia is due to its isolation from other continents. (2)

4. In line 2 the phrase **unique to** most nearly means

a. unparalleled in b unequaled in c. found only in d. distinctive in

Though in looks the twins cannot be told apart, in temperament they could not be more different—one as meek as a lamb, the other as peevish as a mule. (2)

5. In line 2 the word **peevish** is used to mean

a. obstinate b. irritable c. complaining d. cross

Antonyms

*In each of the following groups, circle the word or expression that is most nearly the **opposite** of the word in **boldface** type.*

1. adjacent
a. nearby
b. well-lit
c. remote
d. stuffy

2. transparent
a. muddy
b. clear
c. drinkable
d. dangerous

3. miscellaneous
a. valuable
b. similar
c. colorful
d. used

4. verify
a. read
b. confirm
c. disprove
d. type

5. indignant
a. delighted
b. long
c. offended
d. sleepy

6. trivial
a. new
b. puzzling
c. important
d. minor

7. animated
a. lively
b. dull
c. well-informed
d. unpleasant

8. culminated
a. displaced
b. began
c. announced
d. ended

9. unique
a. commonplace
b. matchless
c. modern
d. popular

11. vicious
a. bitter
b. inaccurate
c. nasty
d. kind

13. retard
a. hold back
b. speed up
c. account for
d. observe

15. interminable
a. pleasant
b. unimportant
c. difficult
d. brief

10. peevish
a. irritable
b. agreeable
c. snobbish
d. puzzling

12. luster
a. value
b. dullness
c. appeal
d. glow

14. sullen
a. strange
b. ugly
c. thoughtful
d. sociable

16. disrupt
a. upset
b. dismount
c. organize
d. disorder

Word Families

A. *On the line provided, write the word you have learned in Units 1–3 that is related to each of the following nouns.*

EXAMPLE: culmination—**culminate**

1. catering, caterer _____

2. trivia, triviality _____

3. yearning, yearner _____

4. uniqueness _____

5. viciousness, vice _____

6. lubricant, lubricator, lubrication _____

7. transparentness, transparency _____

8. verification, verifier, verifiableness, verifiability _____

9. custom, customariness _____

10. insinuation, insinuator _____

11. renovation, renovator _____

12. indignation _____

13. literacy, literati, literature _____

14. indulgence, indulger _____

15. germination, germinability, germ _____

B. *On the line provided, write the word you have learned in Units 1–3 that is related to each of the following verbs.*

EXAMPLE: interrogate—**interrogation**

16. avail _____

17. animate _____

18. dispense _____

19. poise _____

20. orate _____

Two-Word Completions

Circle the pair of words that best complete the meaning of each of the following passages.

1. When I was very young, I truly _____ a life of excitement, adventure, and danger. But now that I'm a good deal older, I'm perfectly content with my rather _____ existence.

a. brooded about . . . interminable
b. yearned for . . . humdrum

c. alighted on . . . trivial
d. indulged in . . . hazardous

2. At one point in last night's hockey game, home-team fans became so angry with the referee that they began to _____ him with refuse. Programs, paper cups, and even a dead fish _____ through the air and landed at his feet.

a. pelt . . . hurtled
b. disrupt . . . droned

c. indulge . . . loomed
d. singe . . . trickled

3. Running our country is full of all kinds of hidden _____ and traps for the unwary. For that reason, no President, no matter how alert or cautious he may be, ever leaves office entirely _____ by the experience.

a. regimes . . . lubricated
b. firebrands . . . poised

c. ingredients . . . animated
d. hazards . . . unscathed

4. When the new _____ took office, its first order of business was to pacify the country by arranging a _____ with the rebel forces that had been waging all-out war against the previous administration.

a. dynasty . . . plague
b. drone . . . homicide

c. firebrand . . . loom
d. regime . . . truce

5. Though crabmeat is one of the _____ mentioned in the classic recipe for a New Orleans fish stew, it isn't always "in season." Accordingly, professional chefs often replace it with whatever shellfish is _____ at the time without any noticeable damage to the dish.

a. résumés . . . adjacent
b. broods . . . indispensable

c. ingredients . . . available
d. orations . . . customary

6. Strong winds fanned the flames, and the fire in the factory quickly spread to _____ buildings. Though the firefighters worked very hard to _____ its progress, the blaze soon engulfed the entire block.

a. available . . . goad
b. adjacent . . . retard

c. miscellaneous . . . animate
d. upright . . . germinate

Building with Classical Roots

pend, pens—to hang, weigh; to pay; to set aside

This root appears in **indispensable** (page 29), literally "not able to be set aside or done away with." The word now has the meaning "essential or necessary." Some other words based on the same root are listed below.

dependent	dispense	expenditure	perpendicular
dispensary	expendable	pension	suspense

From the list of words above, choose the one that corresponds to each of the brief definitions below. Write the word in the blank space in the illustrative sentence below the definition.

1. relying on another for help or support; determined or conditioned by something else; a person who is supported by another

A lion cub is _____ on its mother for nourishment and protection.

2. to give out, distribute

It is a judge's duty to _____ justice with an even hand.

3. replaceable, nonessential

It is difficult for some employees to realize that they are _____ and can be let go at any time.

4. at right angles; exactly upright, vertical

The wall is _____ to the floor.

5. the state of being uncertain or undecided; anxiety, nervous uncertainty

The audience was kept in _____ until the winner was announced.

6. the amount of money spent; spending, using up ("*paying out*")

Worrying is a needless _____ of energy.

7. a place where medicines are made or given out ("*place from which things are weighed out*")

The nurse obtained the medicine she needed in the hospital

_____ .

8. a fixed amount paid to retired employees or their families

At age 65 he will receive a small _____ from his company.

From the list of words on page 48, choose the one that best completes each of the following sentences. Write the word in the blank space provided.

1. Rescue workers set up a makeshift _____, where medical supplies were provided to the survivors of the disaster.

2. As the value of the dollar shrinks, my grandmother finds it harder and harder to live on the small _____ she receives from the government.

3. A section of the bookstore in my neighborhood is devoted to novels of mystery and _____.

4. Because drugs can be dangerous, only trained pharmacists are licensed to _____ prescription medicines.

5. This tremendous project will represent an enormous _____ of public money.

6. "Unlike human beings," said the captain, "supplies and equipment are _____, since they can be replaced."

7. Whether or not we have our picnic tomorrow is _____ on the weather.

8. In italic type the letters are slanted to the right, but in Roman type they are _____.

---

*Circle the **boldface** word that more satisfactorily completes each of the following sentences.*

1. Last year, our school's (**expenditure, dispensary**) on software was five times greater than that of the year before.

2. A retiree's (**dependent, pension**) may not provide enough money to cover all living expenses.

3. Certain fish are (**perpendicular, dependent**) on the sea anemone for protection.

4. As automation becomes widespread, unskilled laborers become (**expendable, expenditure**).

5. You can have this prescription filled at the (**pension, dispensary**) in the clinic.

6. The traffic light should be (**perpendicular, expendable**) to the sidewalk.

7. Many doctors (**dispense, suspense**) both good advice and expert medical care.

8. Theatergoers were kept in (**dispensary, suspense**) by the well-constructed plot of the thrilling play.

Writer's Challenge

Read the following sentences, paying special attention to the words and phrases underlined. From the words in the box below, find better choices for these underlined words and phrases. Then use these choices to rewrite the sentences.

WORD BANK				
alight	drone	loom	poised	unscathed
brood	homicide	lubricate	regime	upright
culminate	humdrum	mutual	seethe	vicious
downright	hurtle	plague	trickle	yearn

Luge

1. Did you ever wonder how it might feel to <u>rush forcefully</u> down an icy slope at 60 or 70 miles an hour? If so, you might enjoy the chance to ride a luge.

_____

_____

2. The luge is a <u>completely, utterly, and totally</u> simple sled-like racing vehicle with runners. Riders zoom down a steep, winding track as fast as possible.

_____

_____

3. Luge riders get <u>ready for action</u> for a run by donning skin-tight suits to decrease air resistance.

_____

_____

4. The luge competitor starts off sitting <u>in a perpendicular position</u>, and then lies back as the sled gains speed. The sled is controlled by pressure of the shoulders and legs on the runners.

_____

_____

5. A luge requires nothing to <u>oil or grease</u> it for its rapid descent, since the course is covered with ice.

_____

_____

6. Luge accidents are not uncommon, but most experienced luge riders emerge <u>wholly unharmed</u> and eager to learn from their mistakes.

_____

_____

7. Top-level luge racers hope to <u>reach a high point of development in</u> their vigorous training by earning a spot to compete in the Winter Olympic Games.

_____

_____

Definitions

Note carefully the spelling, pronunciation, part(s) of speech, and definition(s) of each of the following words. Then write the word in the blank space(s) in the illustrative sentence(s) following. Finally, study the lists of synonyms and antonyms given at the end of each entry.

1. alliance
(ə lī′ əns)

(*n.*) a joining together for some common purpose

The two nations formed an _____ to defend each other in case of attack.

SYNONYMS: pact, league, coalition
ANTONYMS: rift, split

2. bewilder
(bi wil′ dər)

(*v.*) to puzzle completely, confuse

The captain continues to _____ his troops by giving contradictory orders.

SYNONYMS: baffle, perplex
ANTONYMS: set straight, enlighten

3. buffoon
(bə fün′)

(*n.*) a clown; a coarse, stupid person

Some students think that they need to play the _____ in order to entertain their classmates.

SYNONYMS: jester, fool

4. controversial
(kän trə vər′ shəl)

(*adj.*) arousing argument, dispute, or disagreement

The school board waited until all members were present before issuing the _____ proposal to ban after-school programs.

SYNONYMS: arguable, debatable

5. dishearten
(dis härt′ ən)

(*v.*) to discourage

Do not let your low score on the math test _____ you.

SYNONYMS: dismay, demoralize, dispirit
ANTONYMS: encourage, hearten

6. fruitless
(früt′ ləs)

(*adj.*) not producing the desired results, unsuccessful

When their efforts to fight the infection with penicillin proved _____, the doctors tried a different antibiotic.

SYNONYMS: useless, vain, unproductive, futile
ANTONYMS: productive, effective

7. hostile
(häs' təl)

(*adj.*) unfriendly; unfavorable; warlike, aggressive

Relations between the two nations have been _____ for decades.

ANTONYMS: friendly, cordial, peaceful

8. inflammable
(in flam' ə bəl)

(*adj.*) easily set on fire; easily angered or aroused

Always be cautious when using _____ cleaning solvents.

SYNONYMS: combustible, flammable, excitable
ANTONYMS: fireproof, fire-resistant, calm

9. inflict
(in flikt')

(*v.*) to give or cause something unpleasant, impose

Despite all the jokes, doctors do not like to _____ pain on their patients.

SYNONYMS: deal out, visit upon
ANTONYMS: suffer, undergo, sustain

10. malignant
(mə lig' nənt)

(*adj.*) deadly, extremely harmful, evil; spiteful, malicious

Much to the patient's relief, the X ray revealed no _____ growth.

SYNONYMS: lethal, wicked
ANTONYMS: wholesome, beneficial, benign

11. mortify
(môrt' ə fī)

(*v.*) to hurt someone's feelings deeply; to cause embarrassment or humiliation; to subdue or discipline by self-denial or suffering

The teacher was _____ by the students' childish behavior on the field trip.

SYNONYMS: humiliate, embarrass, abash

12. orthodox
(ôr' thə däks)

(*adj.*) in agreement with established or generally accepted beliefs or ways of doing things

Our principal, who believes in proven teaching methods, takes an _____ approach to education.

SYNONYMS: traditional, standard, customary
ANTONYMS: unusual, unconventional, heretical

13. procure
(prə kyür')

(*v.*) to obtain through special effort; to bring about

The hospital held a raffle to _____ the necessary funds for the new children's wing.

SYNONYMS: gain, acquire, achieve

14. scurry
(skər' ē)

(*v.*) to run quickly, scamper, hurry

The reappearance of the teacher caused the students in the class to _____ back to their seats.

SYNONYMS: rush, dash, scramble
ANTONYMS: trudge, plod, creep, crawl

15. sodden
(säd′ ən)

(*adj.*) soaked with liquid or moisture; expressionless, dull; spiritless, listless

All at once, and with much loud honking, the flock of geese rose from the _____ marshlands.

SYNONYMS: drenched, waterlogged, saturated
ANTONYMS: parched, arid

16. spirited
(spir′ ə tid)

(*adj.*) full of life and vigor; courageous

The royal soldiers put up a _____ defense against the invading army.

SYNONYMS: lively, animated, gallant
ANTONYMS: lifeless, dull, lackluster

17. virtual
(vər′ chü əl)

(*adj.*) having a certain force or effect in fact but not in name; so close as to be equivalent to the real thing

To those who worked in the office, the bossy new manager was a _____ dictator.

SYNONYMS: functioning as, equivalent to

18. void
(void)

(*adj.*) completely empty; having no legal force or effect; (*n.*) empty or unfilled space; (*v.*) to cancel or nullify

I thought that poem was completely _____ of sense.

Grandmother's death left a great _____ in my grandfather's life.

Do you know how to _____ a check?

SYNONYMS: (*adj.*) invalid, vacant, bare
ANTONYMS: (*adj.*) in effect, teeming with; (*v.*) confirm

19. wayward
(wā′ wərd)

(*adj.*) disobedient, willful; unpredictable, capricious

Tracking the _____ path of a comet is no easy matter.

SYNONYM: perverse
ANTONYMS: docile, well-behaved, predictable

20. wince
(wins)

(*v.*) to draw back suddenly, as though in pain or fear; (*n.*) the act of drawing back in this way

The dog's bite made the child _____ in pain.

The patient's _____ told the doctor to press more gently.

SYNONYMS: (*v.*) flinch, shudder, recoil

Completing the Sentence

From the words for this unit, choose the one that best completes each of the following sentences. Write the word in the space provided.

1. The frozen wastes of the Arctic may seem _____ to human life, but in fact thousands of people are able to survive there.

2. After four days of steady rainfall, the _____ ground actually gurgled as we trudged wearily over it.

3. Before we set out on the camping trip, I was given sole responsibility for _____ all the necessary equipment and supplies.

4. Would it be a bad pun if I were to say that our attempts to set up an apple orchard have proved to be _____?

5. In 1949, the United States formed a(n) _____ with eleven other nations, organized into the North Atlantic Treaty Organization.

6. When the Supreme Court finds a law unconstitutional, that law is said to be null and _____.

7. Some parts of the President's proposal were agreeable to everyone; others proved highly _____.

8. We _____ such heavy casualties on the enemy that they were forced to break off the engagement and retreat.

9. Though the gallant defenders of the fort were hopelessly outnumbered, they put up a truly _____ fight.

10. Their behavior is so _____ and unpredictable that I never know what they are going to do next.

11. Since the gas did not burn when we brought a flame to it, the experiment showed that carbon dioxide is not _____.

12. The directions he gave us for driving to the beach were so complicated that I was completely _____ by them.

13. Even though you like to do things in your own way, I suggest that you first learn the _____ method of batting.

14. Despite the fact that she has no official title of any kind, she has become the _____ director of the company.

15. Even though I'm an adult, I still _____ in discomfort at the thought of a trip to the dentist.

16. I was thoroughly _____ when I suddenly stumbled and spilled punch all over the host's tuxedo.

17. If it is allowed to spread unchecked, the poison of racial prejudice will have a decidedly _____ effect on our community.

18. When the naughty children heard their mother's footsteps approaching, they quickly _____ back to bed.

19. The court of many a medieval king or prince was enlivened by the pranks and antics of jesters and other _____ .

20. Refusing to be _____ by her early failures to find a summer job, Lucy made up her mind to try again.

Synonyms

*Choose the word from this unit that is **the same** or **most nearly the same** in meaning as the **boldface** word or expression in the given phrase. Write the word on the line provided.*

1. to **recoil** at the idea of getting up so early _____

2. showed a **perverse** unwillingness to study _____

3. made a **futile** effort to defeat the enemy _____

4. persuaded the partners to **cancel** the contract _____

5. **baffle** friends with their odd reaction _____

6. sank into the grass **drenched** with rain _____

7. would **humiliate** her parents with her crude behavior _____

8. used a highly **combustible** cleaning fluid _____

9. did not become **discouraged** by the lack of money needed _____

10. was **equivalent to** freedom to the inmates _____

11. was suffering from a **deadly** brain tumor _____

12. formed a strong **coalition** with that political party _____

13. tries to **acquire** the freshest produce _____

14. acts like a **clown** in front of his friends _____

15. made the **debatable** call that ended the game _____

Antonyms

*Choose the word from this unit that is **most nearly opposite** in meaning to the **boldface** word or expression in the given phrase. Write the word on the line provided.*

16. would **trudge** up the hill once a day _____

17. gave a **lackluster** performance for the audience _____

18. was introduced to the **friendly** crowd _____

19. held **unconventional** political beliefs _____

20. to **suffer** serious wounds in battle _____

Choosing the Right Word

Circle the **boldface** word that more satisfactorily completes each of the following sentences.

1. In high school, students should (**procure, void**) training in basic skills that they will need to qualify for good jobs in later life.

2. The scrappy coach's (**fruitless, spirited**) pep talk lifted the team out of its "losing-season blues" almost overnight.

3. "It's hard not to be a little (**procured, disheartened**) when your favorite team is in the cellar two weeks before the playoffs," I replied.

4. I can understand that you want to be witty and amusing, but take care not to give everyone the impression that you're a mere (**alliance, buffoon**).

5. I could see from the (**inflicted, bewildered**) expression on the child's face that he was quite lost.

6. Because I no longer go to high school, my student bus pass has been (**voided, disheartened**).

7. Instead of being so (**mortified, hostile**), why don't you try to show some friendliness to those newcomers?

8. Our supervisor gives the impression of being an easygoing man, but we have learned that he has a very (**orthodox, inflammable**) temper.

9. A severe cold spell in December (**inflicted, bewildered**) heavy losses on the Florida citrus crop.

10. When his army seemed (**virtually, soddenly**) defeated by the British, George Washington crossed the Delaware and won a major victory.

11. (**Fruitless, Controversial**) political figures are likely to have as many critics as they have supporters.

12. On the hottest night of the entire summer, the sheets on my bed became so (**sodden, malignant**) with perspiration that I had to change them.

13. Though her views about the role of women in society are far from (**hostile, orthodox**), even conservatives and traditionalists listen to them.

14. Walking through the meadow at night, we could hear mice and other small animals (**scurrying, wincing**) about in the grass.

15. "Whenever you find (**wayward, controversial**) children," the speaker said, "you also find ineffective parents."

16. All our efforts to control pollution will be (**fruitless, inflammable**) unless we work out a careful, detailed plan in advance.

17. Being scolded for my shortcomings in front of the entire basketball squad was a truly (**mortifying, wayward**) experience for me.

18. (**Malignant, Virtual**) gossip has unjustly damaged their reputation.

19. I still (**scurry, wince**) when I think of the two bad errors that cost us the championship game.

20. We are going to form a broad (**void, alliance**) among all the groups that are working to improve life in our community.

Vocabulary in Context

*Read the following passage, in which some of the words you have studied in this unit appear in **boldface** type. Then complete each statement given below the passage by circling the letter of the item that is **the same** or **almost the same** in meaning as the highlighted word.*

The Lewis and Clark Expedition

(Line)

In 1803 President Thomas Jefferson sent his friend James Monroe to Paris to try to buy the port of New Orleans in the French-owned Louisiana Territory. Yet when the French response came, it would **bewilder** both men.

(5) Shortly after negotiations had begun, an impatient French official asked Monroe, "How much will you give for the whole of Louisiana?" France needed money for its war with Great Britain. An agreement between France and the United States was soon reached. For just $15 million, about three cents an acre, the United States

(10) would **procure** this huge piece of land.

Once the Louisiana Purchase had been made, Jefferson asked Meriwether Lewis to lead an expedition to explore the territory. The President also hoped that

(15) Lewis would find a safe water route to the Pacific. To ready himself for the journey, Lewis engaged in a **spirited** study of scientific techniques. He also asked his friend William Clark to join him on the trip.

Sacajawea Leading Lewis and Clark by Alfred Russell

(20) On May 14, 1804, Lewis and Clark and a group of 42 men, calling itself the "Corps of Discovery," left from St. Louis.

As the men followed the Missouri River and struggled to cross the Rockies, much happened to **dishearten** them. They suffered from all the hazards associated with crossing a rugged and often **hostile** wilderness. For all their troubles, however, they

(25) never found a fully navigable water route to the Pacific Ocean.

Yet the strenuous journey was far from **fruitless**. After eighteen months, Lewis and Clark reached the Pacific Ocean. Along the way, they had mapped more than 3,000 miles. They had learned about new plants and animals. With the help of Sacajawea, a Shoshone woman, they had met many Native American groups. In

(30) the words of Thomas Jefferson, the Lewis and Clark expedition had shown that the United States was "a rising nation, spread over a wide and fruitful land."

---

1. The meaning of **bewilder** (line 3) is
a. scramble
b. puzzle
c. enlighten
d. flinch

2. Procure (line 10) most nearly means
a. give
b. confirm
c. gain
d. provide

3. Spirited (line 17) is best defined as
a. lively
b. lackluster
c. wicked
d. gallant

4. Dishearten (line 23) most nearly means
a. fool
b. cheer
c. discourage
d. inform

5. The meaning of **hostile** (line 24) is
a. hospitable
b. arguable
c. cordial
d. unfriendly

6. Fruitless (line 26) most nearly means
a. effective
b. unproductive
c. useful
d. productive

Definitions

Note carefully the spelling, pronunciation, part(s) of speech, and definition(s) of each of the following words. Then write the word in the blank space(s) in the illustrative sentence(s) following. Finally, study the lists of synonyms and antonyms given at the end of each entry.

1. anecdote
(an' ek dōt)

(*n.*) a short account of an incident in someone's life

The governor told a humorous _____ about her first day in office.

SYNONYMS: tale, story, sketch, vignette, yarn

2. consolidate
(kən säl' ə dāt)

(*v.*) to combine, unite; to make solid or firm

The generals agreed to _____ their forces for the invasion.

SYNONYMS: strengthen, firm up, merge
ANTONYMS: scatter, disperse, dissipate, separate

3. counterfeit
(kaùn' tər fit)

(*n.*) an imitation designed to deceive; (*adj.*) not genuine, fake; (*v.*) to make an illegal copy

The painting was a _____ of Gainsborough's *Blue Boy.*

The forger was selling _____ postage stamps.

It is a crime to _____ money.

SYNONYMS: (*adj.*) false, phony, bogus
ANTONYMS: (*adj.*) genuine, real, authentic

4. docile
(däs' əl)

(*adj.*) easily taught, led, or managed; obedient

She was a _____ child, eager to learn and to please.

SYNONYMS: manageable, teachable, pliant
ANTONYMS: unruly, wayward, intractable, disobedient

5. dominate
(däm' ə nāt)

(*v.*) to rule over by strength or power, control; to tower over, command due to height

History shows us that powerful nations tend to _____ weaker ones.

SYNONYMS: control, govern, overlook

6. entreat
(en trēt')

(*v.*) to beg, implore, ask earnestly

The dog's eyes seemed to _____ me for an extra helping of dinner.

SYNONYMS: plead, beseech
ANTONYM: clamor for

7. fallible
(fal′ ə bəl)

(*adj.*) capable of being wrong, mistaken, or inaccurate

The researcher's _____ methods led to faulty conclusions.

SYNONYMS: imperfect, errant
ANTONYMS: foolproof, unfailing, flawless

8. fickle
(fik′ əl)

(*adj.*) liable to change very rapidly, erratic; marked by a lack of constancy or steadiness, inconsistent

My aunt's interests change with the weather, showing she is a truly _____ person.

SYNONYMS: capricious, inconstant, faithless
ANTONYMS: constant, steady, invariable

9. fugitive
(fyü′ jə tiv)

(*n.*) one who flees or runs away; (adj.) fleeting, lasting a very short time; wandering; difficult to grasp

That thief is a _____ from justice, wanted in several states.

The couple had a few _____ moments together before the wife boarded the train.

SYNONYMS: (*n.*) runaway, deserter; (*adj.*) elusive
ANTONYMS: (*adj.*) lasting, enduring, permanent

10. grimy
(grī′ mē)

(*adj.*) very dirty, covered with dirt or soot

The miners emerged from the pits with _____ hands and faces.

SYNONYMS: filthy, sooty, soiled, dirt-encrusted
ANTONYMS: spotless, spick-and-span, immaculate

11. iota
(ī ō′ tə)

(*n.*) a very small part or quantity

The employer had not an _____ of proof, but he blamed the new clerk for the theft anyway.

SYNONYMS: speck, dab, jot, bit, smidgen
ANTONYMS: flood, deluge, avalanche, glut

12. maul
(môl)

(*v.*) to beat or knock about, handle roughly; to mangle; (*n.*) a heavy hammer

The tiger was about to _____ its victim when the zookeeper intervened.

SYNONYMS: (*v.*) rough up, manhandle, batter

13. potential
(pə ten′ chəl)

(*adj.*) possible, able to happen; (*n.*) something that can develop or become a reality

Hurricanes are a _____ threat to this area in the late summer and early fall.

They were a football team with _____.

SYNONYMS: (*n.*) possibility, capability
ANTONYMS: (*adj.*) actual, real, unlikely, impossible

14. radiant
(rā′ dē ənt)

(*adj.*) shining, bright; giving forth light or energy

A model needs to have a _____ smile in order to advertise toothpaste.

SYNONYMS: glowing, brilliant, dazzling, resplendent
ANTONYMS: dull, tarnished, lackluster

15. rural
(rür′ əl)

(*adj.*) relating to farm areas and life in the country

They settled in a _____ community that was miles from the nearest large city.

SYNONYMS: countrified, rustic
ANTONYMS: urban, metropolitan, citified

16. substantial
(səb stan′ shəl)

(*adj.*) large, important; major, significant; prosperous; not imaginary, material

Expecting a _____ raise in salary, the employee put a down payment on a new car.

SYNONYMS: considerable, tangible, big
ANTONYMS: minor, insignificant, negligible

17. tactful
(takt′ fəl)

(*adj.*) skilled in handling difficult situations or people, polite

A _____ approach is usually the wisest one to take with coworkers.

SYNONYMS: skillful, diplomatic, discreet
ANTONYMS: clumsy, gauche, boorish, indiscreet

18. tamper
(tam′ pər)

(*v.*) to interfere with; to meddle rashly or foolishly with; to handle in a secret and improper way

Please don't _____ with our baggage.

SYNONYMS: monkey with, fool with, mess with

19. ultimate
(əl′ tə mət)

(*adj.*) last, final; most important or extreme; eventual; basic, fundamental

California is the _____ destination on our cross-country trip.

SYNONYMS: farthest, furthest, terminal
ANTONYMS: first, initial, most immediate, nearest

20. uncertainty
(ən sər′ tən tē)

(*n.*) doubt, the state of being unsure

It was the _____ about the future that was of the greatest concern to the immigrants.

SYNONYMS: doubtfulness, unsureness, hesitation
ANTONYMS: sureness, certainty, confidence

Completing the Sentence

From the words for this unit, choose the one that best completes each of the following sentences. Write the word in the space provided.

1. The new book of presidential _____ contains many amusing stories involving our Chief Executives, both past and present.

2. Though the UN has many lesser objectives, its _____ goal is to achieve lasting world peace.

3. The wily old senator had such a forceful and aggressive personality that he soon came to _____ his entire party.

4. Since I had expected the children to be hard to handle, I was pleasantly surprised by their _____ behavior.

5. To be _____ in everyday life means doing whatever you can to avoid hurting the feelings of other people.

6. As she told us the good news, her face was _____ with joy.

7. Trying desperately to avoid the police, the _____ hid in the cellar of the abandoned house.

8. The boat has been so badly _____ by the storm that it will have to be overhauled before it can be used again.

9. Despite the doctor's best efforts, there has been no _____ change in the patient's condition for weeks.

10. The windows had become so _____ and spotted that it took me some time to get them clean.

11. Since all our cashiers handle large sums of money, we have given them special training in recognizing _____ bills.

12. "As a mother," the woman said to the judge, "I _____ you to show leniency toward my son."

13. There is an old saying that pencils are made with erasers because human beings are _____ .

14. Unwilling to bear the _____ any longer, I called the Dean of Admissions to find out if I had been accepted.

15. We discovered that there was not a(n) _____ of truth in the rumors that they had spread so eagerly.

16. Though Company A has very little chance of expanding in the near future, the _____ growth rate of Company B is staggering.

17. I took my broken TV set to a qualified repair service, rather than run the risk of damaging it further by _____ with it myself.

18. The taste of the public is so _____ that a TV performer who is a big hit one season may be out of a job the next.

19. The Board of Education believes it would save considerable money to _____ three small schools into one big school.

20. After having lived for so long in a large city, I was happy to spend a few weeks in those beautiful _____ surroundings.

Synonyms

*Choose the word from this unit that is **the same** or **most nearly the same** in meaning as the **boldface** word or expression in the given phrase. Write the word on the line provided.*

1. saw a **dazzling** sunrise _____

2. avoid a **possible** source of trouble _____

3. to **meddle** with the truth _____

4. made **significant** progress last week _____

5. watched the lion **rough up** its prey _____

6. made a **diplomatic** remark _____

7. is **capricious** in her affections _____

8. found the plan to be **imperfect** _____

9. paid with a **bogus** $50 bill _____

10. will **control** the game with their speed _____

11. found a way to **combine** several companies _____

12. would **implore** me to contribute money _____

13. moved forward with no **hesitation** _____

14. was a **runaway** from oppression _____

15. shared a charming **story** from her childhood _____

Antonyms

*Choose the word from this unit that is **most nearly opposite** in meaning to the **boldface** word or expression in the given phrase. Write the word on the line provided.*

16. held a **spotless** handkerchief _____

17. owned a **disobedient** pet _____

18. lives in a **metropolitan** area _____

19. does not have an **avalanche** of evidence against her _____

20. reached the **initial** stop on the journey _____

Choosing the Right Word

*Circle the **boldface** word that more satisfactorily completes each of the following sentences.*

1. Throughout the course of its history, the United States has opened its gates to (**fugitives, counterfeits**) from tyranny in other lands.

2. Although the ideals of my youth have been (**entreated, mauled**) by hard experience, they have not been totally destroyed.

3. The (**ultimate, rural**) population of the United States is growing smaller, but the people living on farms are as important as ever to the nation.

4. The mayor has no chance for reelection unless she can (**consolidate, maul**) the different groups and forces supporting her.

5. There, in the very heart of the noisy and (**grimy, fallible**) city was a truly beautiful little park with green lawns, flowers, and a fountain.

6. Rarely in our history has a single man so (**dominated, entreated**) the federal government as Franklin D. Roosevelt did during his four terms.

7. The only certain thing in life is that there will always be many (**fugitives, uncertainties**).

8. It wasn't very (**docile, tactful**) of you to tell her that she seemed to have gained weight.

9. I found his (**anecdotes, entreaties**) amusing, but I fail to see what they had to do with the central idea of his talk.

10. The young man who seemed so quiet and (**docile, substantial**) turned out to be very well informed and to have strong opinions of his own.

11. I suspected that his expression of happiness was (**potential, counterfeit**) and that he was really jealous of our success.

12. Evidence showed that the lawyer had tried to (**consolidate, tamper**) with the witnesses by offering them bribes to change their testimony.

13. Imagine someone as changeable as George having the nerve to say that I'm (**radiant, fickle**)!

14. Larry got good grades on the midterm tests, but he is headed for trouble because he hasn't done an (**anecdote, iota**) of work since then.

15. I know from personal experience how much harm smoking can do, and I (**dominate, entreat**) you not to get started on that miserable habit.

16. As soon as 300-pound Horace settled down in that delicate little chair, we realized he should have something more (**grimy, substantial**) to sit on.

17. If you want to see the (**iota, ultimate**) in shoe styles, ask Beth to show you the new sandals she bought for the spring dance.

18. How can we properly direct the (**uncertainties, potential**) for good and evil in each of us into useful channels?

19. In modern hospitals, everything possible is done to prevent and control mistakes resulting from human (**fallibility, fickleness**).

20. One of our best hopes of solving the energy problem lies in making direct use of (**radiant, fugitive**) energy from the sun.

Read the following passage, in which some of the words you have studied in this unit appear in **boldface** *type. Then complete each statement given below the passage by circling the letter of the item that is* **the same** *or* **almost the same** *in meaning as the highlighted word.*

A Giant Find

(Line)

In 1869, near the town of Cardiff, in a **rural** area of New York State, workers digging a well unearthed a giant humanlike figure. The Cardiff Giant, as it came to be known, was more than 10 feet tall and appeared to be of ancient origin. The discovery created a national sensation. Was the Cardiff Giant one of the greatest scientific discoveries of the century? (5)

A number of people thought that it was. Newspaper reporters called it the "eighth wonder of the world." William Newell, who owned the farm on which the discovery was made, erected a tent around the Giant and charged admission to view it. Thousands came. Then a group of prominent Syracuse, New York, businesspeople saw the **potential** for making even greater profits. They purchased (10)

Cardiff Giant on display

a three-fourths interest in the Cardiff Giant for $30,000 and moved it to Syracuse, where it could attract even larger crowds.

At this point, some anthropologists began to express **uncertainty** about the authenticity (15) of the Giant. Shortly thereafter, it was exposed as a **counterfeit**, a hoax engineered by George Hull, a tobacco farmer and cigar manufacturer. Hull had bought a large block of gypsum, a white (20) mineral, and had had two sculptors carve from it the likeness of a human being. He then attended to every detail to give the statue an aged look. When the Giant was complete, Hull and Newell had buried it.

Hull's Cardiff Giant was the **ultimate** American anthropological hoax. Ironically, (25) people still wanted to see the fake. It was moved to Albany and then to New York City. Thwarted in his attempt to buy the giant, the great promoter P.T. Barnum had an imitation made. Barnum's fake was soon drawing larger crowds than the original!

Over the years, the Cardiff Giant has been displayed by its many owners. In 1948 the Giant was moved to the Farmers' Museum in Cooperstown, New York, (30) where you can still see it today.

---

1. The meaning of **rural** (line 1) is
a. urban　　　　c. rustic
b. majestic　　　d. metropolitan

2. Potential (line 10) most nearly means
a. danger　　　　c. strength
b. possibility　　d. uncertainty

3. Uncertainty (line 15) is best defined as
a. confidence　　c. doubt
b. importance　　d. sureness

4. The meaning of **counterfeit** (line 17) is
a. fake　　　　c. discovery
b. coin　　　　d. game

5. Ultimate (line 25) most nearly means
a. imperfect　　c. first
b. lasting　　　d. most extreme

Definitions

Note carefully the spelling, pronunciation, part(s) of speech, and definition(s) of each of the following words. Then write the word in the blank space(s) in the illustrative sentence(s) following. Finally, study the lists of synonyms and antonyms given at the end of each entry.

1. anonymous
(ə nän′ ə məs)

(*adj.*) unnamed, without the name of the person involved (writer, composer, etc.); unknown; lacking individuality or character

The detective received an _____ tip that helped to narrow the search for the thief.

SYNONYM: nameless

2. browse
(braüz)

(*v.*) to nibble, graze; to read casually; to window-shop

I like to _____ through a book before I buy it.

SYNONYMS: skim, scan, dip into, graze
ANTONYMS: pore over, scrutinize

3. dupe
(düp)

(*n.*) a person easily tricked or deceived; (*v.*) to deceive

He played the _____ in one of Shakespeare's comedies.

The villain in the play tried to _____ the hero out of his money.

SYNONYMS: (*v.*) fool, mislead, hoodwink, delude
ANTONYMS: (*v.*) undeceive, disabuse

4. dynamic
(dī nam′ ik)

(*adj.*) active, energetic, forceful

The advertising agency was looking to hire a creative person with a _____ personality.

SYNONYMS: vigorous, high-powered
ANTONYMS: lazy, lackadaisical, lethargic, sluggish

5. eradicate
(i rad′ ə kāt)

(*v.*) to root out, get rid of, destroy completely

The team of doctors and researchers worked tirelessly to _____ the disease.

SYNONYMS: wipe out, uproot
ANTONYMS: implant, instill, foster, promote

6. frustrate
(frəs′ trāt)

(*v.*) to prevent from accomplishing a purpose or fulfilling a desire; to cause feelings of discouragement

Nothing could _____ our plans to storm the fort.

SYNONYMS: thwart, foil, baffle, disappoint
ANTONYMS: help, assist, abet

7. grim
(grim)

(*adj.*) stern, merciless; fierce, savage, cruel

Many Third World nations face the

_____ prospect of famine.

SYNONYMS: dreadful, frightful, ferocious
ANTONYMS: mild, merciful, delightful

8. inimitable
(in im' ə tə bəl)

(*adj.*) not capable of being copied or imitated

The young performer stole the show with her

_____ charm.

SYNONYMS: matchless, incomparable, unique

9. makeshift
(māk' shift)

(*n.*) a temporary substitute for something else; (*adj.*) crude, flimsy, or temporary

The boards and cinder blocks are only a

_____ until the bookcase arrives.

That army cot serves as a _____ bed for guests.

SYNONYMS: (*n.*) stopgap, substitute
ANTONYMS: (*adj.*) permanent, durable, solid, sturdy

10. marginal
(märj' ən əl)

(*adj.*) in, at, or near the edge or margin; only barely good, large, or important enough for the purpose

During times of economic hardship, many people have

only a _____ standard of living.

SYNONYMS: borderline, minimal, peripheral
ANTONYMS: central, pivotal, focal

11. pending
(pen' diŋ)

(*adj.*) waiting to be settled; (*prep.*) until

Curiosity about the _____ trial builds with each day.

Sentencing of the convicted criminal was postponed

_____ the judge's decision.

SYNONYMS: (*adj.*) undecided, unsettled
ANTONYMS: (*adj.*) settled, decided, resolved

12. prescribe
(pri skrīb')

(*v.*) to order as a rule or course to be followed; to order for medical purposes

The doctor was quick to _____ complete bed rest.

SYNONYMS: specify, appoint, recommend

13. preview
(prē' vyü)

(*n.*) something seen in advance; (*v.*) to view beforehand

The critics saw a _____ of the new movie.

The teacher wished to _____ the video before showing it to the class.

SYNONYM: (*n.*) foretaste

14. prominent
(präm′ ə nənt)

(*adj.*) standing out so as to be easily seen; important, well-known

Some famous authors are _____ figures in society.

SYNONYMS: conspicuous, noticeable
ANTONYMS: inconspicuous, unnoticeable, obscure

15. quaint
(kwānt)

(*adj.*) odd or old-fashioned in a pleasing way; clever, ingenious; skillfully made

My parents stayed at a _____ old inn in Vermont.

SYNONYMS: picturesque, peculiar, strange, curious
ANTONYMS: familiar, commonplace, modern, contemporary

16. reluctant
(ri lək′ tənt)

(*adj.*) unwilling, holding back

The attorney called the _____ witness to the stand.

SYNONYMS: hesitant, loath, disinclined
ANTONYMS: willing, eager, inclined

17. scrimp
(skrimp)

(*v.*) to handle very economically or stingily; to supply in a way that is small, short, or scanty

When the factory closed and other work was scarce, many people were forced to _____.

SYNONYM: economize
ANTONYM: splurge

18. snare
(snâr)

(*v.*) to trap, catch; (*n.*) a trap or entanglement

They set a trap to _____ the rodents that were getting into the garden.

The unsuspecting spy was caught in a _____ set by the other side.

SYNONYMS: (*n.*) pitfall; (*v.*) entrap
ANTONYM: liberate

19. utmost
(ət′ most)

(*adj.*) greatest, highest, farthest; (*n.*) the extreme limit

The voters had the _____ regard for her ability as a leader.

SYNONYMS: (*adj., n.*) maximum, supreme, best
ANTONYM: least

20. vengeance
(ven′ jəns)

(*n.*) punishment in return for an injury or a wrong; unusual force or violence

History is filled with examples of wronged rulers seeking _____ against their enemies.

SYNONYMS: revenge, retaliation, reprisal
ANTONYMS: forgiveness, pardon

Completing the Sentence

From the words for this unit, choose the one that best completes each of the following sentences. Write the word in the space provided.

1. The most _____ feature of the skyline of that little town in Iowa is the four-story grain elevator.

2. When we visited Salem, Massachusetts, last year, we were charmed by the _____ 18th-century houses in the town.

3. After the angler _____ the fish, he unhooked it from his line and threw it back into the stream.

4. We may not be able to _____ crime in our community, but if we go about it in the right way, I am sure we can reduce it greatly.

5. Instead of seeking personal _____ for the wrong that has been done to you, why don't you look for justice under the law?

6. When unexpected guests turned up on the doorstep, I hurriedly made a few _____ arrangements to accommodate them.

7. After several unsuccessful attempts to catch the waiter's eye, I began to become a little _____ .

8. When we saw the _____ expression on the poor man's face, we realized that the situation was indeed serious.

9. Safety measures are of the _____ importance when you are planning a canoe trip over rivers filled with dangerous rapids.

10. For weeks I _____ on everything to save enough money to buy the replacement tires for my bicycle.

11. There is quite a contrast between the _____ administration that now runs that country and the "do-nothing" regime that preceded it.

12. Many books have been written about boys, but none of them can match the _____ qualities of *Tom Sawyer* and *Huckleberry Finn*.

13. Although we know who wrote such famous epics as the *Aeneid* and the *Iliad*, the author of *Beowulf* remains _____ .

14. The suspect was held in the local police station _____ the outcome of the investigation.

15. The eyewitness was _____ to tell the police all that she had seen, but we convinced her that it was the only right thing to do.

16. I was _____ into trusting him, and I have paid a heavy price for being misled so easily.

17. I like to write _____ notes in a book alongside important material, but I never do so unless the book belongs to me.

18. Each unit in the textbook opens with a section that _____ and highlights the material in the chapters that follow.

19. It took the pharmacist about an hour to prepare the medicine that the doctor had _____ for my cold.

20. Is there any sight in the world more restful than cows _____ in a meadow alongside a little brook?

Synonyms

*Choose the word from this unit that is **the same** or **most nearly the same** in meaning as the **boldface** word or expression in the given phrase. Write the word on the line provided.*

1. has an **incomparable** sense of humor _____

2. had a **foretaste** of the new spring clothing _____

3. wanted to **wipe out** poverty _____

4. was of **minimal** help to the team _____

5. is an issue that is still **undecided** _____

6. tried to **economize** on nonessential items _____

7. set a **trap** for the gophers _____

8. waited to hear what the doctor would **order** _____

9. gave a very **vigorous** effort _____

10. will demand swift **revenge** _____

11. likes to **skim** through the books on the shelves _____

12. attempted to **thwart** his opponent _____

13. received a card from an **unknown** admirer _____

14. is of the **highest** priority _____

15. was unable to **fool** the audience _____

Antonyms

*Choose the word from this unit that is **most nearly opposite** in meaning to the **boldface** word or expression in the given phrase. Write the word on the line provided.*

16. was **eager** to join the others _____

17. remained a very **obscure** playwright _____

18. amused by the guest's **modern** notions _____

19. built a **permanent** shelter _____

20. heard the **delightful** news on the radio _____

Choosing the Right Word

*Circle the **boldface** word that more satisfactorily completes each of the following sentences.*

1. As I was (**previewing, browsing**) my way lazily through the newspaper, I was shocked to see my own name in a headline!

2. He still doesn't realize that he has been used as a (**dupe, snare**) by our opponents to do their dirty work for them.

3. The mistaken idea that the most important thing in life is to "have fun" is a (**snare, vengeance**) that leads to serious trouble for many young people.

4. We have many good musicians in our school orchestra, but they need a (**makeshift, dynamic**) conductor to make them play as a unit.

5. Although the announcement had promised us "a (**prominent, reluctant**) speaker," the person turned out to be a very minor public official.

6. Although we cannot mention her by name, we want to express our heartfelt gratitude to the (**quaint, anonymous**) donor who gave us this generous gift.

7. I understand your (**reluctance, vengeance**) to be our candidate in the next election, but I think it is your duty to accept the nomination.

8. (**Pending, Eradicating**) the outcome of our national election, none of the foreign governments is willing to take any definite action.

9. His reference to a "historic downfall" after I had failed the history test struck me as a rather (**dynamic, grim**) joke.

10. For months the winter was unusually mild, but when the cold weather did come, it struck with a (**vengeance, prominence**).

11. The new parking regulations are only a (**snare, makeshift**) that will have to be replaced by a better plan within a few years.

12. The exhibition at the fair is intended to give people a (**preview, dupe**) of what life may be like fifty years from now.

13. To improve your unsatisfactory school record, I would (**browse, prescribe**) regular doses of study, to be taken every day for as long as is necessary.

14. It is very easy to say that our city government should (**scrimp, snare**) to balance its budget, but which departments should spend less?

15. You must realize that, although we may find the customs of other lands (**anonymous, quaint**), they are just part of everyday life in those areas.

16. The wily champion used every tennis trick she knew to (**frustrate, scrimp**) her opponent's attempts to come to the net and hit a winner.

17. Landing a man on the moon was a great achievement, but it is far from being the (**utmost, pending**) limit of our space program.

18. Since my job is only (**marginal, inimitable**), I'm afraid that if business falls off a little, my employer may let me go.

19. Even before we saw Alice, we heard her (**inimitable, grim**) high-pitched giggle and knew she was at the party.

20. Nothing can (**eradicate, scrimp**) the love of liberty from the hearts of a free people!

Vocabulary in Context

*Read the following passage, in which some of the words you have studied in this unit appear in **boldface** type. Then complete each statement given below the passage by circling the letter of the item that is **the same** or **almost the same** in meaning as the highlighted word.*

More Than an Explorer

(Line)

The **dynamic** John Wesley Powell was perhaps the greatest example of the fearless American explorer of the nineteenth century. Powell maintained that he was neither an adventurer nor just an explorer. To Powell, it was the pursuit of science that was of the **utmost** importance. Indeed, his exploration of the Colorado River
(5)   and the Grand Canyon actually led to the development of some of the principles of geology. It also prompted the settlement of the American Southwest.

In 1869, Powell, who had lost an arm during the Civil War, and nine companions set out to explore and map the largely
(10)   uncharted canyons of the Green and Colorado rivers. The party had just four flimsy wooden boats and a meager supply of rations. The hazards of the **grim** journey challenged the group at every turn. In fact,
(15)   Powell and his party surprised even the local Native Americans, who were themselves **reluctant** to navigate the dangerous Grand Canyon River Gorge. Yet Powell would not let anything **frustrate** his
(20)   plans for exploration—not even the three reports of his death!

Majestic Grand Canyon in Arizona

Fortunately, Powell did not die on the river, and the one-thousand-mile journey was a success, as was a second trip he led two years later. Powell's book about the Grand Canyon region, as well as the photographs, topographic map, diaries,
(25)   and field notes prepared by several other members of his party, provided valuable information about the area.

Soon after his second expedition, Powell became a **prominent** government official, involved in the management of arid western lands. He went on to become the Director of the Bureau of Ethnology, which collected data about fast
(30)   disappearing North American Indian groups, and later, the Director of the U.S. Geological Survey.

---

1. The meaning of **dynamic** (line 1) is
a. explosive
b. energetic
c. lethargic
d. sturdy

2. Utmost (line 4) is best defined as
a. strangest
b. high-powered
c. greatest
d. least

3. Grim (line 13) most nearly means
a. merciful
b. short
c. dirty
d. frightful

4. Reluctant (line 17) is best defined as
a. hesitant
b. willing
c. undecided
d. delighted

5. Frustrate (line 19) most nearly means
a. assist
b. foil
c. settle
d. mislead

6. The meaning of **prominent** (line 27) is
a. inconspicuous
b. curious
c. central
d. well-known

Analogies

In each of the following, circle the item that best completes the comparison.

1. fugitive is to **flee** as
a. buffoon is to browse
b. lawyer is to scrimp
c. beggar is to entreat
d. doctor is to wince

2. scurry is to **fast** as
a. maul is to slow
b. tamper is to fast
c. browse is to slow
d. dominate is to fast

3. anecdote is to **incident** as
a. lyric is to emotion
b. opera is to ambition
c. drama is to opinion
d. epic is to concern

4. sheen is to **radiant** as
a. blemish is to splendid
b. tarnish is to dull
c. luster is to grimy
d. glow is to inflammable

5. mountain is to **prominent** as
a. valley is to virtual
b. marsh is to sodden
c. orchard is to potential
d. desert is to makeshift

6. barn is to **rural** as
a. skyscraper is to urban
b. subway is to rural
c. corral is to urban
d. tenement is to rural

7. dynamic is to **energy** as
a. fickle is to courage
b. malignant is to benefit
c. spirited is to vigor
d. makeshift is to substance

8. substantial is to **much** as
a. marginal is to little
b. pending is to much
c. utmost is to little
d. void is to much

9. procure is to **obtain** as
a. consolidate is to disperse
b. inflict is to observe
c. eradicate is to implant
d. snare is to trap

10. racehorse is to **spirited** as
a. pony is to malignant
b. mule is to reluctant
c. donkey is to controversial
d. colt is to tactful

11. blunder is to **mortify** as
a. victory is to frustrate
b. agreement is to bewilder
c. pleasure is to wince
d. defeat is to dishearten

12. con artist is to **dupe** as
a. patient is to prescribe
b. buffoon is to amuse
c. fugitive is to reward
d. ally is to dominate

13. puzzle is to **bewilder** as
a. iota is to delight
b. anecdote is to dishearten
c. uncertainty is to comfort
d. stalemate is to frustrate

14. inimitable is to **copy** as
a. unpredictable is to foresee
b. uncomfortable is to remove
c. undesirable is to avoid
d. undeniable is to prove

15. fallible is to **err** as
a. anonymous is to discover
b. wayward is to obey
c. dynamic is to delay
d. fickle is to change

16. wayward is to **docile** as
a. ultimate is to final
b. void is to empty
c. hostile is to friendly
d. quaint is to charming

17. alliance is to **agree** as
a. preview is to disagree
b. anecdote is to agree
c. controversy is to disagree
d. vengeance is to agree

18. fruitless is to **result** as
a. heartless is to skill
b. aimless is to direction
c. tactless is to merit
d. priceless is to value

Word Associations

In each of the following groups, circle the word that is best defined or suggested by the given phrase.

1. something that the doctor does
   a. prescribe   b. preview   c. bewilder   d. wince

2. taking pains not to hurt someone's feelings
   a. wayward   b. tactful   c. reluctant   d. virtual

3. "Ouch!"
   a. wince   b. tamper   c. void   d. dupe

4. a court jester
   a. prominent   b. vengeance   c. pending   d. buffoon

5. a whole lot of nothing
   a. void   b. anecdote   c. vengeance   d. snare

6. "I'm afraid that I won't to able to find a job this summer."
   a. substantial   b. malignant   c. grimy   d. disheartened

7. like a sheep
   a. fallible   b. docile   c. dynamic   d. reluctant

8. "I haven't got a clue."
   a. inflict   b. dominate   c. preview   d. bewilder

9. rather badly chewed up by a tiger
   a. consolidate   b. maul   c. frustrate   d. inflammable

10. The North Atlantic Treaty Organization (NATO)
   a. iota   b. snare   c. alliance   d. uncertainty

11. "Have you heard the story about _____?"
   a. grim   b. makeshift   c. anecdote   d. controversial

12. not at all foolproof
   a. inflict   b. inimitable   c. fallible   d. utmost

13. to pull something out by the roots
   a. browse   b. scrimp   c. entreat   d. eradicate

14. stray from the straight and narrow
   a. rural   b. marginal   c. wayward   d. orthodox

15. find the equipment we need for the trip
   a. procure   b. mortify   c. scurry   d. dominate

16. given to sudden and unexpected changes of mood
   a. fickle   b. docile   c. dynamic   d. potential

17. not the real thing
   a. inimitable   b. orthodox   c. marginal   d. counterfeit

18. not yet decided
   a. sodden   b. pending   c. potential   d. virtual

19. to interfere with, as evidence or a witness
   a. consolidate   b. inflict   c. tamper   d. dominate

20. like greasy, dirty overalls
   a. grimy   b. fruitless   c. fickle   d. grim

Vocabulary in Context

Read the following passage, in which some of the words you have studied in Units 4–6 appear in **boldface** type. Then complete each statement given below the passage by circling the item that is **the same** or **almost the same** in meaning as the highlighted word.

Byline: "Nellie Bly"

(Line)

It wasn't her real name, but in 1885 when 18-year-old Elizabeth Cochrane, a **spirited** young woman from a small town in Pennsylvania,
(5) moved to Pittsburgh to become a writer, the aspiring reporter knew she would need a catchy new name. She chose Nellie Bly, from the title of a popular Stephen Foster tune, and
(10) turned out stories on **controversial** subjects that would sell more newspapers than ever imagined.

Under the byline "Nellie Bly," the young woman wrote articles for the
(15) *Pittsburgh Dispatch* that were spiced with shocking **anecdotes** she heard from the older women living in her boardinghouse. Nellie's writing rang true, and soon she was exposing the
(20) **grim** conditions in Pittsburgh's slums, jails, and factories. When her stories became too sensational for her editors, Nellie left Pittsburgh for New York City, where she joined the staff
(25) of Joseph Pulitzer's *New York World*.

Once again, there was nothing typical about the topics Nellie chose to write about, and nothing **orthodox** about the way she researched them.
(30) To expose the dreadful conditions in

New York's insane asylum, Bellevue, she threw a fit and got admitted to this hospital. To test the capabilities of a ferry rescue crew, she jumped
(35) overboard into the Hudson River. To expose shameful prison conditions, Nellie framed herself on a robbery charge and landed in jail. Her stories both thrilled and **mortified** readers.
(40) Some of her work led to social reform. It also made her famous.

In the name of grabbing headlines, Nellie had her share of adventures. Yet a stunt she pulled in 1889 would
(45) be the greatest adventure of her career. Responding to the fame of Jules Verne's novel *Around the World in Eighty Days*, Nellie proposed to outdo the book's fictional character,
(50) Phileas Fogg, and circle the globe in less time. Pulitzer accepted her idea, and as readers breathlessly followed her course, Nellie made her way around the world. In the end, she
(55) bested Fogg. Her time: 72 days. People had said that it couldn't be done, but then Nellie Bly, still only 21, was used to beating the odds.

---

1. The meaning of **spirited** (line 3) is
   a. lifeless
   b. aggressive
   c. saturated
   d. lively

2. Controversial (line 10) most nearly means
   a. ordinary
   b. arguable
   c. agreeable
   d. discouraging

3. Anecdotes (line 16) is best defined as
   a. stories
   b. prescriptions
   c. novels
   d. disappointments

4. Grim (line 20) is most nearly means
   a. grimy
   b. dreadful
   c. benign
   d. predictable

5. Orthodox (line 28) is best defined as
   a. unusual
   b. debatable
   c. traditional
   d. borderline

6. The meaning of **mortified** (line 39) is
   a. elated
   b. disheartened
   c. dismayed
   d. embarrassed

Choosing the Right Meaning

Read each sentence carefully. Then circle the item that best completes the statement below the sentence.

Perhaps the hectic touring schedule had taken its toll on the cast; at any rate I found last night's performance of the play decidedly sodden. (2)

1. The word **sodden** in line 2 is used to mean
a. drenched   b. brilliant   c. listless   d. soaked

In some early religious orders, members mortified their bodies by fasting and even, in some cases, by voluntarily suffering physical pain. (2)

2. In line 1 the word **mortified** is best defined as
a. embarrassed   b. disciplined   c. humiliated   d. strengthened

The suburban building boom of the 1950s saw entire developments of anonymous tract houses spring up practically overnight. (2)

3. The word **anonymous** in line 1 most nearly means
a. nameless   b. indistinguishable c. unknown   d. inexpensive

Physicists use huge devices called particle accelerators to explore the ultimate building blocks of matter. (2)

4. In line 1 the word **ultimate** most nearly means
a. basic   b. final   c. eventual   d. most important

With three straight primary victories the candidate consolidated her position as front-runner for the nomination of her party. (2)

5. The best definition for **consolidated** in line 1 is
a. strengthened   b. united   c. merged   d. combined

Antonyms

*In each of the following groups, circle the word or expression that is most nearly the **opposite** of the word in **boldface** type.*

1. grim
a. happy
b. sad
c. horrified
d. stern

2. substantial
a. large
b. small
c. generous
d. personal

3. spirited
a. amusing
b. lackluster
c. bitter
d. firm

4. grimy
a. mild
b. soiled
c. immaculate
d. matchless

5. scurry
a. scamper
b. fly
c. run
d. trudge

6. orthodox
a. familiar
b. heretical
c. interesting
d. puzzling

7. fruitless
a. successful
b. well-planned
c. exhausted
d. failing

8. uncertainty
a. doubtfulness
b. newness
c. strangeness
d. sureness

9. iota
a. glut
b. result
c. smidgen
d. failure

10. potential
a. possible
b. real
c. new
d. minor

11. prominent
a. wealthy
b. unselfish
c. famous
d. obscure

12. rural
a. urban
b. foreign
c. sizable
d. new

13. malignant
a. harmless
b. dangerous
c. ugly
d. unexplained

14. makeshift
a. temporary
b. durable
c. worthless
d. complicated

15. snare
a. capture
b. kill
c. release
d. feed

16. marginal
a. central
b. laughable
c. secondary
d. unworthy

Word Families

A. On the line provided, write the word you have learned in Units 4–6 that is related to each of the following nouns.

EXAMPLE: reluctance—**reluctant**

1. quaintness _____

2. entreaty, entreatment _____

3. domination, dominator, dominance _____

4. tact, tactfulness _____

5. malignancy (malignance) _____

6. hostility _____

7. consolidation, consolidator _____

8. spirit, spiritedness _____

9. bewilderment _____

10. orthodoxy _____

11. mortification _____

12. prescription, prescriber, prescript _____

13. waywardness _____

14. fallibility _____

15. controversy, controversialist, controversialism, controverter _____

B. On the line provided, write the word you have learned in Units 4–6 that is related to each of the following verbs.

EXAMPLE: begrime—**grimy**

16. controvert _____

17. inflame _____

18. avenge _____

19. radiate _____

20. ally _____

Two-Word Completions

Circle the pair of words that best complete the meaning of each of the following passages.

1. The book is full of highly amusing stories involving many people who were _____ at the time. One of these witty little _____ tells how a famous director once used glue to get an actor to stand on his mark.

a. utmost . . . previews
b. inimitable . . . iotas
c. dominant . . . snares
d. prominent . . . anecdotes

2. "His methods are hardly what I'd call _____ but they do get results," the sales manager remarked about her star salesperson. "If he took a more traditional approach to his job, the company's profits might not be so _____."

a. dynamic . . . disheartening
b. quaint . . . marginal
c. orthodox . . . substantial
d. controversial . . . fruitless

3. I know that an injection of novocaine doesn't normally _____ a great deal of pain. Still, the mere thought of the dentist's sharp needle is enough to make me _____ in imaginary discomfort.

a. inflict . . . wince
b. consolidate . . . scurry
c. eradicate . . . maul
d. procure . . . scrimp

4. "The President's new economic program has stirred up a good deal of _____ on Capitol Hill," the reporter observed. "Some of the members of Congress are clearly in favor of the plan; others are definitely _____ to it."

a. vengeance . . . anonymous
b. controversy . . . hostile
c. bewilderment . . . malignant
d. uncertainty . . . reluctant

5. Despite setbacks that would have _____ a less determined person, she continued to do her _____ to become the top tennis player in the world. As she herself admitted, she knew that she wouldn't succeed unless she gave the task her "very best shot."

a. mortified . . . potential
b. entreated . . . ultimate
c. frustrated . . . virtual
d. disheartened . . . utmost

6. Two convicts escaped from the state prison last week. The police managed to recapture one of the _____ in a matter of hours. Yet their efforts to catch the other have so far proved _____.

a. buffoons . . . fallible
b. counterfeits . . . void
c. fugitives . . . fruitless
d. dupes . . . wayward

Building with Classical Roots

scrib, scribe, script—to write

This root appears in **prescribe** (page 66). Literally "to write before," this word means "to set down as a rule, order for medical treatment, or give medical advice." Some other words based on the same root are listed below.

circumscribe	inscription	proscribe	subscribe
indescribable	postscript	script	transcribe

From the list of words above, choose the one that corresponds to each of the brief definitions below. Write the word in the blank space in the illustrative sentence below the definition.

1. handwriting; a manuscript of a play or movie

The actor read the _____ before he decided to star in the new movie.

2. to draw a line around, encircle; to confine within limits, restrict

Some students need to _____ their after-school activities.

3. to write out or make a typewritten copy of; to write in another alphabet

The assistant will need to _____ her shorthand notes before inputting the information.

4. that which is written on a monument, coin, building; a dedication in a book

The _____ on the monument is short and to the point.

5. to sign one's name; to express agreement or approval; to promise to take or to pay for

My parents _____ to several newsmagazines.

6. beyond description

The joy the winning team felt was _____ .

7. to outlaw, forbid, prohibit; to banish

Building codes _____ that type of flimsy construction.

8. an addition to a letter written after the writer's name has been signed

The _____ that she added to her letter was so long that it took up an entire page.

From the list of words on page 78, choose the one that best completes each of the following sentences. Write the word in the space provided.

1. The _____ in the book identifies it as a birthday gift my father gave to his father 40 years ago!

2. We cannot _____ to a plan that would be unfair to so many teenagers.

3. Because I had forgotten to ask a key question in the letter, I added it as a(n) _____ at the bottom.

4. The police inspector _____ an area of the street map in which the suspect most likely would be found.

5. The director made several changes in the _____ to adapt the play to a smaller cast.

6. The foreign language specialist will _____ the Russian names into our alphabet.

7. The dictator will _____ all public meetings other than the ones he himself orders.

8. It is impossible to portray in words the way that the sunset filled the sky with those _____ colors!

---

*Circle the **boldface** word that more satisfactorily completes each of the following sentences.*

1. Our coach used chalk to (**subscribe, circumscribe**) the boundaries of the playing field.

2. Interviewers know that it is important to (**proscribe, transcribe**) their notes soon after the interview is completed.

3. The duke was exiled from his country and (**proscribed, circumscribed**) from ever returning.

4. It is the job of the poet to put the (**indescribable, postscript**) into words.

5. The (**postscript, inscription**) on the pharaoh's tomb had been written in hieroglyphics.

6. The information in the (**inscription, postscript**) is so important that it should have been included in the actual body of the letter.

7. My parents heartily (**subscribe, proscribe**) to the idea of strict discipline.

8. It was difficult for the performer to recite her lines without glancing at the (**script, postscript**).

Writer's Challenge

Read the following sentences, paying special attention to the words and phrases underlined. From the words in the box below, find better choices for these underlined words and phrases. Then use these choices to rewrite the sentences.

		WORD BANK		
alliance	dishearten	pending	rural	ultimate
anecdote	entreat	potential	scurry	utmost
anonymous	fickle	prominent	spirited	void
controversial	grim	reluctant	tactful	wince

Casey Jones

1. A full of life and vigor song about a heroic railroad engineer turned J. L. "Casey" Jones into an American legend.

   _____

   _____

2. Engine wiper Wallace Saunders wrote a popular musical account describing Jones, a man with years of experience as a railroad worker, doing his highest on his last fateful trip.

   _____

   _____

3. On April 29, 1900, Casey Jones headed south from Memphis on a routine run of the Cannonball Express that normally might have been canceled of excitement.

   _____

   _____

4. Jones left late that night, but he believed that his skill and a light load gave him the possible capability to arrive on schedule.

   _____

   _____

5. As Engine 382 neared Vaughan, Mississippi, a warning blast alerted Casey Jones to the ferocious reality that a freight train lay stalled on the track directly ahead.

   _____

   _____

6. Jones nagged Sim Webb, the fireman, to jump to safety, but Casey himself stayed on, trying desperately to stop the train.

   _____

   _____

7. Jones paid the most extreme price that morning—but his heroic actions prevented any other deaths when the trains crashed.

   _____

   _____

Analogies *In each of the following, circle the item that best completes the comparison.*

1. quaint is to **charm** as
a. marginal is to bulk
b. anonymous is to interest
c. malignant is to use
d. animated is to liveliness

2. inimitable is to **unique** as
a. makeshift is to potential
b. customary is to strange
c. interminable is to endless
d. miscellaneous is to indignant

3. lead is to **docile** as
a. separate is to mutual
b. preview is to orthodox
c. overlook is to prominent
d. dupe is to gullible

4. fruitless is to **barren** as
a. substantial is to trivial
b. grimy is to immaculate
c. adjacent is to distant
d. transparent is to clear

5. missile is to **pelt** as
a. feather is to maul
b. net is to snare
c. firebrand is to douse
d. hose is to singe

6. anecdote is to **biography** as
a. homicide is to forgery
b. epic is to lyric
c. alliance is to treaty
d. toast is to oration

7. dissuade is to **stubborn** as
a. dishearten is to confident
b. retard is to slow
c. indulge is to selfish
d. dupe is to shallow

8. bewilder is to **uncertain** as
a. irritate is to peevish
b. control is to wayward
c. procure is to reluctant
d. dominate is to hostile

9. humdrum is to **stimulation** as
a. spirited is to energy
b. literate is to intelligence
c. grim is to charm
d. sullen is to anger

10. poised is to **mortify** as
a. determined is to frustrate
b. certain is to verify
c. fallible is to recompense
d. controversial is to counterfeit

Choosing the Right Meaning *Read each sentence carefully. Then circle the item that best completes the statement below the sentence.*

When we open *Alice in Wonderland*, we leave behind the trivial world to which we are accustomed and inhabit for a time the fantastical, topsy-turvy universe of the author's (2) imagination.

1. In line 1 the word **trivial** most nearly means
  a. minor   b. petty   c. ordinary   d. real

Alice's adventures in Wonderland begin when she chases after a white rabbit, dressed in a waistcoat, that has come pelting by. (2)

2. The phrase **pelting by** in line 2 is used to mean
  a.shedding its fur   b. throwing things   c. nibbling   d. hurrying by

No matter how vivid and lifelike it may seem, "virtual reality" is no more substantial than a dream. (2)

3. The word **substantial** in line 1 is best defined as

a. important   b. prosperous   c. tangible   d. affordable

Of all the notions that humankind has ever pondered, is there any so fugitive as time?

4. The word **fugitive** in line 1 is best defined as

a. wandering   b. elusive   c. fleeting   d. puzzling

The quaint machines that Leonardo da Vinci sketched in his notebooks show him to have been as accomplished an inventor as he was a painter. (2)

5. In line 1 the word **quaint** most nearly means

a. old-fashioned   b. picturesque   c. odd   d. ingenious

Two-Word Completions

Circle the pair of words that best complete the meaning of each of the following sentences.

1. Just as a surgeon might remove a(n) _____ tumor from our bodies, we must _____ the cancer of racial and religious prejudice from our hearts and minds.

a. fugitive . . . singe
b. wayward . . . germinate
c. indispensable . . . void
d. malignant . . . eradicate

2. She used to be a very cheerful and confident young woman, but she has been so _____ of late by ill health and financial worries that she has lost a good deal of her _____ good humor and optimism.

a. disheartened . . . sullen
b. unscathed . . . virtual
c. plagued . . . customary
d. frustrated . . . vicious

3. Eventually, I _____ them from attempting to retaliate for the wrong done to them by reminding them of a famous passage in the Bible, in which God says, "_____ is mine; I will repay."

a. animated . . . Truce
b. dissuaded . . . Vengeance
c. culminated . . . Homicide
d. seethed . . . Recompense

4. Gaius Julius Caesar's rivals in the Senate bitterly criticized the political _____ he formed with Pompey and Crassus as a thinly veiled attempt to overthrow the Republic and _____ the Roman world by becoming its undisputed masters.

a. dynasty . . . eradicate
b. alliance . . . dominate
c. regime . . . hurtle
d. iota . . . disrupt

5. The _____ of Cicero's reputation as one of the foremost public speakers of his day shines as bright today as it did on the day he first delivered that famous _____ more than 2000 years ago.

a. luster . . . oration
b. uncertainty . . . anecdote
c. radiance . . . ingredient
d. prominence . . . résumé

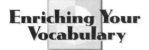

Enriching Your Vocabulary

Read the passage below. Then complete the exercise at the bottom of the page.

Once Upon a Time . . .

Stories have been called the building blocks of knowledge and the foundation of learning. The hearing and telling of stories has been an essential part of life for as far back in human history as we can imagine. Stories allow us to pass on accumulated wisdom, beliefs, and values. Stories can instruct, entertain, amaze, prompt, and inspire us.

At their core, all stories are words linked together to convey ideas. Because there are so many kinds of stories and purposes for their telling, our language has evolved to include a range of story-related words. An *anecdote* (Unit 5) is a short account of an incident in someone's life. A biography is the true story of someone's lifetime. What would you expect to hear in a saga?

Have you even been chatting with others when someone says, "That reminds me of the time . . ." and the pleasant give-and-take of storytelling begins? Perhaps your cousin recalls the occasion of catching a trout last

A whopper!

summer. As the story is retold and embellished, the modest one-pound fish soon evolves into a ten-pound whopper. Now, that's a fish story! After you stop rolling your eyes, you may counter with the instructive fable about the boy who cried wolf. Or you may seek out a scientific article that provides facts about the largest fish ever measured.

In Column A below are 10 more story-related words. With or without a dictionary, match each of these words with its meaning in Column B.

Column A	Column B
_____ **1.** fable	**a.** an informal story "spun" out in a casual way
_____ **2.** allegory	**b.** a short literary scene or description
_____ **3.** tall tale	**c.** a story that illustrates a moral or religious lesson
_____ **4.** memoir	**d.** a story about a memorable character—real or fictional
_____ **5.** yarn	**e.** a recollection of events in a writer's own life
_____ **6.** vignette	**f.** a symbolic story told to represent principles or ideas
_____ **7.** parable	**g.** a story, often with animal characters, that teaches a moral
_____ **8.** legend	**h.** a hard-to-believe story filled with exaggeration
_____ **9.** narrative	**i.** a long story of adventure and heroic events
_____ **10.** saga	**j.** a recounting of events and experiences in story form

Definitions

Note carefully the spelling, pronunciation, part(s) of speech, and definition(s) of each of the following words. Then write the word in the blank space(s) in the illustrative sentence(s) following. Finally, study the lists of synonyms and antonyms given at the end of each entry.

1. amiss
(ə mis′)

(*adj.*) faulty, imperfect, not as it should be; (*adv.*) in a mistaken or improper way, wrongly

Under the circumstances it would not be

_____ to offer our congratulations.

SYNONYM: (*adj., adv.*) awry
ANTONYM: (*adv.*) properly

2. brawl
(brôl)

(*n.*) a noisy quarrel or fight; (*v.*) to quarrel or fight noisily

The noise coming from the classroom sounded more like a

_____ than a debate.

SYNONYMS: (*n.*) scuffle, donnybrook; (*v.*) spar, scrap

3. detest
(di test′)

(*v.*) to hate, dislike very much, loathe

Children who dislike green vegetables often

_____ spinach.

SYNONYMS: despise, abhor
ANTONYMS: relish, love, admire, esteem

4. domestic
(də mes′ tik)

(*adj.*) native to a country, not foreign; relating to the life or affairs of a household; (*n.*) a household servant

The newspaper is filled with information about our country's

_____ affairs.

When my grandmother first came to this country, she took a

job as a _____.

SYNONYMS: (*adj.*) household, native; (*n.*) servant
ANTONYMS: (*adj.*) foreign, alien

5. flagrant
(flā′ grənt)

(*adj.*) extremely bad, glaring; scandalous, notorious

Crossing against the light shows a

_____ disregard for the law.

SYNONYMS: blatant, gross, outrageous
ANTONYMS: petty, piddling, trifling, inconsequential

6. flaw
(flô)

(*n.*) a slight fault, defect, crack

We noticed a _____ in the plan to
start building the house before the spring rains.

SYNONYMS: imperfection, blemish
ANTONYMS: faultlessness, perfection

7. fledgling
(flej′ liŋ)

(*n.*) an inexperienced person, beginner; a young bird about to leave the nest; (*adj.*) inexperienced, budding

We placed the _____ back in its nest.

A _____ police officer appeared on the scene and wisely called for assistance.

SYNONYMS: (*n.*) novice, tyro, neophyte
ANTONYMS: (*n.*) pro, expert, veteran

8. fluster
(fləs′ tər)

(*v.*) to make or become confused, agitated, or nervous; (*n.*) a state of confusion or agitation

During the trial, the judge told the attorney not to

_____ the witness.

SYNONYMS: (*v.*) agitate, rattle, disconcert
ANTONYMS: (*v.*) reassure, soothe, quiet

9. foremost
(fôr′ mōst)

(*adj.*) chief, most important, primary; (*adv.*) in the first place

Music is _____ among my interests.

First and _____ , you must call home to let your family know you'll be late.

SYNONYMS: (*adj.*) leading, principal, paramount
ANTONYMS: (*adj.*) hindmost, last, secondary

10. momentum
(mō ment′ əm)

(*n.*) the force or speed with which something moves

The presidential campaign gained

_____ once the first primary was over.

SYNONYMS: drive, thrust, impetus

11. notable
(nōt′ ə bəl)

(*adj.*) striking, remarkable; (*n.*) a person who is well known, distinguished, or outstanding in some way

Being chosen for the team was a

_____ event in our lives.

The party was attended by _____ from the film world.

SYNONYMS: (*adj.*) noteworthy, impressive
ANTONYMS: (*adj.*) undistinguished, unremarkable; (*n.*) unknown

12. nurture
(nər′ chər)

(*v.*) to bring up, care for, train, nourish; (*n.*) rearing, training, upbringing

It is wonderful to watch chimpanzees

_____ their young.

The _____ they received as children served them well as they grew into adulthood.

SYNONYMS: (*v.*) raise, rear, foster
ANTONYMS: (*v.*) neglect, ignore, discourage, hinder

13. paradox
(par′ ə däks)

(*n.*) a self-contradictory statement that on closer examination proves true; a person or thing with seemingly contradictory qualities

It is a _____ to say that youth is wasted on the young.

SYNONYMS: riddle, enigma, anomaly, absurdity

14. perjury
(pər′ jə rē)

(*n.*) the act of swearing to a lie

The witness was convicted of _____ and was sentenced to serve two years in prison.

SYNONYM: false witness

15. presume
(pri züm′)

(*v.*) to take for granted, assume or suppose; to dare, take upon oneself, take liberties

The counselors _____ that the job they had last summer will be theirs this summer as well.

SYNONYMS: surmise, trespass, infringe

16. prior
(prī′ ər)

(*adj.*) earlier, former

Unfortunately, the governor had a _____ appointment and could not meet with the class.

SYNONYMS: previous, anterior
ANTONYMS: subsequent, later, ensuing, following

17. proficient
(prə fish′ ənt)

(*adj.*) skilled, expert, or capable in any field or activity

Dad knows his way around the kitchen and is quite a _____ cook.

SYNONYMS: competent, adept, able
ANTONYMS: incompetent, inept, unskilled, ignorant

18. salvo
(sal′ vō)

(*n.*) a burst of gunfire or cannon shot, often as a tribute or salute; a sudden burst of anything; a spirited verbal attack

The audience erupted in a _____ of laughter.

SYNONYMS: barrage, volley

19. vigilant
(vij′ ə lənt)

(*adj.*) wide-awake, alert, watchful

The _____ guards paced back and forth in front of the barracks.

SYNONYMS: attentive, on one's toes
ANTONYMS: sleepy, inattentive, unobservant

20. wrath
(rath)

(*n.*) intense anger

In Greek and Roman myths characters fear the _____ of the gods.

SYNONYMS: rage, fury, ire, choler, indignation
ANTONYMS: favor, approval, pleasure, blessing

 **Completing the Sentence**

From the words for this unit, choose the one that best completes each of the following sentences. Write the word in the space provided.

1. In the old days, wooden battleships saluted their victorious admiral by repeatedly firing _____ of cannon shot from their decks.

2. It's a fact that some important battles of the American Revolution occurred _____ to the signing of the Declaration of Independence.

3. I must warn you again that if you fail to tell the truth, you may lay yourself open to a charge of _____.

4. I wouldn't call such a(n) _____ and premeditated lie merely a "minor lapse of memory."

5. The minister saw from the statistics that imported goods were cutting into the _____ market.

6. Her parents _____ her musical talents by hiring the finest teachers and taking her to hear the performances of great musicians.

7. Some people truly love the music of such modern composers as Arnold Schoenberg or Igor Stravinsky; others absolutely _____ it.

8. We must be _____ in recognizing the early signs of decay in our community and move quickly to improve conditions.

9. I have no way of knowing for sure why she left, but I _____ that she had a good reason for doing so.

10. I well remember how often during my childhood I felt the full force of my parents' _____ when I had done something wrong.

11. In most respects she is a fine person, but excessive stubbornness is the one important _____ in her character.

12. We suspected that something was _____ when he did not return home from school at the usual time.

13. Like a(n) _____ eagle about to leave the nest for the first time, our son is preparing to spend his first summer away from home.

14. At what point does a spinning top lose sufficient _____ to topple over?

15. When two players suddenly started to throw punches at each other during last night's game, an ugly bench-clearing _____ ensued.

16. The speaker went right on with his speech, in no way _____ or disturbed by the jeers and catcalls of a few rowdy hecklers.

17. Though his career as a whole was not particularly distinguished, he did score one _____ success on Broadway a few years ago.

18. How do you explain the fact that some students who do poorly in math are highly

_____ in figuring out batting averages?

19. _____ among her many outstanding qualities is her ability to understand the points of view of other people.

20. That terrible instruments of war should in fact prove useful as guardians of the peace is one of the _____of modern life.

Synonyms

*Choose the word from this unit that is **the same** or **most nearly the same** in meaning as the **boldface** word or expression in the given phrase. Write the word on the line provided.*

1. felt his enemy's **fury** _____

2. continued to roll due to its own **force** _____

3. under the eye of the **watchful** officer _____

4. did not **rattle** the experienced pilot _____

5. was responsible for a variety of **household** chores _____

6. witnessed a violent street **scuffle** _____

7. committed the act of **lying** during the trial _____

8. a really **impressive** effort _____

9. became a **skilled** gymnast after much practice _____

10. not trust the script to **inexperienced** screenwriters _____

11. was **supposed** to be an expert on dolphins _____

12. sought to **foster** the fragile relationship _____

13. a philosophy steeped in **enigma** _____

14. suspected that something had gone **awry** _____

15. released a **barrage** of rockets _____

Antonyms

*Choose the word from this unit that is **most nearly opposite** in meaning to the **boldface** word or expression in the given phrase. Write the word on the line provided.*

16. began to **admire** the new leader's policies _____

17. had no **subsequent** arrests _____

18. noticed the **perfection** in her character _____

19. committed a **petty** violation of the law _____

20. an issue of **secondary** importance _____

Choosing the Right Word

Circle the **boldface** word that more satisfactorily completes each of the following sentences.

1. Under the American system of justice, any person accused of a crime is (**presumed, flawed**) to be innocent until proven guilty.

2. She may have given wrong information in court, but this was an honest mistake and certainly does not make her guilty of (**perjury, wrath**).

3. How can you expect the court to excuse your repeated and (**flagrant, vigilant**) violations of the traffic laws?

4. As support for our candidate continued to gain (**momentum, salvo**), it soon became clear that she would win the election by a landslide.

5. Please don't take it (**amiss, notably**) if I suggest that your French accent sounds more like Paris, Texas, than Paris, France.

6. I can forgive an honest mistake, but I (**presume, detest**) any attempt to cover up errors by lying.

7. I am disturbed by the (**momentum, paradox**) of impoverished people in the richest land on Earth.

8. Since there had been no (**prior, proficient**) notice of the scholarship competition, we had practically no time to prepare for it.

9. *Romeo and Juliet* opens with members of the rival houses of Montague and Capulet (**brawling, perjuring**) in the streets of Verona.

10. Abraham Lincoln had very little formal schooling, but his mind was (**nurtured, flawed**) by such great works as the Bible and the plays of Shakespeare.

11. The easternmost tip of Cuba was the first populated area in the region to feel the (**paradox, wrath**) of Hurricane Zelda.

12. She worked so easily and quietly that at first we did not realize how remarkably (**proficient, amiss**) she was in the laboratory.

13. It was hard to believe that the small, rather ordinary-looking person who was standing before us was a world-famous (**notable, fledgling**).

14. The charges of incompetence the candidate leveled at her opponent were but the opening (**brawl, salvo**) in her campaign to become mayor.

15. No parent can ever be (**vigilant, amiss**) enough to prevent a small child from taking many a painful tumble.

16. The rather skinny boy whom we had noticed only two years before as a (**prior, fledgling**) quarterback was now an all-American!

17. A happy (**domestic, nurture**) life can afford an executive a great deal of relief from the everyday strains of running a large company.

18. To say that the U.S. Constitution is one of the greatest documents of all time does not mean that it is entirely without (**momentum, flaws**).

19. Though I hadn't expected to be treated quite so unkindly by the audience, I didn't become (**flustered, nurtured**) or lose my professional cool.

20. (**Foremost, Flagrant**) among the reasons that so many millions of immigrants have come to the United States is the desire for freedom.

Vocabulary in Context

Read the following passage, in which some of the words you have studied in this unit appear in **boldface** type. Then complete each statement given below the passage by circling the letter of the item that is **the same** or **almost the same** in meaning as the highlighted word.

The Space Race

(Line)

Have you ever heard of the Cold War? If so, then you are familiar with one of the greatest **paradoxes** of the twentieth century: from 1948 to 1989, a war without warfare existed between the United States and the Soviet Union.

A **notable** feature of the Cold War was the race to explore space. On October 4, (5) 1957, the Soviets launched the space race by putting the world's first satellite, *Sputnik*, into orbit around the earth. Not to be outdone, the United States retaliated by sending into space a satellite of its own. Also in 1958, Congress established the National Aeronautics and Space Administration (NASA). The main task of the **fledgling** agency was to keep up with the Soviets in the space race.

NASA faced its first great challenge in (10) 1961. In April the Soviet cosmonaut Yuri Gagarin became the first person to orbit the earth, giving the space race new **momentum**.

Less than a month after Gagarin's flight, (15) Alan Shepard became the first American to make a space flight. Nine months later, John Glenn made three orbits of the earth. During this time, President John F. Kennedy proclaimed that the **foremost** goal of the (20) nation's space program was to land a man on the moon before the end of the decade. The question in the minds of Americans was, could the nation meet the President's challenge? Americans also wondered if (25)

Buzz Aldrin on the moon, July 20, 1969

NASA could land an astronaut on the moon *before* the Soviets.

Then just as the decade was ending, NASA achieved its greatest triumph. On July 20, 1969, the spacecraft *Eagle* landed on the surface of the moon. With millions watching around the world, Neil Armstrong took his famous moonwalk. With Armstrong's first step, the Americans had won the space race. (30)

1. The meaning of **paradoxes** (line 2) is
   a. statements
   b. lies
   c. contradictions
   d. donnybrooks

2. Notable (line 4) is best defined as
   a. trifling
   b. noteworthy
   c. petty
   d. foreign

3. Fledgling (line 9) most nearly means
   a. budding
   b. high-flying
   c. birdlike
   d. experienced

4. Momentum (line 14) is best defined as
   a. perfection
   b. minute
   c. importance
   d. impetus

5. The meaning of **foremost** (line 20) is
   a. paramount
   b. secondary
   c. last
   d. valued

Definitions

Note carefully the spelling, pronunciation, part(s) of speech, and definition(s) of each of the following words. Then write the word in the blank space(s) in the illustrative sentence(s) following. Finally, study the lists of synonyms and antonyms given at the end of each entry.

1. abnormal
(ab nôr′ məl)

(*adj.*) not usual, not typical, strange

For my sister, who is always late, being early for an appointment would constitute an

_____ situation.

SYNONYMS: freakish, unnatural, irregular, anomalous
ANTONYMS: normal, usual, regular, typical

2. capsize
(kap′ sīz)

(*v.*) to turn bottom side up, upset

Anyone watching could see that it was our inexperience that caused us to _____ the canoe.

SYNONYMS: overturn, upend, tip over
ANTONYM: remain upright

3. catastrophe
(kə tas′ trə fē)

(*n.*) a large-scale disaster, misfortune, or failure

During the Cold War, the United States did everything possible to avoid a nuclear _____ .

SYNONYMS: calamity, tragedy, cataclysm
ANTONYMS: triumph, victory, success

4. decrease
(*v.*, di krēs′;
n., dē′ krēs)

(*v.*) to become or make less; (*n.*) a lessening

The manager hopes that theft will

_____ once the new security system is installed.
Because of a sharp _____ in sales, the company had to lay off two-thirds of its workers.

SYNONYMS: (*v.*) lessen, reduce, dwindle, diminish
ANTONYMS: (*v.*) increase, grow, develop, wax

5. disputatious
(dis pyü ta′ shəs)

(*adj.*) inclined to argue or debate; provoking debate

The _____ senator had engaged in filibusters to block the passage of many a bill.

SYNONYMS: argumentative, quarrelsome, contentious
ANTONYMS: nonargumentative, peaceable, pacific

6. eject
(i jekt′)

(*v.*) to drive or throw out, evict

The security guards arrived to _____ the troublesome spectator from the stands.

SYNONYMS: oust, expel, kick out
ANTONYMS: admit, let in, insert

7. flourish
(flər' ish)

(v.) to grow, thrive, be prosperous; to wave in the air;
(n.) a dramatic gesture; a fanfare of horns

It is fortunate for lovers of the arts that painting and opera still _____ in Italy.

Actors often enter the stage with a

_____ .

SYNONYMS: (v.) prosper, burgeon, increase
ANTONYMS: (v.) wither, die, fade, shrivel up

8. incentive
(in sen' tiv)

(n.) a reason for doing something; something that stimulates action

Because career advancement is such a strong

_____, adults are usually eager and hard-working students.

SYNONYMS: stimulus, spur, motive, inducement
ANTONYMS: curb, check, restraint, hindrance

9. insubordinate
(in sə bôrd' ən ət)

(adj.) disobedient, rebellious

The _____ soldier repeatedly interrupted his commanding officer.

SYNONYMS: defiant, unruly, mutinous
ANTONYMS: obedient, submissive, docile, tractable

10. legible
(lej' ə bəl)

(adj.) easily read

In keeping with the jokes, pharmacists will tell you that most doctors' handwriting is barely

_____ .

SYNONYMS: readable, clear, decipherable
ANTONYMS: unreadable, indecipherable

11. nub
(nəb)

(n.) the central point or heart of a matter; a knob

After seemingly endless digressions, the speaker finally got to the _____ of his argument.

SYNONYMS: core, kernel, nucleus, crux
ANTONYMS: fringe, periphery, edge

12. onslaught
(än' slôt)

(n.) a violent attack; a sudden rush of something

To prepare for the _____ of winter, we replenished our supply of firewood and rock salt.

SYNONYMS: assault, charge, foray, onset

13. ordain
(ôr dān')

(v.) to establish by law; to order or command; to appoint as a priest or minister; to destine

Ancient astrologers believed that the stars could

_____ one's future.

SYNONYMS: anoint, consecrate, enact, decree
ANTONYMS: forbid, veto, cancel

14. outstrip
(aút strip′)

(v.) to get ahead of, do better than, exceed

By offering customers low prices and good terms, the new store hopes to ——————————— the competition.

SYNONYMS: outdo, outperform, outdistance, surpass
ANTONYMS: trail, lag behind

15. pervade
(pər vād′)

(v.) to spread throughout

Pollutants ——————————— the atmosphere of many of our nation's large cities.

SYNONYMS: saturate, permeate, diffuse, imbue

16. prudent
(prüd′ ənt)

(adj.) cautious, careful, showing good sense

It pays to make ——————————— investments.

SYNONYMS: wary, sensible, judicious
ANTONYMS: foolish, unwise, rash, reckless

17. quench
(kwench)

(v.) to put out, extinguish, end

The firefighters will ——————————— the flames with water.

SYNONYMS: douse, stifle, slake
ANTONYMS: ignite, kindle

18. remnant
(rem′ nənt)

(n.) a small part remaining behind

By the end of the war, the rebels had but a ——————————— of their former strength.

SYNONYMS: remainder, residue, leftover, fragment

19. simultaneous
(si məl tā′ nē əs)

(adj.) happening or existing at the same time

The diplomats put on headphones so that they could listen to a ——————————— translation of the speech.

SYNONYM: occurring at the same time, concurrent
ANTONYM: occurring at different times

20. swerve
(swərv)

(v.) to turn aside sharply; (n.) a sharp or sudden turn

Be aware that if you ——————————— too sharply, you may lose control of the car.

The sudden ——————————— of the bus caused some passengers to fall out of their seats.

SYNONYMS: (v.) veer, digress, sheer off

Completing the Sentence

From the words for this unit, choose the one that best completes each of the following sentences. Write the word in the space provided.

1. Even the most _____ businessperson knows that there are times when it is necessary to take chances.

2. American farms continue to produce more and more food, even though the number of people working on them has actually _____.

3. Though we are still the leading producers of various industrial products, other countries are catching up fast and may soon _____ us.

4. Do you really believe that making money is the only _____ that leads people to work hard and try to excel?

5. Let's ignore minor side issues and get to the _____ of the problem as quickly as possible.

6. The secret of the trick is to remove the first card and pick up the second so quickly that the two actions seem to be _____.

7. Trying to avoid an argument with that _____ fellow is like trying to nail oatmeal to the wall.

8. By landing the damaged plane in an open field, the pilot prevented a major _____ from occurring.

9. When my canoe unexpectedly hit a tree stump and _____, I suddenly found myself neck-deep in some very cold and dirty water.

10. The writing on the curious old document had faded badly, but it was still perfectly _____ when held up to the light.

11. As the holidays approached, a feeling of excitement and anticipation seemed to _____ the entire school.

12. The only thing that ever really _____ my thirst on a stifling summer afternoon is a glass of ice-cold lemonade.

13. Although we are used to severe winters, a heavy snowfall this early in the season is quite _____.

14. My brother was _____ a priest after he had completed his studies at the seminary.

15. At the first shock of the enemy's _____, our lines wavered a bit, but they soon recovered and held firm.

16. "If that _____ young hothead had followed my orders to the letter," the general remarked sourly, "we wouldn't be in this fix!"

17. When you want to remove the cassette from the tape deck, just push this button, and the cartridge will _____ automatically.

18. When a deer suddenly ran onto the road, the car _____ quickly to avoid hitting it.

19. After I had eaten my fill, I threw the _____ of my dinner into the dog's bowl.

20. After our team won the last big game of the season, we all ran out onto the field, _____ our pennants and banners jubilantly.

Synonyms

*Choose the word from this unit that is **the same** or **most nearly the same** in meaning as the **boldface** word or expression in the given phrase. Write the word on the line provided.*

1. finally got to the **core** of the matter _____

2. would **outdo** our competitors _____

3. no **stimulus** to continue her studies _____

4. was forced to **veer** to the right _____

5. wants to **oust** the corrupt officials _____

6. two events that were **happening at the same time** _____

7. witnessed the **calamity** of war _____

8. has **readable** handwriting _____

9. tried to **slake** her thirst with water _____

10. strong winds that could **overturn** the boat _____

11. had nothing left but a **fragment** of her pride _____

12. a chance meeting that only fate could **decree** _____

13. clothing **saturated** with the liquid _____

14. held their ground after the initial **assault** _____

15. was reprimanded for being **disobedient** _____

Antonyms

*Choose the word from this unit that is **most nearly opposite** in meaning to the **boldface** word or expression in the given phrase. Write the word on the line provided.*

16. a treaty marked by **peaceable** negotiations _____

17. began to **increase** in size _____

18. was **reckless** in managing her affairs _____

19. plants that will **wither** under your care _____

20. exhibits **natural** behavior _____

*Circle the **boldface** word that more satisfactorily completes each of the following sentences.*

1. To get a good grade, make sure that your composition is interesting in content, correct in grammar and spelling, and (**abnormal, legible**).

2. The high spirits with which we had begun the hike were soon (**pervaded, quenched**) when it began to rain.

3. The only advice I can give you is to take the problems one at a time and deal with each in a sensible and (**prudent, disputatious**) way.

4. After the officials had put a stop to the fight that had broken out, they (**ejected, ordained**) the offending players from the game.

5. As we returned to the dressing room after that terrible first half, the whole atmosphere seemed to be (**pervaded, capsized**) by defeat.

6. "We have become so engrossed in the minor details of the situation that we have left no time to consider the (**nub, incentive**) of the matter," I said.

7. Two of the more (**abnormal, disputatious**) members of the committee soon got into an argument about where to build the new facility.

8. We have made some progress in cleaning up the slums in our community, but that is certainly no reason to (**decrease, eject**) our efforts.

9. The train and the car approached the crossing almost (**simultaneously, prudently**), and a terrible accident seemed unavoidable.

10. When the musicians failed to arrive and the air-conditioning conked out, we realized that the party was becoming a (**nub, catastrophe**).

11. As (**ordained, flourished**) in the U.S. Constitution, the President must be a native-born American at least 35 years old when he or she takes office.

12. The possibility of getting a summer job in an office is all the (**incentive, onslaught**) I need to improve my computer skills.

13. All our hopes and plans were (**capsized, outstripped**) when we learned that we would not be able to attend the music festival.

14. The first (**onslaught, remnant**) of the disease is marked by a severe fever and the appearance of an ugly rash all over the body.

15. With eager students and able teachers, learning will (**flourish, decrease**), even though the school building may be old and shabby.

16. When the elderly pianist began to play, we were saddened to observe that he had only a(n) (**incentive, remnant**) of his once great skill.

17. Even though you may think your supervisor is wrong, you won't be able to hold your job if you act (**simultaneously, insubordinately**).

18. I'm following a very strict study schedule, but I must admit that I (**swerved, flourished**) from it when the play-offs were televised.

19. Doesn't it seem (**abnormal, insubordinate**) for a bright young person to show no interest in taking part in any school activities?

20. Has the ability of human beings to produce new inventions (**quenched, outstripped**) our ability to use them wisely?

*Read the following passage, in which some of the words you have studied in this unit appear in **boldface** type. Then complete each statement given below the passage by circling the letter of the item that is **the same** or **almost the same** in meaning as the highlighted word.*

Also a Woman's War

(Line)

By almost any standards, the Civil War was the greatest **catastrophe** in U.S. history. Destruction **pervaded** the South and led to its economic ruin. More than 600,000 soldiers died in the conflict, and the war left a **disputatious** legacy of racial and sectional bitterness that would last for more than a century. Yet the Civil

(5) War also left another legacy. It opened the way for American women to serve with honor in war. For the first time in U.S. history, scores of women, from the North and the South, actively took part in the war effort.

With the **onslaught** of battle, women came forward in droves to pitch in on the soldiers' behalf. Some, like Sally

(10) Tompkins, established small hospitals. Others, like Mary Livermore and Mary Ann Bickerdyke, organized or ran chapters of soldiers' aid societies.

(15) Even the famous Dorothea Dix, known for being **prudent** in her care of the mentally ill, took charge of the nursing services for all the Federal armies. A great number of women

(20) also looked after their farms or took jobs formerly held by men.

Women caring for wounded Civil War soldiers

Many women, particularly nurses, came dangerously close to the fighting. Clara Barton, who later founded the American Red Cross, regularly put

(25) her life on the line while tending a wounded soldier. Some Northern women disguised themselves as men so that they could fight with Union regiments. For some, the **incentive** was patriotism. For other women, it was to be with their husbands.

Regardless of the role they played in the war, women demonstrated loyalty, bravery,

(30) and skill. They also showed that the Civil War was not just a man's war. It was also a war in which women could serve both on the battlefield and on the home front.

---

1. The meaning of **catastrophe** (line 1) is
  a. triumph   c. tragedy
  b. success   d. battle

2. Pervaded (line 2) most nearly means
  a. ignited   c. outdid
  b. trailed   d. permeated

3. Disputatious (line 3) is best defined as
  a. peaceable   c. burgeoning
  b. contentious   d. triumphant

4. Onslaught (line 8) is best defined as
  a. onset   c. slaughter
  b. ending   d. horrors

5. The meaning of **prudent** (line 16) is
  a. rash   c. lagging
  b. sensible   d. successful

6. Incentive (line 27) most nearly means
  a. pressure   c. hindrance
  b. restraint   d. inducement

Definitions

Note carefully the spelling, pronunciation, part(s) of speech, and definition(s) of each of the following words. Then write the word in the blank space(s) in the illustrative sentence(s) following. Finally, study the lists of synonyms and antonyms given at the end of each entry.

1. accelerate
(ak sel′ ə rāt)

(*v.*) to speed up, cause to move faster; to bring about more quickly

The hikers needed to _____ their pace once it became clear that it would soon rain.

SYNONYMS: step up, quicken, hasten
ANTONYMS: slow down, retard, decelerate

2. bystander
(bī′ stan dər)

(*n.*) one who looks on or observes, a person present but not taking part

The _____ who had witnessed the collision gave his statement to the police.

SYNONYMS: observer, spectator, onlooker
ANTONYM: active participant

3. canvass
(kan′ vəs)

(*v.*) to go through an area in order to procure votes, sales, or opinions; to go over in detail; to discuss

The students volunteered to _____ the neighborhood for our candidate.

SYNONYMS: poll, survey, solicit

4. casual
(kazh′ ə wəl)

(*adj.*) happening by chance or on an irregular basis; showing little concern; informal

A _____ remark made by the mayor was taken out of context and used against him by the press.

SYNONYMS: accidental, haphazard, offhand
ANTONYMS: formal, serious, premeditated, intentional

5. downtrodden
(daůn′ träd ən)

(*adj.*) treated unfairly and cruelly, oppressed

Most of the immigrants at Ellis Island represented the _____ masses yearning to be free.

SYNONYMS: mistreated, ground underfoot
ANTONYMS: uplifted, liberated

6. entice
(en tīs′)

(*v.*) to attract, tempt

To _____ shoppers into the store, salespersons were giving away coupons for free gifts.

SYNONYMS: lure, beguile
ANTONYMS: nauseate, sicken, revolt, repel

7. erode
(i rōd')

(v.) to wear away gradually, eat away

Storms and mud slides _____ the road so that eventually it became impassible.

SYNONYMS: corrode, abrade
ANTONYMS: nurture, promote, encourage

8. flounder
(flaún' dər)

(v.) to thrash about in a clumsy or ineffective way

After suffering much damage in the storm, the small craft was left to _____ about helplessly.

SYNONYMS: wallow, struggle

9. graphic
(graf' ik)

(adj.) lifelike, vivid; relating to the pictorial arts

A witness gave the reporter a _____ account of the destruction caused by the tornado.

SYNONYMS: lively, colorful, descriptive
ANTONYMS: dull, boring, unrealistic, colorless

10. gruesome
(grü' səm)

(adj.) horrible, revolting, ghastly

The _____ crime rocked the ordinarily quiet neighborhood.

SYNONYMS: gory, hideous, grisly
ANTONYMS: pleasant, delightful, appealing

11. melancholy
(mel' ən käl ē)

(adj.) sad, gloomy, unhappy; (n.) sadness, gloominess

It must have been the gloom of the house and the steady rain that made me feel so _____ .

The tune and the lyrics of the song were filled with

_____ .

SYNONYMS: (adj.) depressed, dejected; (n.) dejection, depression
ANTONYMS: (adj.) merry, happy, cheerful; (n.) joy, elation

12. ordeal
(ôr dēl')

(n.) a difficult or painful experience, a trial

The climbers were exhausted by the

_____ .

SYNONYMS: test, hardship
ANTONYMS: pleasure, cinch

13. parch
(pärch)

(v.) to make dry and thirsty; to shrivel with heat

The fields of Oklahoma were _____ by drought in the 1930s.

SYNONYMS: dry up, dehydrate, desiccate
ANTONYMS: soak, drench, saturate, waterlog

14. persist
(pər sist′)

(v.) to continue steadily in a course of action, refuse to stop or be changed; to last, remain

Despite stern warnings from their doctor, the brothers _____ in their bad habits.

SYNONYMS: persevere, keep at it, endure
ANTONYMS: give up, discontinue

15. puny
(pyü′ nē)

(adj.) of less than normal strength or size; of no importance

The wrestler let out a coarse burst of laughter when his _____ opponent entered the ring.

SYNONYMS: undersized, pint-size, small, weak
ANTONYMS: robust, brawny, mammoth, gigantic

16. quibble
(kwib′ əl)

(v.) to evade or belittle a point by twisting words or raising minor objections; (n.) a petty objection

Let's not _____ over details.
The buyer's _____ notwithstanding, the parties soon came to an agreement.

SYNONYMS: (v.) nitpick, split hairs, cavil; (n.) squabble

17. ratify
(rat′ ə fī)

(v.) to approve, give formal approval to, confirm

The legislatures of three fourths of the states must _____ an amendment to the U.S. Constitution.

SYNONYMS: endorse, sanction, uphold
ANTONYMS: cancel, repeal, annul, veto

18. regal
(rē′ gəl)

(adj.) royal, kinglike; fit for a king

The two families pooled their resources to give the bride and groom a truly _____ wedding.

SYNONYMS: majestic, stately, princely, august
ANTONYMS: lowly, humble, abject, servile

19. stifle
(stī′ fəl)

(v.) to smother, prevent from breathing; to hold back or choke off

Unable to _____ her anger, the sculptor lashed out at her harshest critic.

SYNONYMS: strangle, suppress, snuff
ANTONYMS: nurture, promote, encourage

20. vital
(vīt′ əl)

(adj.) having life, living; necessary to life, essential; key, crucial

The treaty is of _____ importance to the security of our nation.

SYNONYMS: indispensable, fundamental
ANTONYMS: nonessential, unnecessary

Completing the Sentence

From the words for this unit, choose the one that best completes each of the following sentences. Write the word in the space provided.

1. In our environment class, we learned that in much of the United States, the topsoil has been badly _____ by natural forces.

2. She gave us a clear, detailed, and _____ picture of what is likely to happen if we fail to come to grips with the pollution problem.

3. As we fought the forest fire, we were practically _____ by the extreme heat and heavy smoke.

4. The President's powers in foreign affairs are limited by the fact that any treaty he may negotiate must be _____ by a two-thirds vote of the Senate.

5. When the inexperienced swimmer realized that he was in very deep water, he panicked and began to _____ about wildly.

6. According to Greek mythology, the Sirens used their remarkable singing voices to _____ unwary sailors to watery graves.

7. Some poets are at their best when dealing with happy events, while others seem to prefer the more _____ side of life.

8. A group of reporters from the local TV station _____ our district for reactions to the proposed changes in the law.

9. As soon as he learned that he was to play the king in the play, his whole personality took on an almost _____ air.

10. The _____ sight that greeted my eyes at the scene of that awful traffic accident gave me nightmares for weeks.

11. He now claims that he was just an innocent _____, but I saw him actually taking part in the fight.

12. If you were spending your own money, rather than mine, you would be more inclined to _____ over the price of the repairs.

13. Though the new halfback looked a little _____ to us, he managed to hold his own against players twice his size and build.

14. Regular visits to the dentist are _____ if you wish to have healthy, good-looking teeth.

15. How can he _____ in denying that he was at the scene of the crime when several people saw him there?

16. Since the twins' birthday party is by no means a formal affair, _____ clothing is in order.

17. The sled _____ with alarming speed as it went down the steep slope.

18. At that tender age I was so shy that I found it a(n) _____ to be introduced to people I'd never met before.

19. After an hour of trudging along the dusty road under the hot sun, we were so _____ that all we could think of was cold water.

20. Although these workers were _____ in their native land, in the United States they are entitled to a fair wage and safe working conditions.

Synonyms

*Choose the word from this unit that is **the same** or **most nearly the same** in meaning as the **boldface** word or expression in the given phrase. Write the word on the line provided.*

1. described the devastation in **vivid** detail   _____

2. a blistering sun that will **desiccate** the land   _____

3. attempted to **hold back** a sob   _____

4. a meeting that seemed **accidental**   _____

5. chastised for a **weak** effort   _____

6. horrified by the **grisly** sight   _____

7. pain that will **endure** despite medication   _____

8. acids that **corrode** its strength   _____

9. could always **tempt** them with homemade cookies   _____

10. was just a **spectator**, not a participant   _____

11. would **nitpick** over the smallest details   _____

12. to **poll** voters for their opinion   _____

13. survived the painful **test**   _____

14. will **hasten** the growth of industry   _____

15. would **wallow** about in the mud   _____

Antonyms

*Choose the word from this unit that is **most nearly opposite** in meaning to the **boldface** word or expression in the given phrase. Write the word on the line provided.*

16. was in a **cheerful** mood after the play   _____

17. expected Congress to **repeal** the legislation   _____

18. read about the **liberated** masses   _____

19. is a **humble** affair from beginning to end   _____

20. thought those details **unnecessary**   _____

Choosing the Right Word

*Circle the **boldface** word that more satisfactorily completes each of the following sentences.*

1. With her (**regal, graphic**) bearing and imperious manner, Elizabeth I looked every inch the queen she in fact was.

2. The soundness of the basic ideas of the U.S. Constitution has been (**ratified, enticed**) by the experience of more than 200 years.

3. "How can you compare a union employee," the factory owner asked, "to the (**downtrodden, melancholy**) serfs and slaves of earlier times?"

4. In a democracy, the average citizen should be an active participant in public affairs, not just a quiet (**bystander, enticer**).

5. She made what proved to be a (**vital, parched**) mistake when she gave the job to one of the applicants without checking his references.

6. In spite of all the setbacks we have had, we must (**persist, quibble**) in our efforts to achieve the goal we have set for ourselves.

7. Aided by diagrams on the chalkboard, she gave a summary of her plan so clear and (**graphic, regal**) that it won the full support of the audience.

8. I find your offer most (**gruesome, enticing**), but my better judgment tells me to have nothing to do with it.

9. Do her efforts to (**accelerate, flounder**) our departure mean that she is trying to help us, or just get rid of us?

10. You will never do well in school so long as your attitude toward your studies remains (**downtrodden, casual**) and unconcerned.

11. If you have prepared properly for the exams, there will be no reason to regard them as a terrible (**quibble, ordeal**).

12. Instead of continuing to (**flounder, accelerate**), we must decide on a goal and start to move toward it.

13. It is hard to believe that this sturdy, six-foot basketball star was a (**vital, puny**) 100-pounder only a few years ago.

14. No doubt he has our best interests at heart, but my faith in him has been (**eroded, persisted**) by repeated evidence of his poor judgment.

15. In spite of the bright sunshine and the happy crowds, a strange mood of (**ordeal, melancholy**) seemed to take possession of me.

16. The dictator used fear and violence to (**stifle, canvass**) discontent among the people he ruled.

17. After weeks of no rain, the (**parched, graphic**) earth turned to dust that was blown away by the strong winds.

18. When I asked you what you meant by those words, I wasn't (**quibbling, ratifying**) but trying to discover what the problem was.

19. I think it showed bad judgment on your part to tell such a (**gruesome, puny**) story to a child who is so easily frightened.

20. The assistant principal (**canvassed, quibbled**) the faculty for ways of improving the educational standards of the school.

*Read the following passage, in which some of the words you have studied in this unit appear in **boldface** type. Then complete each statement given below the passage by circling the letter of the item that is **the same** or **almost the same** in meaning as the highlighted word.*

Giants of the Desert

(Line)

Visitors to the **parched** Sonoran Desert of southern Arizona and northern Mexico marvel at the many-armed giants that give the landscape its unique appearance. These are the giant saguaro cacti. In the dry, rugged desert a saguaro cactus can live for more than 200 years, grow to a height of 60 feet, and have as many as 50 arms.

Amazingly, saguaro cacti **persist** despite the harsh, unforgiving desert climate. Those (5) that have grown to old age have survived drought, freezes, flash floods, and brush fires, as well as the pack rats that eat their seedlings. Like all desert plants, saguaros hoard water. These leafless plants absorb the water through their long roots and store it for use during the desert's long (10) dry spells.

Saguaro cactus in bloom

Naturally, the mighty saguaro is a **vital** part of desert life. In fact, this giant may be home to many animals, including woodpeckers, owls, doves, bats, and insects. In addition, after a (15) saguaro reaches the age of fifty or so, hardy flowers appear at the top of the plant once a year. These flowers **entice** birds, bats, and bees, who come for the nectar and for the tasty flowers with their black seeds. (20)

Although the **regal** saguaros are plentiful in the Southwest, they are, unfortunately, in danger. These giant cacti have great value in landscape gardening, and poachers can earn thousands of dollars by uprooting them and selling them to (25) nurseries. To protect these Southwestern treasures from poachers, agents for the Arizona Department of Agriculture patrol the desert. Theirs is a hard but important job, for without the saguaro many desert creatures would suffer food shortages and loss of nesting sites. The Southwest, too, would lose something of unique importance, since these desert giants have come to symbolize the very essence of this rugged region. (30)

---

1. The meaning of **parched** (line 1) is
a. saturated
b. rugged
c. enclosed
d. dry

2. Persist (line 5) most nearly means
a. expire
b. persevere
c. give up
d. fight

3. Vital (line 12) is best defined as
a. useless
b. humble
c. crucial
d. unique

4. Entice (line 18) most nearly means
a. lure
b. repel
c. sicken
d. uproot

5. The meaning of **regal** (line 21) is
a. tall
b. hardy
c. majestic
d. lowly

Visit us at www.sadlier-oxford.com
for interactive puzzles and games.

REVIEW UNITS 7–9

Analogies

In each of the following, circle the item that best completes the comparison.

1. swerve is to **sideways** as
a. presume is to backwards
b. erode is to inside out
c. ordain is to forwards
d. capsize is to upside down

2. quench is to **wet** as
a. capsize is to dry
b. nurture is to wet
c. parch is to dry
d. flourish is to wet

3. legible is to **read** as
a. audible is to see
b. portable is to carry
c. lovable is to detest
d. notable is to write

4. prudent is to **wisdom** as
a. legible is to sense
b. honest is to perjury
c. wrathful is to patience
d. proficient is to skill

5. foreign is to **domestic** as
a. gruesome is to pleasant
b. regal is to princely
c. foremost is to backhanded
d. simultaneous is to timely

6. eject is to **expel** as
a. presume is to know
b. fluster is to disconcert
c. canvass is to paint
d. pervade is to avoid

7. enraged is to **wrath** as
a. contented is to jealousy
b. downtrodden is to joy
c. detested is to interest
d. depressed is to melancholy

8. prior is to **before** as
a. subsequent is to after
b. simultaneous is to before
c. amiss is to after
d. flagrant is to before

9. bystander is to **observe** as
a. fledgling is to instruct
b. domestic is to referee
c. activist is to participate
d. paradox is to report

10. accelerate is to **faster** as
a. decrease is to slower
b. retard is to faster
c. outstrip is to slower
d. persist is to faster

11. vigilant is to **favorable** as
a. notable is to unfavorable
b. gruesome is to favorable
c. disputatious is to unfavorable
d. abnormal is to favorable

12. brawl is to **war** as
a. setback is to catastrophe
b. movement is to momentum
c. salvo is to salute
d. withdrawal is to onslaught

13. treaty is to **ratify** as
a. trust is to erode
b. check is to countersign
c. goal is to outstrip
d. cane is to flourish

14. dwarf is to **puny** as
a. ogre is to flagrant
b. giant is to colossal
c. fledgling is to proficient
d. bystander is to foremost

15. insubordinate is to **obedience** as
a. prudent is to caution
b. vigilant is to perception
c. foremost is to position
d. casual is to formality

16. vital is to **life** as
a. amiss is to knowledge
b. vigilant is to size
c. graphic is to vividness
d. gruesome is to concern

17. disputatious is to **quibble** as
a. stubborn is to persist
b. slow is to outstrip
c. peaceful is to brawl
d. wrathful is to canvass

18. practice is to **proficient** as
a. experience is to talented
b. dieting is to chubby
c. ability is to sincere
d. study is to knowledgeable

Word Associations

In each of the following groups, circle the word that is best defined or suggested by the given phrase.

1. fit for a king
   a. vital   b. regal   c. proficient   d. disputatious

2. be ever watchful
   a. flagrant   b. persistent   c. vigilant   d. domestic

3. the heart of the problem
   a. ordeal   b. onslaught   c. nub   d. remnant

4. to outdo the competition
   a. outstrip   b. eject   c. erode   d. nurture

5. a sudden or violent attack
   a. onslaught   b. incentive   c. ordeal   d. paradox

6. what is left over
   a. bystander   b. nub   c. remnant   d. incentive

7. something essential
   a. abnormal   b. vital   c. prudent   d. puny

8. could not find a defect
   a. flaw   b. perjury   c. paradox   d. quibble

9. trial by fire or water
   a. incentive   b. quibble   c. ordeal   d. paradox

10. a noisy quarrel or fight
   a. ordeal   b. incentive   c. catastrophe   d. brawl

11. to wear away one's confidence
   a. swerve   b. erode   c. stifle   d. fluster

12. to permeate the house with cooking smells
   a. entice   b. pervade   c. flourish   d. quench

13. to take their innocence for granted
   a. presume   b. pervade   c. quench   d. persist

14. to suppress a yawn
   a. detest   b. stifle   c. entice   d. capsize

15. to douse the flames with water
   a. parch   b. eject   c. outstrip   d. quench

16. a burst of laughter, cheers, or applause
   a. salvo   b. fledgling   c. catastrophe   d. brawl

17. the oppressed masses
   a. fledgling   b. downtrodden   c. insubordinate   d. casual

18. has gone awry
   a. properly   b. well   c. amiss   d. slowly

19. an inducement to make one work harder
   a. salvo   b. momentum   c. nub   d. incentive

20. to bring up and care for a child
   a. ratify   b. nurture   c. ordain   d. flourish

Vocabulary in Context

Read the following passage, in which some of the words you have studied in Units 7–9 appear in **boldface** type. Then complete each statement given below the passage by circling the item that is **the same** or **almost the same** in meaning as the highlighted word.

High Marks for the CCC

(Line)

During the Great Depression of the 1930s, the **domestic** economy was all but destroyed. Joblessness was widespread, and millions of

(5) Americans were hungry. In an effort to address the economic **catastrophe** gripping the nation, President Franklin D. Roosevelt created several ambitious programs

(10) under a policy known as the New Deal. These programs were aimed not only at building the nation's economy but also at uplifting the American spirit.

(15) Although the New Deal provided help to banks, farmers, and failing businesses, perhaps its most **notable** achievement was in the creation of programs to **decrease** the

(20) number of the nation's unemployed. By 1932, 12 million people were jobless, and Roosevelt knew he had to put Americans back to work. Promising "direct, vigorous action" in

(25) his Inaugural Address, the President created a variety of programs to help the jobless and **downtrodden**.

One of the first and most successful of these programs was

(30) the Civilian Conservation Corps, or CCC, which operated from 1933 to 1942. This was a massive public works project that addressed two of the President's interests: promoting

(35) conservation and providing jobs for the nation's unemployed youth. Calling the CCC a civilian "tree army," Roosevelt put the program under the Army's control. Guided by

(40) engineers and experts in forestry and agriculture, nearly 3 million young men between the ages of 17 and 28 went to work. They planted trees, dug canals, conserved soil, cleared

(45) beaches and campgrounds, stocked lakes and rivers with fish, and even restored historic battlefields—and they did it for just $30 a month, warm clothing, and three meals a day.

(50) While the CCC proved an **ordeal** for some, it gave others a lifeline. Unexpectedly, it also proved to be a boon for the nation. As the future would show, it gave the Army much-

(55) needed experience in managing large numbers of recruits, while it also prepared the nation's youth for the military discipline they would soon face in the Second World War.

---

1. The meaning of **domestic** (line 2) is
a. national
b. foreign
c. blatant
d. oppressed

2. Catastrophe (line 7) most nearly means
a. success
b. attack
c. disaster
d. quarrel

3. Notable (line 18) is best defined as
a. competent
b. mammoth
c. attentive
d. striking

4. Decrease (line 19) is most nearly means
a. reduce
b. increase
c. develop
d. tip over

5. Downtrodden (line 27) is best defined as
a. uplifted
b. unhappy
c. oppressed
d. inexperienced

6. The meaning of **ordeal** (line 50) is
a. cinch
b. hardship
c. pleasant experience
d. challenging game

Read each sentence carefully. Then circle the item that best completes the statement below the sentence.

Heavy losses during the Battle of Britain forced the Royal Air Force sometimes to send fledglings up against the German formations. (2)

1. In line 2 the word **fledglings** is best defined as

a. young birds　　b. novice pilots　　c. veteran flyers　　d. damaged fighters

According to the principle of Manifest Destiny—first advanced in the 1840s—the United States was ordained to expand westward to the Pacific. (2)

2. In line 2 the word **ordained** is used to mean

a. ordered　　b. appointed　　c. enacted　　d. fated

I think that the chairperson is doing me an injustice by dismissing my contribution to the project as "puny." (2)

3. The word **puny** in line 2 most nearly means

a. sickly　　b. unimportant　　c. undersized　　d. off the wall

Far from being only casual acquaintances, as they claimed, the two had secretly been in cahoots for years. (2)

4. The word **casual** in line 1 most nearly means

a. occasional　　b. personal　　c. unconcerned　　d. accidental

"There will be no response to the proposal," remarked the diplomat, "until my government has had an opportunity to canvass the terms and conditions." (2)

5. The best definition for the word **canvass** in line 2 is

a. gather　　b. solicit　　c. examine　　d. poll

Antonyms

In each of the following groups, circle the word or expression that is most nearly the **opposite** of the word in **boldface** type.

1. foremost
a. chief
b. last
c. first
d. most popular

2. abnormal
a. strange
b. new
c. interesting
d. commonplace

3. decrease
a. shrivel
b. dwindle
c. change
d. grow

4. fledgling
a. veteran
b. wealthy
c. painless
d. clumsy

5. ratify
a. honor
b. cancel
c. write
d. endorse

6. nurture
a. beguile
b. esteem
c. neglect
d. foster

7. detest
a. adore
b. notice
c. avoid
d. loathe

8. notable
a. experienced
b. up-to-date
c. unimpressive
d. demanding

9. vital
a. unimportant
b. interesting
c. difficult
d. life-or-death

11. prudent
a. sensible
b. wealthy
c. demanding
d. foolish

13. melancholy
a. sleepy
b. sad
c. happy
d. weird

15. proficient
a. fast
b. unskilled
c. expert
d. fearless

10. puny
a. brawny
b. wise
c. intelligent
d. small

12. flagrant
a. youthful
b. petty
c. serious
d. unexplained

14. legible
a. elegant
b. unreadable
c. childish
d. neat

16. wrath
a. favor
b. intelligence
c. position
d. anger

Word Families

A. *On the line provided, write the word you have learned in Units 7–9 that is related to each of the following nouns.*

EXAMPLE: persistence—**persist**

1. proficiency, proficientness   _____

2. priority, prioress, priory   _____

3. flagrancy (flagrance)   _____

4. ratification, ratifier   _____

5. detester, detestastion, destestability, detestableness   _____

6. vigil, vigilance, vigilantness, vigilante, vigilantism   _____

7. presumption, presumer, presumptuousness   _____

8. erosion, erodibility, erosiveness, erosivity   _____

9. enticement   _____

10. abnormality, abnormalness, abnormalcy   _____

11. ejection, ejector, ejectment, ejecta   _____

12. insubordination   _____

13. legibility   _____

14. prudence   _____

15. simultaneity, simultaneousness   _____

B. *On the line provided, write the word you have learned in Units 7–9 that is related to each of the following verbs.*

EXAMPLE: pervade—**pervasive**

16. note   _____

17. perjure   _____

18. domesticate   _____

19. vitalize   _____

20. dispute   _____

Two-Word Completions

Circle the pair of words that best complete the meaning of each of the following passages.

1. As we _____ violently to the right to avoid some rocks that suddenly sprang into view, our canoe _____ and pitched us headlong into the churning waters of the river.

a. flourished . . . flustered
b. canvassed . . . ejected
c. swerved . . . capsized
d. brawled . . . nurtured

2. If you want to stop your automobile, apply the brakes. If you want it to gain _____, step on the _____.

a. momentum . . . accelerator
b. salvo . . . nub
c. wrath . . . flaw
d. incentive . . . paradox

3. When prices go up, the value of our money _____. The higher the cost of living climbs, the more deeply inflation _____ the purchasing power of the dollar.

a. accelerates . . . entices
b. decreases . . . erodes
c. persists . . . perjures
d. flourishes . . . parches

4. My throat became so _____ during that long trek over dusty trails on the hottest day of summer that I firmly believed nothing would ever _____ my thirst!

a. flawed . . . nurture
b. puny . . . decrease
c. parched . . . quench
d. flagrant . . . pervade

5. "An experienced worker doesn't usually have trouble handling a new job with _____," the personnel manager observed. "A beginner, however, will normally _____ around until he or she learns the ropes."

a. prudence . . . quibble
b. proficiency . . . flounder
c. incentive . . . flourish
d. vigilance . . . swerve

6. "It isn't _____ to spend more than you make," I observed. "Only a fool would allow expenses to _____ income."

a. vital . . . fluster
b. amiss . . . stifle
c. abnormal . . . nurture
d. prudent . . . outstrip

Building with Classical Roots

graph, graphy—to write

This root appears in **graphic** (page 99), literally "having to do with writing." The word now means "lifelike or vivid," "relating to graphs or diagrams," or "having to do with the visual arts." Some other words based on the same root are listed below.

autobiography	biography	graphite	pictograph
autograph	geography	graphology	seismograph

From the list of words above, choose the one that corresponds to each of the brief definitions below. Write the word in the blank space in the illustrative sentence below the definition.

1. an account of a person's life written by another person; such writings, collectively

A famous _____ of Abraham Lincoln was written by Carl Sandburg.

2. to write in one's own handwriting; to write one's signature on or in; a signature

Fans hounded the actor for his _____ .

3. the study of handwriting

Police investigators often rely on _____ to help them unlock clues to a criminal's personality.

4. an instrument that records the direction, force, and duration of earthquakes and other earth tremors

A _____ measures the intensity of an earthquake.

5. the story of one's own life written by oneself

Helen Keller's _____ is entitled *The Story of My Life.*

6. the study of the earth's surface, climate, plants, animals, natural resources, people, and industries; the physical features of a place or region

Maps are important tools in the study of _____ .

7. a picture or symbol used to represent an idea in a system of picture writing; a diagram using pictures to represent data

The Lakota used _____ to record important events from their past.

8. a soft, black form of carbon

The "lead" in lead pencils is actually _____ .

From the list of words on page 111, choose the one that best completes each of the following sentences. Write the word in the blank space provided.

1. On Career Day our teacher's handwriting was analyzed by a guest speaker who had studied _____.

2. The _____ of Frederick Douglass, covering his early years, became an instant bestseller.

3. The university's _____ detected that a moderate earthquake had occurred in the Pacific Ocean.

4. _____ can be used as a lubricant when mixed with oil.

5. The young woman begged the star of the musical to _____ her program.

6. A good _____ of Ulysses S. Grant or Robert E. Lee can provide valuable information about the important battles of the Civil War.

7. Our teacher advised us to draw a _____ to help us chart the latest information about population growth in Asia.

8. The _____ of Central America includes rugged mountains.

---

*Circle the **boldface** word that more satisfactorily completes each of the following sentences.*

1. Certain ancient peoples, such as the Egyptians, used (**pictographs, autographs**) in their written messages.

2. Although vacationers might not realize it, they are studying our country's (**autobiography, geography**) when they take to the roads in the summer.

3. (**Autographs, Graphologies**) of famous people such as Abraham Lincoln can fetch high prices at auctions.

4. Networks of (**pictographs, seismographs**) can sometimes help to warn of approaching tidal waves—which are caused by earthquakes.

5. "This (**biography, geography**) gives an accurate history of Leo Tolstoy's life," the librarian said.

6. Old school desks often had a groove into which hot liquid (**graphite, seismograph**) could be poured and then used for writing when cooled.

7. An expert in (**graphology, geography**) once told me that my signature showed me to be a very generous person.

8. *The Diary of a Young Girl* is an example of a(n) (**biography, autobiography**) since it was written by Anne Frank herself.

Writer's Challenge

Read the following sentences, paying special attention to the words and phrases underlined. From the words in the box below, find better choices for these underlined words and phrases. Then use these choices to rewrite the sentences.

		WORD BANK		
capsize	flourish	onslaught	puny	simultaneous
downtrodden	foremost	ordain	quench	vigilant
flagrant	gruesome	prior	regal	vital
fledgling	incentive	proficient	remnant	wrath

Jacques Cousteau (1910–1997)

1. Environmentalists who are <u>on their toes</u> about protecting the oceans and seas owe a great debt to Jacques Cousteau.

_____

_____

2. Cousteau had a lifelong passion for the water, and became quite <u>skilled, expert, or capable</u> at making films as a teenager.

_____

_____

3. His work in the French Navy during World War II helped to further his <u>budding, inexperienced</u> career as an oceanographer.

_____

_____

4. Cousteau made <u>necessary to life</u> contributions to the field of underwater science, including the co-invention of the Aqua-Lung, better known as scuba gear.

_____

_____

5. <u>Earlier</u> to Cousteau's perfection of the breathing device that let divers stay under water for long periods of time, the only way to explore the deep was in a diving bell or a hulking diving suit.

_____

_____

6. Cousteau was a complex, driven man, and <u>things that stimulate action</u> for him were many—patriotism, fame, and a genuine concern for the environment.

_____

_____

7. In time, Cousteau became internationally regarded as the <u>number one</u> explorer and defender of the quiet and unique mysteries of the undersea world.

_____

_____

Analogies

In each of the following, circle the item that best completes the comparison.

1. foretaste is to **preview** as
a. luster is to radiance
b. recompense is to ingredient
c. salvo is to snare
d. iota is to nub

2. incentive is to **goad** as
a. potential is to mortify
b. quibble is to dishearten
c. flaw is to entice
d. hazard is to dissuade

3. drought is to **parched** as
a. deluge is to sodden
b. blizzard is to transparent
c. trickle is to drenched
d. heat wave is to unscathed

4. paradox is to **bewilder** as
a. pleasure is to wince
b. failure is to animate
c. triumph is to brood
d. mishap is to fluster

5. plague is to **catastrophe** as
a. operation is to entertainment
b. vacation is to danger
c. cross-examination is to ordeal
d. appointment is to emergency

6. perjury is to **lie** as
a. forgery is to kidnap
b. robbery is to cheat
c. larceny is to envy
d. homicide is to kill

7. substantial is to **weight** as
a. dynamic is to momentum
b. trivial is to importance
c. makeshift is to solidity
d. marginal is to leeway

8. counterfeit is to **inimitable** as
a. douse is to inflammable
b. replace is to indispensable
c. continue is to interminable
d. see is to inaudible

9. eradicate is to **nurture** as
a. germinate is to flourish
b. browse is to maul
c. stifle is to foster
d. dupe is to hoodwink

10. notable is to **prominent** as
a. tactful is to spirited
b. barren is to void
c. graphic is to simultaneous
d. sullen is to poised

Choosing the Right Meaning

Read each sentence carefully. Then circle the item that best completes the statement below the sentence.

Though Lee's surrender brought to an end the terrible bloodshed of the Civil War, hard feelings between North and South persisted for generations. (2)

1. The best definition for the word **persisted** in line 2 is
a. were unchanged
b. slowly disappeared
c. stubbornly endured
d. flared up

In the plays of Shakespeare, the entrance of a king is often announced by a flourish of trumpets. (2)

2. In line 1 the word **flourish** most nearly means
a. prosperity   b. gesture   c. waving   d. fanfare

"May I presume upon your patience," I inquired of my boss, "to ask you to explain once again why I can't have that raise?" (2)

3. In line 1 the phrase **presume upon** most nearly means
a. safely assume
c. dare
b. take liberties with
d. completely exhaust

The gunnery officer concluded the drill by ordering the launching crew to fire at a drone.

4. In line 1 the word **drone** is used to mean
a. swarm of bees
c. loud humming noise
b. remote-control target
d. loafer

Try as they might, negotiators could not persuade the hostile parties to sit down and talk, much less patch up their differences. (2)

5. The word **hostile** in line 1 is best defined as
a. warring
b. unfavorable
c. suspicious
d. restless

Two-Word Completions

Circle the pair of words that best complete the meaning of each of the following sentences.

1. The little camper's _____ expression and mournful voice told me more eloquently than words could ever have just how much she _____ for home.
a. fickle . . . canvassed
c. melancholy . . . yearned
b. anonymous . . . scurried
d. prudent . . . catered

2. Sometimes, public opinion is so _____ and unpredictable that a candidate who is the darling of the crowd one day may find himself or herself roundly _____ the next.
a. fickle . . . detested
c. proficient . . . prescribed
b. miscellaneous . . . presumed
d. orthodox . . . dominated

3. The violence of the enemy's _____ at first threatened to turn our position and drive us from the field, but we quickly regrouped and _____ a stunning defeat on the foe.
a. vengeance . . . entreated
c. wrath . . . eroded
b. onslaught . . . inflicted
d. remnant . . . consolidated

4. When police _____ the man about his movements on that night, he claimed to have been at a ball game. But officials have failed to _____ his alibi.
a. indulged . . . ratify
c. canvassed . . . pelt
b. ordained . . . swerve
d. interrogated . . . verify

5. The study of history teaches us that laziness and indifference may slowly _____ the rights and privileges of a free people. For that reason, we must be ever _____ in protecting and defending our liberties.
a. hurtle . . . transparent
c. eradicate . . . docile
b. erode . . . vigilant
d. nurture . . . tactful

Enriching Your Vocabulary

Read the passage below. Then complete the exercise at the bottom of the page.

Our Debt to the Greeks

In Greek mythology, Atlas was one of the Titans, a race of mythical giants characterized by brute strength and primitive force. Atlas stood atop a mountain

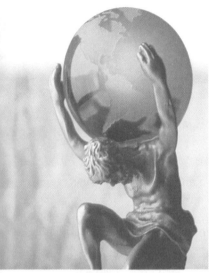

Atlas holding up the world

separating the earth from the heavens. This myth inspired the great 16th-century Flemish geographer Gerhardus Mercator to illustrate the cover of his new book of maps with a drawing of the mighty Atlas balancing a globe on his shoulders.

Classical Greek was the language of ancient Greece. The English language owes a tremendous debt to the Greeks for hundreds of words that have become part of our living language. A *dynasty* (Unit 1) is a powerful family or group of rulers that maintains its position or power for some time. A critic who describes a dance performance as *dynamic* (Unit 6) is conveying that it was vigorous and forceful. Both of these words are based on the Greek root *dyna-* (from the Greek word *dynamikos*), which means power.

Greek mythology has been the source of many English words. For example, Hygeia was the Greek goddess of vigor and well-being. What weakness could you claim as your Achilles heel?

In Column A below are 9 more words borrowed from the Greeks. With or without a dictionary, match each word with its meanings in Column B.

Column A

_____ **1.** tyrant

_____ **2.** titanic

_____ **3.** hygiene

_____ **4.** tragedy

_____ **5.** monopoly

_____ **6.** mosaic

_____ **7.** strategy

_____ **8.** sphere

_____ **9.** chorus

Column B

a. a round, solid figure in which any point on its surface is the same distance from its center; an area of interest

b. a serious play that has a sad ending; any event that is disastrous or terrible

c. a plan of action intended to attain a specific goal

d. a group of people trained to sing together; the part of a song repeated after each verse

e. the science that deals with maintaining good health

f. a decorative picture or pattern made from the artful arrangement of small pieces of tile, glass, wood, or stone

g. total control of a service or product by one company

h. one who exercises power unfairly or cruelly

i. having great size, power, or strength; colossal, gigantic

Definitions

Note carefully the spelling, pronunciation, part(s) of speech, and definition(s) of each of the following words. Then write the word in the blank space(s) in the illustrative sentence(s) following. Finally, study the lists of synonyms and antonyms given at the end of each entry.

1. bellow
(bel′ ō)

(*v.*) to make a sound similar to that of a bull, roar; (*n.*) a loud, angry roar

The wounded buffalo began to _____ in pain.

The troop commander's _____ could be heard a mile away.

SYNONYMS: (*v.*) yell, bawl, holler; (*n.*) howl
ANTONYMS: (*v.*) whisper; (*n.*) murmur

2. beneficiary
(ben ə fish′ ē er ē)

(*n.*) one who benefits from something; a person who is left money or other property in a will or the like

The _____ of the dead man's will was the main suspect in the murder case.

SYNONYMS: recipient, heir

3. botch
(bäch)

(*v.*) to repair or patch poorly; make a mess of; (*n.*) a hopelessly bungled job

The unsupervised laborers proceeded to _____ the job badly.

SYNONYMS: (*v.*) foul up, bungle, mangle

4. clutter
(klət′ ər)

(*v.*) to fill or cover in a disorderly way; (*n.*) a state of disorder, mess

When we moved into our new house, we unloaded the truck and began to _____ up the dining room with boxes.

Attics are often filled with _____.

SYNONYMS: (*v.*) litter; (*n.*) confusion
ANTONYMS: (*n.*) order, tidiness, neatness

5. dilapidated
(də lap′ ə dā tid)

(*adj.*) falling apart or ruined, run-down

The old house had become so _____ that no one could live in it anymore.

SYNONYMS: in disrepair, deteriorated, gone to seed
ANTONYMS: shipshape, trim

6. dismantle
(dis man′ təl)

(*v.*) to take apart; to strip of something

After the final performance, all the actors worked with the stagehands to _____ the set.

SYNONYM: disassemble
ANTONYMS: put together, assemble, construct

7. farce
(färs)

(*n.*) a play filled with ridiculous or absurd happenings; broad or far-fetched humor; a ridiculous sham

The humor in the play was so broad and the plot so ridiculous that the critic termed the play a

_____.

SYNONYMS: buffoonery, mockery
ANTONYMS: tragedy, melodrama, tearjerker

8. futile
(fyüt′ əl)

(*adj.*) not successful, failing to have any result; useless; unimportant, frivolous

After several _____ attempts to save it, the captain ordered the ship abandoned.

SYNONYMS: fruitless, vain, ineffective
ANTONYMS: successful, effective

9. grueling
(grü′ liŋ)

(*adj.*) very tiring, calling for an extreme effort

After the _____ climb, two of the mountaineers collapsed, exhausted.

SYNONYMS: exhausting, punishing, taxing
ANTONYMS: easy, effortless

10. hospitable
(häs pit′ ə bəl)

(*adj.*) offering friendly or generous treatment to guests; open to anything new or strange

Known for their generosity to strangers, the local inhabitants offered a _____ welcome to our tour group.

SYNONYMS: gracious, cordial, courteous
ANTONYMS: unfriendly, cold, icy, chilly

11. lair
(lâr)

(*n.*) the home or den of a wild animal; any hideout

The police were making careful preparations to trap the smugglers in their _____ .

SYNONYMS: nest, burrow, hideaway

12. lavish
(lav′ ish)

(*adj.*) overly generous, extravagant; abundant; (*v.*) to spend or give freely or without limit

The couple received _____ wedding gifts from their closest friends.

SYNONYMS: (*adj.*) excessive, profuse
ANTONYMS: (*adj.*) stingy, meager; (*v.*) begrudge, stint, deny

13. morbid
(môr′ bid)

(*adj.*) in an unhealthy mental state, extremely gloomy; caused by or related to disease, unwholesome

The police captain was afraid that the officer was taking a _____ interest in the crime.

SYNONYMS: depressed, unsound, "sick"
ANTONYMS: wholesome, healthy, cheerful, blithe

14. notorious
(nō tôr′ ē əs)

(*adj.*) widely known because of bad conduct

Chicago had its share of _____ gangsters in the 1930s.

SYNONYMS: disgraceful, infamous, disreputable
ANTONYMS: unknown, obscure, respectable

15. pamper
(pam′ pər)

(*v.*) to allow too many privileges, be too generous and easygoing toward

If my aunt continues to _____ that child, he may grow into an irresponsible adult.

SYNONYMS: coddle, cater to, indulge
ANTONYMS: abuse, maltreat, mistreat, discipline

16. parasite
(par′ ə sīt)

(*n.*) an organism that lives in or on another organism; one who lives off another person

Uninvited, he hung around with the players so much that the team considered him a real _____.

SYNONYMS: sponger, freeloader, leech

17. shirk
(shərk)

(*v.*) to avoid or get out of doing work, neglect a duty; to sneak, slink

People who tend to _____ their responsibilities are not to be relied upon.

SYNONYMS: duck, sidestep
ANTONYMS: fulfill, perform, shoulder, take on

18. surplus
(sər′ pləs)

(*n.*) an amount beyond what is required, excess; (*adj.*) more than what is needed or expected

Dad was relieved to find that his business had a _____ at the end of the year.

The Army decided to sell its _____ goods to a group of manufacturers.

SYNONYMS: (*n.*) glut, surfeit, overage
ANTONYMS: (*n.*) shortage, lack, dearth, paucity

19. timidity
(tə mid′ ə tē)

(*n.*) the state of being easily frightened

The shy child's natural _____ had made her afraid to try out for the team.

SYNONYMS: fearfulness, faintheartedness
ANTONYMS: fearlessness, boldness, intrepidity

20. veto
(vē′ tō)

(*n.*) the power to forbid or prevent; (*v.*) to prohibit, reject

The President decided to _____ the bill presented to him by Congress.

SYNONYMS: (*v.*) turn down, nix, forbid
ANTONYMS: (*v.*) approve, endorse, ratify, confirm

Completing the Sentence

From the words for this unit, choose the one that best completes each of the following sentences. Write the word in the space provided.

1. All the members of that family are such _____ people that we are always completely at ease whenever we visit them.

2. They gave me so _____ a helping of dinner that for the first time in my life I was unable to polish off the food on my plate.

3. As a child she was so _____ by her parents that she still seems to think that her wishes should be instantly granted.

4. The practice session was so _____ that we scarcely had the strength to get to the dressing room and take our showers.

5. It is a curious fact of nature that most _____ are unable to survive when they are separated from the organisms they feed on.

6. The _____ of food produced each year in the United States is desperately needed to feed hungry people all over the world.

7. The President can _____ a measure passed by a majority of Congress, but his _____ may be overridden.

8. It is hard to believe that a teenager so courageous and able on a camping trip can show so much _____ when invited to a dance.

9. Though the cabin was a little _____ when we bought it, we were able to spruce it up without going to a great deal of expense.

10. The animals in the zoo are kept in quarters that are designed to imitate their _____ in the wild state.

11. When he realized that he had been tricked by his opponent, he let out a _____ of rage that could be heard all over the gym.

12. Unfortunately, the brave lifeguard's valiant attempts to rescue the drowning swimmer proved _____ .

13. He is such a _____ liar that no one takes anything he says seriously anymore.

14. Since the defendant was never given a chance to prove his innocence, his so-called "trial" was nothing more than a _____ .

15. The inexperienced assistant _____ the business letter he was trying to compose and had to rewrite it.

16. Many people both here and abroad seem to have a _____ fascination with the tragic fate of the Russian royal family.

17. When I accepted the invitation to join them on the vessel, I didn't realize that I had agreed to help _____ the ship.

18. Ever since the new tax laws went into effect, there has been speculation as to who the real _____ of the changes will be.

19. Why must you _____ up your mind with so many trivial and useless scraps of information?

20. I know what it is that I have to do, and you may be certain that I will not _____ my duty.

Synonyms

*Choose the word from this unit that is **the same** or **most nearly the same** in meaning as the **boldface** word or expression in the given phrase. Write the word on the line provided.*

1. cautiously inspected the **ruined** old building _____

2. would **spend** time and money on her favorite hobby _____

3. took up acting to overcome their **fearfulness** _____

4. will **disassemble** the tent before leaving the campsite _____

5. may **bungle** the assignment if not careful _____

6. was reluctant to **coddle** the spoiled child any further _____

7. received a truly **gracious** welcome _____

8. cleaned up the **mess** in Dad's workroom _____

9. a meeting that turned into a **sham** _____

10. a **punishing** race to the finish line _____

11. stared at the **infamous** figures in the wax museum _____

12. suspected that the wolf had returned to its **den** _____

13. would inherit the estate as his father's **heir** _____

14. dwelt on the **gloomy** details of the story _____

15. would hang on like a **leech** _____

Antonyms

*Choose the word from this unit that is **most nearly opposite** in meaning to the **boldface** word or expression in the given phrase. Write the word on the line provided.*

16. planned to **endorse** the amendment _____

17. would **whisper** orders to his assistant _____

18. produced a **shortage** of wheat that year _____

19. a **successful** effort by any account _____

20. will **shoulder** each and every responsibility _____

Choosing the Right Word

*Circle the **boldface** word that more satisfactorily completes each of the following sentences.*

1. When I think back to my days of basic training, I can almost hear the drill sergeant (**pampering, bellowing**) commands across the field.

2. The campaign to eliminate pollution will prove (**futile, grueling**) unless it has the understanding and full cooperation of the public.

3. Since I was led to believe that she would approve my proposal, I was very much taken aback when it was (**lavished, vetoed**) out of hand.

4. He amazed us by reaching into the pile of (**clutter, lair**) on his desk and pulling out exactly the piece of paper he wanted.

5. The modern TV sitcom developed from the type of broad (**surplus, farce**) that slapstick comedians served up in the 1920s and 1930s.

6. What a difference between the (**timidity, farce**) of the typical freshman and the know-it-all confidence of a senior!

7. The best way to avoid those (**grueling, bellowing**) cram sessions just before the exams is to do your work steadily all term long.

8. When he said he would "beard the lion in his (**lair, clutter**)," he merely meant that he was going to have it out with the boss.

9. Even the toughest critics have been (**lavish, dilapidated**) in their praise of the new movie.

10. He is (**hospitable, notorious**) for his habit of taking small loans from his best friends and then conveniently forgetting about them.

11. It would be impossible to (**pamper, dismantle**) our system of governmental checks and balances without destroying American democracy.

12. The courts of many Renaissance princes were jammed with (**parasites, lairs**), toadies, and other idle hangers-on.

13. I sometimes think that he enjoys being sick and having everyone wait on him, sympathize with him, and (**shirk, pamper**) him.

14. Their record is 100% consistent—they have managed to (**botch, clutter**) every job they have undertaken.

15. We who live in the United States today are the chief (**beneficiaries, parasites**) of the rich heritage of freedom left us by the framers of the Constitution.

16. My experience has been that people who cut corners on small matters will also (**shirk, botch**) their obligations.

17. Ever since I was bitten by a stray mutt, I have had a (**morbid, lavish**) fear of dogs.

18. Beneath the (**dismantled, dilapidated**) body of the getaway car, there was a powerful, finely tuned motor, capable of reaching high speeds.

19. She was indeed fortunate to find herself working under a person who was (**notorious, hospitable**) to her novel ideas.

20. After buying all the supplies for the club party, we were delighted to find that we had a grand (**surplus, veto**) of 65 cents.

Vocabulary in Context

*Read the following passage, in which some of the words you have studied in this unit appear in **boldface** type. Then complete each statement given below the passage by circling the letter of the item that is **the same** or **almost the same** in meaning as the highlighted word.*

The Great Chicago Fire

(Line)

Chicago was a sprawling metropolis in 1871. Yet it was also a city ripe for disaster. First, Chicago was built almost entirely of wood. Wooden grain elevators, lumber mills, hotels, **dilapidated** houses and barns, bridges, and even streets, paved with pine blocks, were perfect sources of kindling. Second, Chicago also
(5)   made, stored, bought, and sold a **surplus** of inflammable goods. As a result, in the hot, dry summer of 1871, Chicagoans had a right to be concerned.

By early October, Chicago's crack firefighters were exhausted, having spent a **grueling** week extinguishing 24 fires. However, on the evening of October 8,
(10)   the firefighters' stamina would be tested again. It is rumored that at 8:30 in the evening, Mrs. O'Leary's cow kicked over a lantern in the barn, starting the Great Chicago Fire. In just
(15)   a few minutes the barn was ablaze. In an hour the entire block was burning. In the street the **bellow** of trapped cows could be heard, as building after building burned. The flames simply
(20)   could not be stopped; all efforts proved **futile**. By the following morning, much of Chicago lay in ashes.

Chicago after the Great Fire, 1871

The Great Chicago Fire was finally checked by rainfall and by the use of gunpowder. Yet the losses were staggering. In all, 300 deaths were reported. More
(25)   than 100,000 people were left homeless, and 17,500 buildings were demolished. But nothing could destroy the will of the people to rebuild the city.

Soon, the rebuilding began. Architects flocked to the city in droves, eager for the chance to build high into the sky. City planners also came. As a result, Chicago became the **beneficiary** of bold new ideas in construction, city planning, and
(30)   technology. In just a few years the city became the open-air gallery of skyscrapers, grand boulevards, and parks that it still is today.

---

1. The meaning of **dilapidated** (line 3) is
  a. messy   c. confused
  b. shipshape   d. run-down

2. Surplus (line 5) most nearly means
  a. lack   c. surfeit
  b. shortage   d. dearth

3. Grueling (line 8) is best defined as
  a. eating   c. long
  b. taxing   d. fearful

4. Bellow (line 17) most nearly means
  a. roar   c. murmur
  b. whisper   d. cough

5. The meaning of **futile** (line 21) is
  a. fruitless   c. fruitful
  b. difficult   d. successful

6. Beneficiary (line 29) most nearly means
  a. official   c. target
  b. recipient   d. enemy

Definitions

Note carefully the spelling, pronunciation, part(s) of speech, and definition(s) of each of the following words. Then write the word in the blank space(s) in the illustrative sentence(s) following. Finally, study the lists of synonyms and antonyms given at the end of each entry.

1. adequate
(ad′ ə kwət)

(*adj.*) sufficient, enough

Be sure to allow _____ time to check in at the airport.

SYNONYMS: satisfactory, sufficing
ANTONYM: insufficient

2. ajar
(ə jär′)

(*adj., adv.*) partly open

That night, the children foolishly left the back gate _____ , and the dog escaped.

ANTONYMS: (*adj., adv.*) closed tight, shut, open wide

3. dialogue
(dī′ ə läg)

(*n.*) a conversation between two or more people; an interchange of opinions and ideas, free discussion

The witty _____ in the play kept the audience amused.

SYNONYM: exchange of ideas
ANTONYMS: monologue, soliloquy

4. emblem
(em′ bləm)

(*n.*) a symbol, sign, token

Like the heart, the red rose is an _____ of love.

SYNONYMS: badge, insignia

5. gigantic
(jī gan′ tik)

(*adj.*) huge, giant, immense

When it fell to earth, the meteorite made a _____ hole in the ground.

SYNONYMS: enormous, colossal, mammoth
ANTONYMS: tiny, infinitesimal, diminutive

6. havoc
(hav′ ək)

(*n.*) very great destruction, ruin; great confusion and disorder

The monkey created _____ at the fair as soon as it broke from its leash.

SYNONYMS: devastation, harm, disarray
ANTONYMS: peace and quiet, calm, order

7. hearth
(härth)

(*n.*) the floor of a fireplace; the fireside as a symbol of the home and family

It was our custom to sit by the _____ and listen to my grandfather's stories.

SYNONYM: chimney corner

8. implore
(im plôr')

(*v.*) to beg earnestly for

The attorney proceeded to _____ the judge to show his client mercy.

SYNONYMS: entreat, beseech, pray
ANTONYMS: demand forcefully, clamor for

9. infamous
(in' fə məs)

(*adj.*) very wicked; disgraceful, shameful

Because of the outlaw's _____ deeds, the town was offering a large bounty for his capture.

SYNONYMS: scandalous, villainous, flagrant, heinous
ANTONYMS: glorious, splendid, illustrious, praiseworthy

10. innumerable
(i nüm' ə rə bəl)

(*adj.*) too many to count, without number

The landlord heard _____ complaints about the noisy new tenant.

SYNONYMS: countless, beyond reckoning
ANTONYMS: countable, few in number

11. lax
(laks)

(*adj.*) not strict, careless; lacking discipline; not tense, relaxed

Some players took advantage of the new coach's somewhat _____ control of the team.

SYNONYMS: slack, negligent, remiss
ANTONYMS: strict, vigilant, conscientious, scrupulous

12. mar
(mär)

(*v.*) to spoil, damage, injure

Spilled cleaning fluid will surely _____ the wooden table top.

SYNONYMS: scar, disfigure, deface
ANTONYMS: beautify, embellish, repair

13. misdemeanor
(mis di mē' nər)

(*n.*) a crime or offense that is less serious than a felony; any minor misbehavior or misconduct

He was not only fined for the _____ but also sentenced to serve 30 days in jail.

SYNONYMS: misdeed, petty offense or transgression
ANTONYMS: felony, serious crime

14. mull
(məl)

(*v.*) to think about, ponder; to grind or mix; to heat and flavor with spices

The governor had some time to _____ over the bill before signing it into law.

SYNONYMS: consider, reflect on

15. narrative
(nar′ ə tiv)

(*n.*) a story, detailed report; (*adj.*) having the quality or the nature of a story

The _____ of the West African captive gives us a vivid picture of the horrors aboard a slave ship.

Henry Wadsworth Longfellow is considered a _____ poet because of the stories he tells in his poems.

SYNONYMS: (*n.*) tale, chronicle

16. overture
(o′ vər chùr)

(*n.*) an opening move toward negotiation or action; a proposal or offer; an introductory section or part

Our family enjoyed the _____ to the opera better than the rest of it.

SYNONYMS: prelude, tender
ANTONYMS: finale, postlude

17. pact
(pakt)

(*n.*) an agreement, treaty

All the nations signed the _____ after the war in an effort to ensure world peace.

SYNONYMS: compact, alliance, deal

18. stalemate
(stāl′ māt)

(*n.*) a situation in which further action by either of two opponents is impossible; (*v.*) to bring to a standstill

The negotiations ended in _____, as both sides refused to budge on the main issue.

Recent aggression on the part of one nation threatened to _____ the peace talks.

SYNONYMS: (*n.*) standoff, draw; (*v.*) deadlock
ANTONYMS: (*n.*) victory; (*v.*) defeat

19. vindictive
(vin dik′ tiv)

(*adj.*) bearing a grudge, feeling or showing a strong tendency toward revenge

The mayor was so _____ that he threatened to sue the newspaper for its unflattering remarks about his administration.

SYNONYMS: vengeful, spiteful, malicious
ANTONYMS: forgiving, relenting

20. wilt
(wilt)

(*v.*) to become limp and drooping (as a flower), wither; to lose strength and vigor

Intense heat or lack of water will _____ the flowers.

SYNONYMS: sag, weaken, shrivel up
ANTONYMS: flourish, bloom, sprout, perk up, revive

Completing the Sentence

From the words for this unit, choose the one that best completes each of the following sentences. Write the word in the space provided.

1. The smoke from the logs burning on the _____ curled slowly upward into the chimney.

2. "The Highwayman" by Alfred Noyes is a(n) _____ poem that tells the story of a woman who sacrifices her life for her sweetheart.

3. In most operettas, the musical numbers are connected to one another by spoken _____ .

4. Though some of Verdi's operas begin with short preludes, for others he composed full-length _____ .

5. The flood had wrought such _____ that the governor of the state declared the stricken region a disaster area.

6. The U.S. entry into World War I broke the _____ on the Western Front and tipped the balance in favor of an Allied victory.

7. Though Hitler's Germany and Stalin's Russia were bitter enemies, the two countries signed a nonaggression _____ in 1939.

8. Can any punishment be too severe for someone who has been guilty of such a(n) _____ crime?

9. Who has not gazed with awe at the _____ stars that fill the sky on a clear summer night!

10. Since I have never done him any harm, I don't understand why he should take such a(n) _____ attitude toward me.

11. Before you leave, be absolutely sure that your supplies of food and water are _____ for an eight-day journey across the desert.

12. The dove is often used as a(n) _____ of peace.

13. No one questions the honesty and good intentions of the mayor, but he has been criticized for being _____ in carrying out his duties.

14. Though my sister started out looking as fresh as a daisy, she began to _____ noticeably after only five minutes in that humidity.

15. On our trip to northern California, we felt very small and unimportant as we stood beside the _____ redwood trees.

16. She _____ the doctor to tell her frankly how badly her son had been hurt.

17. You cannot discipline a group of teenagers by making a capital offense of every _____ .

18. Because the front door was ___*ajar*___ , the cat strolled into the living room.

19. One careless mistake can seriously _____ an otherwise perfect record.

20. Let me have some time to _____ over your proposal before I give you a definite answer.

Synonyms

*Choose the word from this unit that is **the same** or **most nearly the same** in meaning as the **boldface** word or expression in the given phrase. Write the word on the line provided.*

1. committed a **vengeful** crime against his accuser   _vindictive_

2. a peaceful scene by the **fireplace**   _hearth_

3. tall buildings that would **spoil** the view   _mar_

4. started to **droop** from the heat   _wilt_

5. will **beg** the officer not to arrest her son   _implore_

6. a match that ended in a **standoff**   _stalemate_

7. wears an **insignia** on his collar   _emblem_

8. refused to make the first **offer**   _____

9. signed the **treaty** that would end the fighting   _____

10. was spellbound by the play's opening **conversation**   _____

11. **negligent** in her duties   _____

12. to treat the crime as a **petty offense**   _____

13. a flock of birds that seemed **beyond reckoning**   _____

14. picked up where the **tale** left off   _____

15. would **think** over the new proposal   _____

Antonyms

*Choose the word from this unit that is **most nearly opposite** in meaning to the **boldface** word or expression in the given phrase. Write the word on the line provided.*

16. photographed the **diminutive** species   _____

17. created **calm** with his music   _____

18. left the windows **shut**   _____

19. has **insufficient** funds to complete the job   _____

20. met the **illustrious** politician   _____

Choosing the Right Word

*Circle the **boldface** word that more satisfactorily completes each of the following sentences.*

1. As long as the door to compromise is even slightly (**ajar, vindictive**), there is a chance that we will be able to reach an understanding.

2. Some parents are quite strict with their children; others are somewhat (**lax, adequate**) and permissive.

3. I was a little miffed when my polite (**stalemates, overtures**) of friendship were so rudely and nastily rejected.

4. The facts of history cannot always be arranged in the form of a smooth and logical (**pact, narrative**).

5. British enlistment posters in World War I assured young men that they would be fighting for "king and country, (**hearth, havoc**) and home."

6. In spite of all the criticism, our flag still stands throughout most of the world as a(n) (**pact, emblem**) of justice and freedom.

7. After World War II the United States was not (**vindictive, lax**) toward its former enemies but tried to help them recover and rebuild.

8. Instead of resorting at once to armed force, the two nations entered into a diplomatic (**dialogue, havoc**) that eventually resolved the conflict.

9. For many years Benedict Arnold served his country faithfully, but then he disgraced his name for all time by an (**ajar, infamous**) act of treason.

10. Our high hopes for an easy victory (**wilted, mulled**) away to nothing as we watched our opponents steadily increase their lead over us.

11. I will not allow our long friendship to be (**marred, implored**) by this unfortunate misunderstanding.

12. Contract talks have been stalled for weeks, and nothing either side has suggested can seem to break the (**stalemate, dialogue**).

13. The man has such a (**vindictive, gigantic**) ego that absolutely nothing ever seems to fluster, faze, or deflate him.

14. Instead of continuing to (**mull, implore**) over the injustices that people have done to you, forget about the past and concentrate on the future.

15. Though jaywalking may be considered a(n) (**misdemeanor, overture**), murder is definitely not!

16. As I look over your record, I get the impression that your background in math and science is not (**adequate, ajar**) for an engineering course.

17. Her insistence on studying the terms of our tutoring agreement made me think that I'd signed a (**pact, hearth**) with a lawyer.

18. Since I am willing to contribute to any worthy cause, there is no need to (**wilt, implore**) me for aid in such an emotional way.

19. The blustery winds on that cold November day played (**havoc, pact**) with my hair all during our sight-seeing tour.

20. The wonders of nature are as (**innumerable, adequate**) as the grains of sand on a seashore or the leaves on the trees in a forest.

Vocabulary in Context

*Read the following passage, in which some of the words you have studied in this unit appear in **boldface** type. Then complete each statement given below the passage by circling the letter of the item that is **the same** or **almost the same** in meaning as the highlighted word.*

"Our Flag Was Still There"
(Line)

Every American has sung "The Star-Spangled Banner" **innumerable** times, but not everyone knows the history of the song. Here is a brief **narrative** of the events that led to the writing of the words to our national anthem.

During the War of 1812, a District of Columbia lawyer named Francis Scott Key boarded a British truce ship in Chesapeake Bay to **implore** the British to release (5) Dr. John Beanes, who had been arrested by British troops after they had sacked Washington, D.C. On the night of September 13, 1814, while Key was aboard the

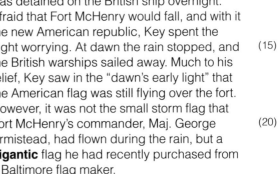

ship during a heavy rain, the British bombarded Fort McHenry, a stronghold guarding Baltimore, causing **havoc** in the fort. (10)

The American cannons returned fire; Key was detained on the British ship overnight. Afraid that Fort McHenry would fall, and with it the new American republic, Key spent the night worrying. At dawn the rain stopped, and (15) the British warships sailed away. Much to his relief, Key saw in the "dawn's early light" that the American flag was still flying over the fort. However, it was not the small storm flag that Fort McHenry's commander, Maj. George (20) Armistead, had flown during the rain, but a **gigantic** flag he had recently purchased from a Baltimore flag maker.

Fourth of July fireworks in Washington, D.C.

Key, an amateur poet, was so inspired by the sight of the "star-spangled banner," a sign that (25) the British had not captured the fort, that although he was still aboard the truce ship, he wrote a poem on the back of a letter he had in his pocket. Key called the poem "In Defense of Fort M'Henry" and had it published anonymously in Baltimore. A little later, he renamed the poem "The Star-Spangled Banner." In the same year the poem was set to the music of a popular English tune, and in 1931 Congress adopted the (30) song as our national anthem.

---

1. The meaning of **innumerable** (line 1) is
  a. numbered   c. several
  b. countless   d. countable

2. Narrative (line 2) is best defined as
  a. dialogue   c. story
  b. essay   d. prelude

3. Implore (line 5) most nearly means
  a. entreat   c. allow
  b. demand   d. signal

4. Havoc (line 10) is best defined as
  a. worry   c. indifference
  b. disfavor   d. disorder

5. Gigantic (line 22) most nearly means
  a. tiny   c. enormous
  b. sufficient   d. diminutive

130 ■ Unit 11

Definitions

Note carefully the spelling, pronunciation, part(s) of speech, and definition(s) of each of the following words. Then write the word in the blank space(s) in the illustrative sentence(s) following. Finally, study the lists of synonyms and antonyms given at the end of each entry.

1. abound
(ə baủnd′)

(*v.*) to be plentiful, be filled

Lush fruit trees _____ in the orchards of Central California.

SYNONYMS: burst with, overflow with, teem with
ANTONYMS: lack, want

2. braggart
(brag′ ərt)

(*n.*) a boaster; *(adj.)* boastful in a loud, annoying way

There seems to be a _____ in every family, who boasts about his or her achievements and worth.

Greek Mythology is filled with _____ gods and heroes who take more than a little pride in their deeds and skills.

SYNONYMS: (*n.*) bigmouth, blowhard

3. cache
(kash)

(*n.*) a hiding place; something hidden or stored

We found a _____ of canned food hidden under the stairs in the cellar.

SYNONYMS: stockpile, hoard, store

4. clarification
(klar ə fə kā′ shən)

(*n.*) the act of making clear or understandable, an explanation

Reporters asked for a _____ of the politician's statement so that they could accurately report her position.

SYNONYMS: elucidation, explication

5. despondent
(di spän′ dənt)

(*adj.*) sad, without hope, discouraged

The doctor was _____ over the loss of his patient and dear friend.

SYNONYMS: dejected, depressed, forlorn
ANTONYMS: jubilant, elated

6. embezzle
(em bez′ əl)

(*v.*) to steal property entrusted to one's care

The senator's aide lost his job when he was caught trying to _____ campaign funds.

SYNONYMS: swindle, defraud

7. heartrending
(härt′ ren diŋ)

(*adj.*) causing mental pain or grief

The survivor told a _____ story about the shipwreck and the days she spent alone on the island.

SYNONYMS: moving, sad, heartbreaking, poignant
ANTONYMS: amusing, funny, hilarious

8. leisurely
(lē′ zhər lē)

(*adj.*) unhurried, taking plenty of time; (*adv.*) in an easygoing or unhurried way

My parents enjoy taking a _____ stroll through the park on Sunday afternoon.

We ate _____ and spent hours talking about old times.

SYNONYMS: (*adj.*) slow, relaxed
ANTONYMS: (*adj.*) hasty, hurried, rushed, hectic

9. lethargic
(lə thär′ jik)

(*adj.*) unnaturally sleepy; dull, slow moving; indifferent

The twins often become _____ after eating a large meal at their grandmother's house.

SYNONYMS: lazy, sluggish, listless
ANTONYMS: wide-awake, alert, energetic, dynamic

10. malady
(mal′ əd ē)

(*n.*) a sickness, illness, disease, disorder

Rheumatic fever, usually a childhood

_____, can cause permanent damage to the heart.

SYNONYMS: ailment, indisposition
ANTONYMS: health, well-being

11. mellow
(mel′ ō)

(*adj.*) ripe, well-matured; soft, sweet, and rich; gentle, pleasant; (*v.*) to become gentle and sweet

Hawaii is known for its _____ fruit, all of which is soft, sweet, ripe, and juicy.

Mom continued to hope that her upstart brother would _____ with age and experience.

SYNONYMS: (*adj.*) dulcet, creamy
ANTONYMS: (*adj.*) unripe, green, harsh, grating, strident

12. nomadic
(nō ma′ dik)

(*adj.*) wandering, moving about from place to place

Many groups in the desert live a

_____ life, moving about in search of water and grazing land.

SYNONYMS: roving, roaming, vagrant, migratory, itinerant
ANTONYMS: stationary, settled, rooted, fixed

13. piecemeal
(pēs′ mēl)

(*adj.*) one piece at a time; (*adv.*) gradually

The committee's _____ approach to the problem was taking more time and money than the school board could afford.

Patchwork quilts are sewn _____ .

SYNONYM: (*adv.*) bit by bit
ANTONYM: (*adv.*) all at once

14. quest
(kwest)

(*n.*) a search, hunt; (*v.*) to search, seek, ask

In _____ of a safe water route to the Pacific, Lewis and Clark journeyed more than three thousand miles.

Diplomats _____ for peaceful solutions to global problems.

SYNONYMS: (*n.*) pursuit, venture

15. random
(ran' dəm)

(*adj.*) by chance, not planned or prearranged; irregular

According to a _____ sampling of voters, Proposition 10 seems to be the most important issue on the ballot.

SYNONYMS: haphazard, arbitrary
ANTONYMS: planned, deliberate, systematic

16. rant
(rant)

(*v.*) to speak wildly and noisily; (*n.*) loud, violent talk

When the speaker began to _____ like a rabble-rouser, the crowd shouted him down.

Listening to the _____ of that radio personality makes me want to give up on talk shows.

SYNONYMS: (*v.*) rave, fume, spout, harangue
ANTONYMS: (*v.*) whisper, mumble

17. reinforce
(rē in fôrs')

(*v.*) to make stronger with new materials or support

They used steel beams to _____ the structure of the building.

SYNONYMS: strengthen, bolster, prop up, support
ANTONYMS: weaken, undermine, sap, impair

18. seclusion
(si klü' zhən)

(*n.*) isolation from others, solitude

Some actors choose to live in _____, away from the prying eyes of journalists.

SYNONYMS: aloneness, solitariness
ANTONYM: the thick of things

19. status
(stā' təs)

(*n.*) a person's condition or position in the eyes of the law; relative rank or standing, especially in society; prestige

Winning the prestigious book award boosted the young writer's literary _____.

SYNONYMS: situation, recognition

20. turmoil
(tər' moil)

(*n.*) a state of great confusion or disorder; mental strain or agitation

For many years after the Civil War, the South remained a society in _____.

SYNONYMS: upheaval, tumult, chaos
ANTONYMS: peace and quiet, order

Completing the Sentence

From the words for this unit, choose the one that best completes each of the following sentences. Write the word in the space provided.

1. After putting up all week with the noise and confusion of life in the big city, I enjoy the _____ of my mountain retreat on weekends.

2. The lake so _____ with trout and pickerel that even a person with my limited skill in fishing can catch them easily.

3. Most detectives solve crimes in a(n) _____ fashion, as clues come to light, rather than all at once.

4. Though Ponce de León's _____ for the Fountain of Youth proved futile, he did discover Florida.

5. The _____ of the French Revolution and the Napoleonic Era was succeeded by 100 years of relative peace and quiet in Europe.

6. Apparently, the man could pay off his staggering gambling debts only by _____ funds from the company that employed him.

7. The park is always full of soapbox orators _____ about the inequality of government or society.

8. The tenor's voice was rich and _____, but the baritone's sounded somewhat harsh and unpleasant.

9. Instead of trying to decide which applicants were best suited for the job, he selected two of them at _____.

10. It's natural to feel a little _____ over not getting the job, but don't let that prevent you from applying for other positions.

11. At first, when I couldn't make out what she wanted me to do, I asked her for some _____ of her instructions.

12. In order to prevent the illegal entry of aliens into the United States, it has been necessary to _____ our border patrols.

13. Yesterday, I read a truly _____ account of the plight of millions of Africans suffering from the effects of a severe famine.

14. The two brothers are both fine athletes, but one is quiet and modest, while the other is an awful _____.

15. When I first entered this country, I was classified as a "resident alien," but my _____ has changed since then.

16. Arthritis is a _____ that attacks many millions of people, especially in middle and old age.

17. During warm months, foxes bury many animals they have killed, with the result that they have _____ to tide them over the winter.

18. Hundreds of homeless people now lead essentially _____ existences on the streets of our major cities.

19. Though I am always full of energy in the morning, I start to become a little _____ as the day wears on.

20. Every once in a while, I like to take time out from my busy schedule to have a _____ dinner with old friends.

Synonyms

*Choose the word from this unit that is **the same** or **most nearly the same** in meaning as the **boldface** word or expression in the given phrase. Write the word on the line provided.*

1. was among the last **roving** groups in Lapland _____

2. achieved a high **standing** among her peers _____

3. students in **pursuit** of knowledge _____

4. will live in **solitude** for the winter _____

5. legal terms that will need **explication** _____

6. attempted to **steal** money from the trust fund _____

7. began to **rave** at the hostile audience _____

8. was caught up in the **chaos** left by the storm _____

9. a **hoard** of gold bullion _____

10. **dejected** over the loss of his job _____

11. to **bolster** belief in our system of government _____

12. is just another conceited **boaster** _____

13. rehearsed the play **bit by bit** _____

14. suffers from a serious **illness** _____

15. inventive minds that **teem with** ideas _____

Antonyms

*Choose the word from this unit that is **most nearly opposite** in meaning to the **boldface** word or expression in the given phrase. Write the word on the line provided.*

16. took a **rushed** trip down the Mississippi River _____

17. is always **energetic** on Monday _____

18. has a **strident** personality _____

19. told a **hilarious** story about their escape _____

20. witnessed a **deliberate** act of kindness _____

Choosing the Right Word

*Circle the **boldface** word that more satisfactorily completes each of the following sentences.*

1. As soon as I opened the book, I realized that I had stumbled on a rich (**cache, braggart**) of useful information for my report.

2. Over the years I have learned one thing about rumors: Where the facts are few, fictions (**abound, clarify**).

3. Since I was in no hurry to get where I was going, I decided to set a rather (**random, leisurely**) pace for myself.

4. Our present policy appears to be so contradictory that I believe some (**clarification, turmoil**) of it is in order.

5. My experience on my summer job has (**reinforced, abounded**) many of the lessons I learned in the classroom.

6. Though he (**rants, embezzles**) and raves about the problems of the world, he has little to offer in the way of solutions to them.

7. Although she appeared calm, her mind was in (**turmoil, status**).

8. The eternal (**quest, seclusion**) for youth and beauty explains the huge sales of cosmetics, to men as well as to women.

9. For weeks a gang of muggers wandered the streets aimlessly, choosing their victims at (**random, piecemeal**) from those who happened by.

10. Only the fact that they cannot see the seriousness of the emergency can explain their (**lethargic, nomadic**) response to our appeal for help.

11. At the time when this event happened, I was very angry, but over the years my emotions have (**mellowed, reinforced**).

12. Many doctors believe that when sick people become (**heartrending, despondent**) over their health, it is more difficult for them to recover.

13. People who waste the natural resources of this country are in a sense (**embezzling, reinforcing**) the wealth of future generations.

14. Instead of such (**mellow, piecemeal**) efforts to prevent air pollution, we need a unified campaign that will be continued for as long as necessary.

15. The President went on the air to inform the general public of the present (**malady, status**) of the negotiations with the enemy.

16. (**Nomadic, Despondent**) groups of horse breeders still wander the plains of Central Asia in search of pasturage for their herds.

17. In the (**heartrending, lethargic**) conclusion of the film, the hero dies in the arms of his beloved.

18. I believe that education, understanding, and experience provide the only cure for the (**malady, status**) of racial prejudice.

19. There is a great difference between being quietly confident of your own ability and being an obnoxious (**nomad, braggart**).

20. Why would a world-famous writer choose to live in the (**quest, seclusion**) of a country village far from the "madding crowd"?

Read the following passage, in which some of the words you have studied in this unit appear in **boldface** type. Then complete each statement given below the passage by circling the letter of the item that is **the same** or **almost the same** in meaning as the highlighted word.

A Museum for Every Taste

(Line)

The United States **abounds with** museums. There are more than 8,000 of them, from the popular, like Chicago's Museum of Science and Industry, to the obscure, like the Devil's Rope Museum, which displays all types of barbed wire, in McLean, Texas. In fact, if your interest is specialized, chances are you can pursue it at one
(5) of the growing number of offbeat museums in our nation.

For example, if wacky airplanes are your cup of tea, you might make your way to the Mid-America Museum, west of Hot Springs, Arkansas, where a **cache** of playful contraptions can be seen and touched. If, on the other hand, your **quest** is for the perfect wave, you can visit "the
(10) world's first surfing museum," in Santa Cruz, California.

If you happen to prefer roller skates to waves, don't be **despondent**—just head to the National Museum of Roller
(15) Skating in Lincoln, Nebraska. There you will find antique roller skates, costumes, motorized skates, and even old skate keys. However, if it's a **mellow** musical experience you're
(20) after, your choice may be the Miles Musical Museum in Eureka Springs, Arkansas. On a **leisurely** tour, the owners will entertain you by cranking up any number of antique musical machines.

Mid-America Museum near Hot Springs, Arkansas

No matter how absurd they may seem, these offbeat museums are true
(25) American treasures. They preserve our shared past by keeping the things that matter to us and also reveal a good deal about our people and country. With these goals in mind, it shouldn't surprise you to know that there is even a museum that honors American know-how—for that's exactly the aim of the Rough and Tumble Engineers' Museum in Kinzers, Pennsylvania. There, old steam engines, threshers,
(30) and tractors are fixed to run almost like new, proving that in this country, no matter how far-out your interest, there is probably a museum just for you.

1. The meaning of **abounds with** (line 1) is
a. bounces with
b. lacks
c. is supplied with
d. overflows with

2. Cache (line 7) most nearly means
a. case
b. store
c. cave
d. cellar

3. Quest (line 8) is best defined as
a. desire
b. need
c. search
d. find

4. Despondent (line 13) is best defined as
a. elated
b. irresponsible
c. discouraged
d. hopeful

5. The meaning of **mellow** in (line 19) is
a. dulcet
b. harsh
c. colorful
d. funny

6. Leisurely (line 22) most nearly means
a. hasty
b. unhurried
c. hectic
d. playful

Analogies *In each of the following, circle the item that best completes the comparison.*

1. braggart is to **boast** as
a. showoff is to strut
b. pickpocket is to botch
c. daredevil is to wilt
d. spoilsport is to mull

2. surplus is to **more** as
a. shortage is to less
b. dearth is to more
c. clutter is to less
d. lack is to more

3. big is to **gigantic** as
a. futile is to random
b. small is to tiny
c. lavish is to adequate
d. ajar is to shut

4. knight is to **quest** as
a. nomad is to herd
b. parasite is to meal
c. soldier is to campaign
d. beneficiary is to will

5. bull is to **bellow** as
a. leopard is to rant
b. elephant is to purr
c. lion is to roar
d. goat is to neigh

6. vindictive is to **revenge** as
a. greedy is to success
b. lazy is to fame
c. envious is to knowledge
d. grasping is to gain

7. hearth is to **fire** as
a. sink is to soap
b. well is to water
c. bucket is to handle
d. floor is to dirt

8. farce is to **laughs** as
a. drama is to yawns
b. tragedy is to tears
c. comedy is to sneezes
d. musical is to groans

9. wolf is to **lair** as
a. tiger is to hearth
b. fox is to cache
c. bear is to seclusion
d. lion is to den

10. cache is to **hidden** as
a. stalemate is to won
b. turmoil is to given
c. loot is to stolen
d. misdemeanor is to forgotten

11. malady is to **sick** as
a. injury is to hurt
b. turmoil is to calm
c. status is to worried
d. problem is to content

12. overture is to **opera** as
a. plot is to novel
b. dialogue is to play
c. preface is to book
d. index is to dictionary

13. embezzler is to **swindle** as
a. dictator is to pamper
b. coward is to veto
c. judge is to mar
d. beggar is to implore

14. narrative is to **told** as
a. dialogue is to thought
b. symphony is to played
c. overture is to sung
d. pact is to spoken

15. mar is to **damage** as
a. dismantle is to disassemble
b. shirk is to fulfill
c. implore is to hire
d. reinforce is to undermine

16. despondent is to **cheer** as
a. morbid is to gloom
b. timid is to courage
c. confident is to clarification
d. hospitable is to courtesy

17. lethargic is to **energy** as
a. mellow is to richness
b. heartrending is to pity
c. lavish is to size
d. leisurely is to speed

18. grueling is to **exhaust** as
a. difficult is to interest
b. knotty is to amaze
c. dull is to bore
d. tiresome is to delight

In each of the following groups, circle the word that is best defined or suggested by the given phrase.

1. a run-down old building
a. despondent   b. morbid   c. dilapidated   d. hospitable

2. to create confusion
a. abound   b. havoc   c. botch   d. shirk

3. got the information a bit at a time
a. piecemeal   b. regularly   c. lethargically   d. ajar

4. like stars that are too many to count
a. mellow   b. innumerable   c. lax   d. dilapidated

5. a person named in a will
a. stalemate   b. misdemeanor   c. beneficiary   d. parasite

6. the search for world peace
a. malady   b. quest   c. havoc   d. cache

7. constantly on the move
a. piecemeal   b. random   c. nomadic   d. despondent

8. to rave or talk wildly
a. veto   b. rant   c. implore   d. bellow

9. extra goods or material
a. random   b. surplus   c. innumerable   d. adequate

10. to ponder their suggestions
a. pamper   b. clutter   c. dismantle   d. mull

11. needs a clear explanation of your remarks
a. pact   b. clarification   c. overture   d. narrative

12. a symbol that stands for something else
a. beneficiary   b. emblem   c. pact   d. overture

13. to litter shelves with books and papers
a. mar   b. dismantle   c. rant   d. clutter

14. a sufficient supply
a. adequate   b. random   c. surplus   d. morbid

15. with the window slightly open
a. dilapidated   b. ajar   c. piecemeal   d. lax

16. a very generous gift
a. lavish   b. adequate   c. grueling   d. gigantic

17. living off someone else
a. parasite   b. braggart   c. beneficiary   d. emblem

18. a dulcet tone
a. leisurely   b. lavish   c. mellow   d. lethargic

19. "Don't bungle the job."
a. embezzle   b. dismantle   c. mar   d. botch

20. to shout a command
a. veto   b. quest   c. implore   d. bellow

Vocabulary in Context

Read the following passage, in which some of the words you have studied in Units 10–12 appear in **boldface** type. Then complete each statement given below the passage by circling the item that is *the same* or *almost the same* in meaning as the highlighted word.

Struggles for Justice

(Line)

Have you ever heard the term *The Great Migration*? If so, then you may know that between 1870 and 1920 hundreds of thousands of African
(5) Americans moved from rural areas in the Southeast to the industrialized urban areas in the Northeast and Midwest. For most, this **gigantic** migration meant an escape from
(10) poverty and the **malady** of discrimination—of being treated unfairly. To these African Americans, the movement north was a **quest** for a better life, as northern factory jobs were
(15) a great improvement over farm work.

As more industrial jobs became available during World War I, about half a million African Americans went north. Although their economic
(20) **status** improved during the war years, African Americans in both the North and the South were still denied many basic rights. As a result, some notable African Americans rose to
(25) the challenge of righting injustices and achieving equal opportunity.

One African American who fought to end injustice was Booker T. Washington. Born enslaved,
(30) Washington taught himself to read.

Years later, in 1891, he founded the Tuskegee Institute in Alabama. There, African Americans were taught skills such as bricklaying,
(35) printing, and teaching, which would help them improve their lives as they worked peacefully toward equality.

African American women also struggled for justice. Ida B. Wells, for
(40) example, strove to end the **notorious** practice of segregation—of separating African Americans from other groups in society—and other forms of racial injustice. For Wells,
(45) her pen and her resolve were her only weapons. As editor of the newspaper *Free Speech*, which she founded in Memphis, Tennessee, Wells fought to end **random** acts of
(50) violence against African Americans. "Can you remain silent," she wrote ". . . when such things are done in your own community and country?"

As these African American leaders
(55) and others lectured across the country, they inspired the growth of the civil rights movement. In fact, even today, their words and deeds still motivate organizations to
(60) continue the struggle for justice.

---

1. The meaning of **gigantic** (line 8) is
a. vigilant
b. splendid
c. immense
d. infinitesimal

2. Malady (line 10) most nearly means
a. pact
b. deadlock
c. fright
d. sickness

3. Quest (line 13) is best defined as
a. victory
b. search
c. finale
d. symbol

4. Status (line 20) most nearly means
a. condition
b. order
c. explanation
d. settlement

5. Notorious (line 40) is best defined as
a. haphazard
b. disgraceful
c. indifferent
d. taxing

6. The meaning of **random** (line 49) is
a. unhurried
b. shameful
c. arbitrary
d. planned

Choosing the Right Meaning

Read each sentence carefully. Then circle the item that best completes the statement below the sentence.

Her lax smile told me that she had not found the vocabulary test as difficult as she had feared. (2)

1. In line 1 the word **lax** most nearly means

a. undisciplined   b. negligent   c. relaxed   d. sarcastic

Edgar Allan Poe's story "The Black Cat" ends with the discovery of the cache in which the narrator has walled up the animal he has slain. (2)

2. In line 1 the word **cache** is used to mean

a. hiding place   b. grave   c. hoard   d. buried coffin

The last words of the 16th-century French author François Rabelais are reported to have been "Draw the curtain; the farce is played." (2)

3. The best definition for the word **farce** in line 2 is

a. sham   b. comedy   c. humor   d. melodrama

As the park rangers approached the carcass left behind by poachers, a few jackals went shirking into the brush. (2)

4. In line 2 the word **shirking** is used to mean

a. neglecting   b. avoiding   c. sidestepping   d. sneaking

Am I guilty of "conspicuous consumption" if I purchase something solely for the status it is supposed to lend me? (2)

5. The word **status** in line 1 is best defined as

a. fame   b. prestige   c. condition   d. position

Antonyms

*In each of the following groups, circle the word or expression that is most nearly the **opposite** of the word in **boldface** type.*

1. veto
a. forbid
b. cancel
c. approve
d. suggest

2. dialogue
a. conversation
b. discussion
c. whisper
d. monologue

3. dismantle
a. explode
b. assemble
c. design
d. destroy

4. shirk
a. describe
b. ignore
c. understand
d. do

5. lethargic
a. dreamy
b. agreeable
c. nasty
d. energetic

6. leisurely
a. well-organized
b. easygoing
c. hasty
d. artistic

7. pamper
a. mistreat
b. educate
c. coddle
d. adopt

8. turmoil
a. flames
b. haste
c. secrecy
d. peace

9. grueling
a. easy
b. tiring
c. long
d. interesting

11. implore
a. demand
b. beg
c. love
d. defend

13. heartrending
a. funny
b. sad
c. modern
d. typical

15. futile
a. large
b. tiring
c. successful
d. new

10. reinforce
a. paint
b. construct
c. test
d. weaken

12. despondent
a. jubilant
b. gloomy
c. unusual
d. sour

14. wilted
a. faded
b. spoiled
c. died
d. bloomed

16. gigantic
a. shaggy
b. tiny
c. fierce
d. new

Word Families

A. *On the line provided, write the word you have learned in Units 10–12 that is related to each of the following nouns.*
EXAMPLE: dilapidation—**dilapidated**

1. despondency (despondence), despond _____
2. futility, futileness _____
3. adequacy, adequateness _____
4. hospitality, hospitableness _____
5. randomness, randomization, randomizer _____
6. embezzlement, embezzler _____
7. vindictiveness _____
8. leisure, leisureliness (leisureness) _____
9. abundance _____
10. reinforcement, reinforcer _____
11. notoriety, notoriousness _____
12. lethargy _____
13. nomad, nomadism _____
14. infamy _____
15. mellowness _____

B. *On the line provided, write the word you have learned in Units 10–12 that is related to each of the following verbs.*
EXAMPLE: seclude—**seclusion**

16. plagiarize _____
17. waste _____
18. indulge _____
19. lament _____
20. contend _____

Two-Word Completions

Circle the pair of words that best complete the meaning of each of the following passages.

1. As he sat by the fire that glowed in the _____, the old sailor entertained the children with a(n) _____ of his adventures on the high seas, beginning when he was a boy of twelve almost sixty years before.

    a. lair . . . farce
                      c. hearth . . . narrative

    b. cache . . . dialogue
                d. clutter . . . overture

2. Since the soil is so remarkably rich and fertile, a variety of crops can be grown in _____. The farmers keep what they need for themselves and sell off the _____ at a handsome profit.

    a. abundance . . . surplus
          c. lavishness . . . hospitality

    b. seclusion . . . reinforcements
      d. leisure . . . adequacy

3. Before we can even think about renovating this _____ old house, we must remove all the worthless _____ that is strewn around the rooms and blocking the entrances.

    a. gigantic . . . cache
              c. mellow . . . havoc

    b. dilapidated . . . clutter
        d. futile . . . surplus

4. "I am still _____ the matter over in my mind," the President told the press. "When I have reached a decision, I will either sign the bill or _____ it."

    a. mellowing . . . botch
          c. mulling . . . veto

    b. narrating . . . dismantle
      d. clarifying . . . mar

5. The earliest inhabitants of North America lived _____ lives. They were constantly moving from place to place in search of the game that made up the greater part of their diet. This endless _____ for food eventually took them to all parts of the continent.

    a. nomadic . . . quest
          c. pampered . . . malady

    b. grueling . . . cache
        d. lethargic . . . status

note, not—to know, recognize

Building with Classical Roots

This root appears in **notorious** (page 119), "widely and unfavorably known." Some other words based on the same root are listed below.

connote	**notary**	**noteworthy**	**notion**
denote	**notation**	**notify**	**notoriety**

From the list of words above, choose the one that corresponds to each of the brief definitions below. Write the word in the blank space in the illustrative sentence below the definition.

1. remarkable, outstanding because of some special excellence ("*worthy of being recognized*")

The senator made _____ remarks about the importance of controlling air pollution.

2. an idea; a foolish idea or opinion; a small useful item

She has the odd _____ that no one in her class likes her.

3. to point out, give notice of, inform

We will _____ an attorney of your intention to sue us.

4. to indicate, be the sign of, mean exactly

The child's high temperature and chills _____ severe illness.

5. to suggest or imply in addition to giving an exact meaning

The name *Angela* means "angel," but it also _____ goodness.

6. a public official who certifies statements and signatures

The _____ public witnessed the signing of Grandfather's will.

7. ill fame; being famous for something bad

Jesse James achieved _____ as an outlaw in the Old West.

8. a record; a note to assist memory, memorandum; a set of symbols or expressions

Good students often write _____ in the margins of books.

From the list of words on page 144, choose the one that best completes each of the following sentences. Write the word in the space provided.

1. The letter I received this morning _____ me that I had been accepted at one of the colleges to which I had applied.

2. Place a _____ on her medical record card to remind the nurse to call her in two months for a follow-up appointment.

3. The deed became a legal document when it was signed by all parties in the presence of a _____ .

4. Do you have any _____ of what he is attempting to do?

5. All the _____ she had received after being a witness in the bribery trial caused her to move to another city.

6. The flashing signals at the crossing _____ the approach of a train.

7. Isn't it fascinating how certain colors have come to _____ strong feelings, such as red for anger?

8. What do you think was the most _____ achievement on behalf of humanity during the past 25 years?

---

*Circle the **boldface** word that more satisfactorily completes each of the following sentences.*

1. The Vikings' (**notation, notoriety**) as bloodthirsty invaders has lasted for more than a thousand years.

2. All the (**noteworthy, notorious**) painters of the Italian Renaissance are represented in the current exhibit at the museum.

3. Symbols such as the plus sign and the minus sign are used in mathematical (**notation, notary**).

4. An inventor has the ability to transform a fleeting (**notation, notion**) into a useful product.

5. Gathering clouds and a dark gray sky (**denote, connote**) rain.

6. In 19th-century novels dark clouds usually (**denote, connote**) that something bad is about to happen.

7. One of the duties of a (**notation, notary**) is to witness the signing of an important document.

8. Please (**denote, notify**) us when the next tryout for the team will be.

Writer's Challenge

Read the following sentences, paying special attention to the words and phrases underlined. From the words in the box below, find better choices for these underlined words and phrases. Then use these choices to rewrite the sentences.

WORD BANK				
abound	embezzle	gigantic	infamous	reinforce
adequate	emblem	havoc	morbid	stalemate
beneficiary	farce	hearth	piecemeal	turmoil
despondent	futile	heartrending	random	wilt

The Triangle Shirtwaist Factory Fire

1. In the <u>upheaval</u> of a disaster that struck on March 25, 1911, 146 young workers lost their lives in 15 minutes, forever changing the laws that govern workplace safety.

_____

_____

2. Late that day, a fire broke out on the eighth floor of a garment factory. The fast-moving blaze—and locked exits—rendered <u>not successful</u> the attempts of the terrified women to escape.

_____

_____

3. Fire prevention procedures were nowhere near <u>okay</u> in those days, nor was fire-fighting equipment designed to reach the higher floors of tall buildings.

_____

_____

4. The fire at New York City's Triangle Shirtwaist Factory was to become a truly <u>villainous</u> reminder of all that could go wrong when immigrant workers were exploited by their employers.

_____

_____

5. Workers (and employers) today are <u>those who have benefited</u>—shielded from such disasters—through laws calling for sprinkler systems, fire drills, and well-marked fire exits.

_____

_____

6. Bessie Cohen, the last survivor of the fire, died in 1999 at the age of 107. To the end, she could vividly recall the terrifying <u>very great destruction</u> of that awful day.

_____

_____

Analogies

In each of the following, circle the item that best completes the comparison.

1. puny is to **gigantic** as
a. foremost is to prominent
b. lethargic is to dynamic
c. grueling is to graphic
d. vicious is to malignant

2. jaywalking is to **misdemeanor** as
a. forgery is to vice
b. homicide is to felony
c. embezzlement is to blunder
d. perjury is to error

3. ratify is to **veto** as
a. mar is to disfigure
b. fluster is to bewilder
c. procure is to ordain
d. renovate is to dilapidate

4. fruitless is to **futile** as
a. spirited is to animated
b. rural is to urban
c. orthodox is to quaint
d. amiss is to upright

5. buffoon is to **farce** as
a. doctor is to patient
b. farmer is to plow
c. acrobat is to circus
d. bystander is to accident

6. innumerable is to **count** as
a. indispensable is to employ
b. interminable is to begin
c. illegible is to read
d. inflammable is to kindle

7. despondent is to **melancholy** as
a. indifferent is to enthusiasm
b. peevish is to courtesy
c. sullen is to joy
d. indignant is to wrath

8. implore is to **entreat** as
a. interrogate is to question
b. parch is to quench
c. accelerate is to decrease
d. nurture is to stifle

9. alliance is to **pact** as
a. truce is to cease-fire
b. dynasty is to brawl
c. anecdote is to oration
d. regime is to onslaught

10. reinforce is to **more** as
a. flourish is to less
b. shirk is to more
c. erode is to less
d. eradicate is to more

Choosing the Right Meaning

Read each sentence carefully. Then circle the item that best completes the statement below the sentence.

The story was so predictable and the characters so dull that it's no wonder the audience's reaction was so lethargic. (2)

1. The word **lethargic** in line 2 is best defined as

a. indifferent   b. lazy   c. enthusiastic   d. critical

One side of the packing material was molded to form a pattern of tiny plastic nubs to absorb shock. (2)

2. In line 1 the word **nubs** most nearly means

a. cores   b. cruxes   c. hearts   d. knobs

The death of Stonewall Jackson in 1863 left a void in the ranks of Lee's generals that no other officer was able to fill. (2)

3. In line 1 the word **void** is used to mean

a. annulment   b. cancellation   c. vacancy   d. promotion

It was the custom in many American homes in the late nineteenth century to serve mulled beverages to guests at holiday time. (2)

4. The best definition for the word **mulled** in line 1 is

a. pondered   c. heated and flavored
b. chilled and diluted   d. homemade

The current was swift in the shallows along the bank, but once we paddled into deeper water, the river turned quite sullen. (2)

5. The word **sullen** in line 2 is used to mean

a. silent   b. sluggish   c. morose   d. surly

Two-Word Completions   *Circle the pair of words that best complete the meaning of each of the following sentences.*

1. Though modern medicine can _____ remedies for many of the _____ that afflict us, it still hasn't found a surefire cure for cancer.
a. prescribe . . . maladies   c. ordain . . . narratives
b. verify . . . remnants   d. presume . . . surpluses

2. The sudden wail of the air-raid siren and the ominous _____ of airplanes overhead sent dozens of civilians _____ for cover.
a. luster . . . floundering   c. rant . . . yearning
b. drone . . . scurrying   d. brood . . . hurtling

3. "Staircases and hallways that are _____ with all kinds of junk constitute a real fire _____," the fire marshal told us when he inspected our plant recently.
a. disrupted . . . ingredient   c. cluttered . . . hazard
b. inflicted . . . momentum   d. retarded . . . stalemate

4. The hunters set various kinds of traps to _____ the beast when it left its mountain lair in _____ of food and water for its young.
a. goad . . . uncertainty   c. plague . . . vengeance
b. snare . . . quest   d. frustrate . . . foretaste

5. During the African dry season the land becomes so _____ that even a mighty river can be reduced to a mere _____.
a. sodden . . . résumé   c. lubricated . . . iota
b. wilted . . . nub   d. parched . . . trickle

Enriching Your Vocabulary

Read the passage below. Then complete the exercise at the bottom of the page.

Bravo!
Words from Italian

It is true that the Roman Empire declined and fell, but it left behind a legacy that includes the five Romance languages: French, Spanish, Portuguese, Romanian, and Italian. English borrowings from Italian are few, but tend to be concentrated in the arts.

Italian words go to the very foundations of the musical arts. *Opera* is an Italian word meaning work or composition (opera was developed in Florence, the center of the Italian Renaissance), as are *piano* and *violin*. The best violins ever created were made not long after the instrument was developed, by Amati and Stradivari (the famous *Stradivarius* violins); a few of these violins still exist today and are extremely valuable. A *soprano* (a very high voice) and a *basso* (a very low voice) make an effort to keep to the *tempo,* or pace, of the music. And the *prima donna* is the female star of an opera.

In the visual arts we find the words *gouache,* for a brilliant opaque water-based paint used in graphics, and *fresco,* for a technique of painting in wet plaster; famous paintings such as *The Last Supper,* by Leonardo Da Vinci, are frescoes.

La Scala opera house in Milan

Other Italian words are scattered throughout English. A *salvo* (Unit 7) is a burst of cannon fire or gunfire, often as a salute, or a spirited verbal attack. To *trill* is to warble, to sing with a fluttering sound like some birds.

In Column A below are 9 more words from Italian. With or without a dictionary, match each word with its meaning in Column B

Column A

_____ **1.** espionage
_____ **2.** inferno
_____ **3.** svelte
_____ **4.** extravaganza
_____ **5.** cavalcade
_____ **6.** corsair
_____ **7.** manifesto
_____ **8.** vista
_____ **9.** maestro

Column B

a. a pirate or pirate ship
b. a distant view, especially from a good viewing point, as from a window or from up high
c. a very large or elaborate display or entertainment
d. a master in an art, especially a musical art
e. the act or practice of spying or of operating a spy network
f. slim or graceful
g. a ceremonial procession; a dramatic series of events
h. a public announcement of aims or intentions
i. a situation or condition of great suffering, resembling hell

Definitions

Note carefully the spelling, pronunciation, part(s) of speech, and definition(s) of each of the following words. Then write the word in the blank space(s) in the illustrative sentence(s) following. Finally, study the lists of synonyms and antonyms given at the end of each entry.

1. agitation
(aj i tā′ shən)

(*n.*) a violent stirring or movement; noisy confusion, excitement; a stirring up of public enthusiasm

The _____ for campaign finance reform was gaining widespread support in Congress.

SYNONYMS: disquiet, uneasiness, upset
ANTONYMS: peace of mind, composure, calm

2. blurt
(blərt)

(*v.*) to say suddenly or without thinking

The detective was fairly certain that after hours of interrogation, the suspect would

_____ out the truth.

SYNONYMS: blab, let slip

3. chronological
(krän əl äj′ i kəl)

(*adj.*) arranged in order of time of occurrence

The importance of a time line is that it arranges historical events in _____ order.

SYNONYMS: in time sequence, consecutive

4. countenance
(kaùn′ tə nəns)

(*n.*) a face, facial expression; (*v.*) to tolerate or approve

The teacher's smiling _____ reassured us that the rehearsal was going well.

The new boss does not _____ lateness or absenteeism.

SYNONYMS: (*v.*) support, condone
ANTONYM: (*v.*) disapprove of

5. diminish
(di min′ ish)

(*v.*) to make or become smaller, reduce in size

It takes no time at all for a fad to

_____ in popularity.

SYNONYMS: lessen, decrease, dwindle
ANTONYMS: increase, enlarge, augment

6. enchant
(en chant′)

(*v.*) to please greatly; to charm, put under a magic spell

The singer proceeded to _____ the audience with her beautiful voice and engaging style.

SYNONYMS: delight, thrill, bewitch
ANTONYMS: bore, nauseate, disgust

7. **fluctuate**
(flək′ chü āt)

(*v.*) to change continually; to move up and down

Stock prices _____ daily.

SYNONYMS: waver, seesaw, oscillate
ANTONYMS: stay put, remain unchanged

8. **foster**
(fôs′ tər)

(*v.*) to bring up, give care to; to promote, encourage;
(*adj.*) in the same family but not related by birth

The American ambassador worked to

_____ positive relations with the
newly formed republic.

It is important for _____ children to
be placed with loving families.

SYNONYMS: (*v.*) support, nurture, cultivate
ANTONYMS: (*v.*) stifle, smother, quash, discourage

9. **grovel**
(gräv′ əl)

(*v.*) to humble oneself, act in a fearful and servile way; to lie
face downward; to indulge in something base or unworthy

Afraid of punishment, the Roman slave began to

_____ at the feet of the emperor.

SYNONYMS: crouch, cower, cringe, wallow

10. **handicraft**
(han′ dē kraft)

(*n.*) work done by hand; a trade requiring hand skill

Making apple-head dolls is a _____
still enjoyed in the Arkansas River Valley, among other
places.

SYNONYMS: handiwork, manual art

11. **hilarious**
(hi lâr′ ē əs)

(*adj.*) extremely funny, causing loud amusement

The comedian told a _____ story that
had the audience laughing hysterically.

SYNONYMS: highly amusing, side-splitting
ANTONYMS: boring, dull, humorless, heartrending

12. **ignite**
(ig nīt′)

(*v.*) to set on fire, cause to burn; to heat up, excite

We used lighter fluid to _____ the
charcoal in the outdoor grill.

SYNONYMS: inflame, light, kindle
ANTONYMS: quench, extinguish, douse, put out

13. **magnitude**
(mag′ nə tüd)

(*n.*) the great size or importance of something

At first, the _____ of the task seemed
to be overwhelming for a group as small as ours.

SYNONYMS: extent, immensity, enormity
ANTONYMS: smallness, unimportance, insignificance

14. massive
(mas′ iv)

(*adj.*) large and heavy; great in size or scope

A _____ boulder still blocks the entrance to the secret cave.

SYNONYMS: bulky, huge, immense, monumental
ANTONYMS: flimsy, frail, thin

15. maternal
(mə tər′ nəl)

(*adj.*) of or like a mother

The kittens' mother took her _____ responsibilities very seriously.

SYNONYMS: motherly, protective, sympathetic
ANTONYMS: fatherly, paternal

16. pall
(pôl)

(*v.*) to lose in interest, attraction, or effectiveness; to become tiresome; (*n.*) a dark covering, something that conceals

The archaeologist's optimism began to _____ when the first excavation yielded only pieces of pottery.

News of the surprise attack on Pearl Harbor cast a _____ over the nation on December 7, 1941.

SYNONYMS: (*v.*) bore, weary; (*n.*) gloom, shadow
ANTONYMS: (*v.*) intrigue, fascinate; (*n.*) light, brightness

17. reputable
(rep′ yət ə bəl)

(*adj.*) well thought of, having a good reputation

A list of _____ lawyers is available through the local bar association.

SYNONYMS: reliable, respectable, trustworthy
ANTONYMS: shady, unsavory, questionable

18. revere
(ri vēr′)

(*v.*) to love and respect deeply, honor greatly

The elderly teacher was _____ by a whole generation of students.

SYNONYMS: admire, esteem, cherish
ANTONYMS: scorn, disdain, mock, deride

19. saga
(säg′ ə)

(*n.*) a narrative of heroic exploits; a long, detailed account

Although written in Old English, *Beowulf* is very much like a Norse _____ in that it details the colorful deeds of a legendary hero.

SYNONYMS: heroic tale, epic, chronicle

20. stodgy
(stäj′ ē)

(*adj.*) dull, boring; old-fashioned, hidebound; lumpy, thick

The _____ politician showed little inclination to listen to the speeches of junior senators.

SYNONYMS: stuffy, tiresome, blah
ANTONYMS: forward-looking, avant-garde, progressive

Completing the Sentence

From the words for this unit, choose the one that best completes each of the following sentences. Write the word in the space provided.

1. The number and the _____ of the problems faced by the President of the United States are almost beyond our imagination.

2. Our study of American history has taught us to _____ the great men and women who founded this nation.

3. In the _____ *of Eric the Red*, there is a very interesting account of the Norse discovery of North America in A.D. 1000.

4. "When I was living in the Australian outback, I learned many curious skills and _____ from the local people," the explorer said.

5. Can you imagine my _____ when I was told I would have to take over the lead role in the play immediately, with no rehearsals!

6. The audience was _____ not only by the lovely voice of the soprano but also by her youthful good looks.

7. She was very fortunate to have had talented and sympathetic teachers who _____ her career.

8. We will donate the proceeds of the cake sale to any _____ charity you may select.

9. We had hoped to have a wonderful time at the party, but the sad news of the principal's accident cast a(n) _____ over the gathering.

10. Statements _____ out in anger may often be regretted for a long time afterward.

11. How can you _____ such rude behavior in a young child!

12. Educators report that there is often a vast difference between a child's mental age and his or her _____ age.

13. The waves of laughter from the audience indicated that those around me found the clown's antics as _____ as I did.

14. The two little girls playing house down in the basement fussed over the doll with all the _____ care and attention that their own mothers bestowed on them.

15. His attitudes are so incredibly _____ and hidebound that they would have been considered old-fashioned 100 years ago!

16. The pilot light of the stove will automatically _____ the burner when the handle is turned to the "on" position.

17. With no money coming in and my daily expenses continuing to mount, my savings have _____ at an alarming rate.

18. Even though I need a job badly, I still have my self-respect, and I am not going to _____ just to get work.

19. Instead of moving steadily upwards or steadily downwards, the price of oil has been _____ all year.

20. All of a sudden, from out of the fog loomed a(n) _____ ocean liner bearing down on our small boat.

Synonyms

*Choose the word from this unit that is **the same** or **most nearly the same** in meaning as the **boldface** word or expression in the given phrase. Write the word on the line provided.*

1. an example of local **handiwork** _____

2. launched a **monumental** attack _____

3. streets filled with a **covering** of black smoke _____

4. will **approve** the President's proposal _____

5. guided by her **motherly** instinct _____

6. to **let slip** the truth _____

7. an earthquake of great **size** _____

8. saw hope **dwindle** with each passing day _____

9. would cause her emotions to **waver** _____

10. narrates events in **consecutive** order _____

11. would **delight** with her smile _____

12. will **cower** before the king _____

13. was left in a state of **uneasiness** _____

14. watched a **highly amusing** play _____

15. read a medieval Icelandic **tale** _____

Antonyms

*Choose the word from this unit that is **most nearly opposite** in meaning to the **boldface** word or expression in the given phrase. Write the word on the line provided.*

16. to **deride** the Romantic poets _____

17. will **extinguish** the flame of rebellion _____

18. can **stifle** pride in their work _____

19. is known for being **progressive** _____

20. was engaged in **questionable** practices _____

Choosing the Right Word

*Circle the **boldface** word that more satisfactorily completes each of the following sentences.*

1. For more than a hundred years, the delightful adventures of Alice in Wonderland have been (**enchanting, palling**) readers young and old.

2. My love of reading, (**fostered, diminished**) by my parents since early childhood, has continued to grow through the years.

3. The cowboy on his trusty quarter horse plays a prominent part in the (**saga, magnitude**) of the Old West.

4. The Tea Act of 1773 was one of the sparks that helped (**ignite, enchant**) the American Revolution.

5. So many different battles took place during the Civil War that I often have difficulty remembering the correct (**chronology, handicraft**).

6. When the Wright brothers made the first successful airplane flight, few people realized the (**pall, magnitude**) of their achievement.

7. As the game proceeded, and the lead continued to change hands, our feelings (**fostered, fluctuated**) from joy to despair and back again.

8. If it were not for the strong (**maternal, hilarious**) instinct to protect the young, many species of animals could not survive.

9. Like everyone else, I want to be well liked, but I will not (**grovel, fluctuate**) before public opinion when I am firmly convinced that it is wrong.

10. The man was such a controversial figure in his own time that he was both (**fostered, revered**) as a saint and despised as a villain.

11. Her charming personality and sparkling wit brought a breath of fresh air into the (**stodgy, hilarious**) atmosphere of the stuffy old club.

12. Though there has of late been a good deal of (**countenance, agitation**) for tax reform, nothing much has come of it so far.

13. Many older people complain that the warm spirit of neighborliness has greatly (**diminished, revered**) under the conditions of city living.

14. The speaker alarmed us when he said that our whole system of handling lawbreakers has (**massive, stodgy**) faults that will be difficult to correct.

15. In my excitement, I accidentally (**blurted, agitated**) out the very thing that I was trying so hard to conceal.

16. Many professionals and executives today have made enjoyable hobbies of such (**handicrafts, sagas**) as carpentry and weaving.

17. Any editorial about pollution appearing in such a (**maternal, reputable**) newspaper is bound to make a strong impression on many citizens.

18. For a long time my favorite TV entertainment was police and detective programs, but now they are beginning to (**pall, enchant**).

19. One of the sure signs of a country that is not free is that the people in power will not (**countenance, blurt**) any criticism of their acts.

20. She kept us in stitches with her (**massive, hilarious**) jokes.

*Read the following passage, in which some of the words you have studied in this unit appear in **boldface** type. Then complete each statement given below the passage by circling the letter of the item that is **the same** or **almost the same** in meaning as the highlighted word.*

The Adams Family

(Line)

No chronicle of American history would be complete without the **saga** of the Adams family, one of our nation's most distinguished clans. Told in **chronological** order, their story begins with Samuel Adams, one of the "radicals" of the American Revolution. Although he began as a brewer, Sam Adams soon found that his true calling was politics. As a founder of the Committees of Correspondence, Adams (5) sought to **ignite** the colonists' passion for self-rule.

Although more moderate, John Adams, Sam Adams' cousin, was also a founder

President John Adams

of the Committees of Correspondence. Like his cousin, John Adams believed that the committees could **foster** unity among the (10) colonists by keeping them informed about political events in each of the colonies, thus becoming a "great political engine," moving the colonies closer toward liberty. When asked some years later about the meaning of the (15) American Revolution, John Adams replied that there really had been two revolutions. One was the war itself. The other "was in the minds and hearts of the people." Indeed, by the end of the war, Adams, like many Americans, would (20) desire not only independence but also a chance to form a new kind of government. As our nation's first Vice President and second President, John Adams would get his chance.

John Adams' son, John Quincy Adams, (25) would also have an opportunity to make his mark in government. The younger Adams held many governmental posts and was our nation's sixth President.

Few families in American history are as **revered** as the Adams family. As the builders of a new nation, this family did, in the words of John Adams, "something notable and striking" that would be remembered. (30)

---

1. The meaning of **saga** (line 1) is
a. home   c. face
b. epic   d. series

2. Chronological (line 2) most nearly means
a. size   c. time
b. importance   d. wavering

3. Ignite (line 6) is best defined as
a. extinguish   c. harden
b. support   d. inflame

4. Foster (line 10) most nearly means
a. promote   c. lessen
b. quash   d. enlarge

5. The meaning of **revered** (line 28) is
a. mocked   c. esteemed
b. scorned   d. liked

Definitions

Note carefully the spelling, pronunciation, part(s) of speech, and definition(s) of each of the following words. Then write the word in the blank space(s) in the illustrative sentence(s) following. Finally, study the lists of synonyms and antonyms given at the end of each entry.

1. affliction
(ə flik′ shən)

(*n.*) a physical ailment; a cause of pain or trouble, misfortune

Lupus is a dreadful _____ that kills nearly 5,000 people, mostly women, each year.

SYNONYMS: illness, woe, torment, anguish
ANTONYMS: blessing, boon, joy

2. akin
(ə kin′)

(*adj.*) related by blood; having similar qualities or character

Our neighbors seem to have ideas _____ to ours about landscaping.

SYNONYMS: kindred, like, comparable
ANTONYMS: unrelated, dissimilar

3. cosmopolitan
(käz mə päl′ ə tən)

(*adj.*) found in most parts of the world; having many fields of interest; of worldwide scope; sophisticated

It does not surprise us that our cousin, a magazine editor and a big-city dweller, has a _____ outlook.

SYNONYMS: global, international, polished
ANTONYMS: narrow, unsophisticated, provincial

4. elongate
(i lôŋ′ gāt)

(*v.*) to grow in length, become longer; to extend the length of

The artist sought to _____ the trunk of the elephant in her caricature in order to amuse the children.

SYNONYMS: lengthen, stretch, protract
ANTONYMS: shorten, abbreviate, contract, curtail

5. gala
(gā′ lə)

(*n.*) a public entertainment marking a special event, a festive occasion; (*adj.*) festive, showy

The reporter had never seen such finery as was worn at the _____ .

The President and the First Lady attended a _____ performance at the Kennedy Center in Washington, D.C.

SYNONYMS: (*n.*) extravaganza, fête; (*adj.*) spectacular, grand

6. gaudy
(gô′ dē)

(*adj.*) flashy, showy; not in good taste

The singer's _____ outfit was totally inappropriate for a command performance before the queen.

SYNONYMS: garish, loud, vulgar
ANTONYMS: restrained, quiet, sober, sedate, tasteful

7. gratitude
('grat ə tüd)

(*n.*) appreciation, thankfulness

Be sure to express your _____ to your teacher for having written you a letter of recommendation.

SYNONYMS: thanks, gratefulness

8. heed
(hēd)

(*v.*) to pay careful attention to, notice; to be guided by; (*n.*) close attention or consideration

My parents are always telling me to _____ their advice.

Pay no _____ to old superstitions.

SYNONYMS: (*v.*) listen to, attend
ANTONYMS: (*v.*) ignore, disregard

9. hoax
(hōks)

(*n.*) an act intended to trick or deceive, a fraud; (*v.*) to trick, deceive

Their plan was to _____ people into believing that they had found a masterpiece.

SYNONYMS: (*n.*) deception, ruse, fake; (*v.*) dupe

10. impartial
(im pär' shəl)

(*adj.*) just, unbiased, fair, not taking sides

The defense attorney knew it would be difficult to find _____ jurors to serve on such a celebrated case.

SYNONYMS: disinterested, neutral, objective
ANTONYMS: one-sided, prejudiced, biased, partial

11. impostor
(im päs' tər)

(*n.*) a swindler, deceiver; one who uses a false name or character in order to cheat

After having posed as a doctor for five years, the man was finally exposed as an _____.

SYNONYMS: cheat, trickster, four-flusher, pretender

12. inflate
(in flāt')

(*v.*) to fill with air or gas; to swell or puff out; to make something appear larger than it is

On the evening before the big parade, we watched the workers _____ the huge balloons.

SYNONYMS: blow up, pump up, enlarge, exaggerate
ANTONYMS: deflate, flatten, diminish

13. meager
(mē' gər)

(*adj.*) poor, scant, unsatisfactory; thin, slight

My brother, a high school student, is always complaining that he cannot live on the _____ allowance my parents give him.

SYNONYMS: scanty, skimpy, sparse
ANTONYMS: ample, plentiful, abundant, lavish

14. meditate
(med′ ə tāt)

(*v.*) to think about deeply and quietly, reflect upon; to plan, intend

Many ancient philosophers would seek peaceful surroundings in which to _____ on the meaning of life.

SYNONYMS: ponder, contemplate, muse, ruminate

15. nutritious
(nü trish′ əs)

(*adj.*) nourishing, valuable and satisfying as food

My mother cooks _____ meals to ensure that we have a balanced diet.

SYNONYMS: healthful, wholesome

16. oppress
(ə pres′)

(*v.*) to govern or rule cruelly or unjustly; to weigh heavily upon

Too many dictators have used their absolute power to _____ the people they govern.

SYNONYMS: mistreat, persecute, grind underfoot
ANTONYMS: pamper, coddle, free, liberate

17. pedestrian
(pə des′ trē ən)

(*n.*) one who goes on foot; (*adj.*) relating to walking; on foot; ordinary, dull, unimaginative

The driver slammed on the brakes and swerved so as not to hit the _____.

Critics denounced his _____ literary style, but his book sales were high.

SYNONYMS: (*adj.*) commonplace, prosaic
ANTONYMS: (*n.*) driver, rider; (*adj.*) original, novel

18. transmit
(tranz mit′)

(*v.*) to send on, pass along, send out

In the Old West local sheriffs would often _____ messages by telegraph to the marshal of the territory.

SYNONYMS: pass on, convey, relay, deliver

19. vanquish
(vaŋ′ kwish)

(*v.*) to defeat in a battle or contest, overthrow; to overcome a feeling or condition

The general's goal was to _____ his country's enemies.

SYNONYMS: beat, conquer, subdue
ANTONYMS: succumb to, yield to

20. wan
(wän)

(*adj.*) unnaturally pale or sickly looking; lacking vitality; dim, faint; weak, ineffectual

The patient was so weak that all she could give the nurse was a _____ smile.

SYNONYMS: ashen, pasty, pallid, bloodless, gaunt
ANTONYMS: rosy, ruddy, blooming, radiant

Completing the Sentence

From the words for this unit, choose the one that best completes each of the following sentences. Write the word in the space provided.

1. Superstars and other celebrities are usually very much in evidence at _____ events such as opening night of a new Broadway show.

2. With a population made up of people from many different lands, New York City is one of the most _____ places in the world.

3. Most of us are so busy with everyday concerns that we can find little or no time to _____ on the larger issues of life.

4. Though the newspapers hailed the find as the "discovery of the century," it turned out to be nothing but an outrageous _____ .

5. The big clown's _____ costume was in sharp contrast to the simple white outfits worn by the trapeze artists.

6. Junk food may look attractive and taste great, but it is by no means as _____ as much plainer fare.

7. Modern medical science can do wonders for people suffering from various physical or emotional _____ .

8. Most cities have now passed laws to discourage _____ from crossing against the light or jaywalking.

9. If you had only _____ my warnings, all this trouble could easily have been avoided.

10. The family lawyer proved that the young man claiming to be the missing heir was no more than a(n) _____ .

11. An earthworm moves by first _____ and then contracting its wonderfully elastic body.

12. I don't expect you to throw yourself on your knees, but I wish you'd show a little _____ for the things I've done for you.

13. Unfortunately, the region cannot support a very large population because its natural resources are so _____ .

14. "Although these two words are not related etymologically," the professor observed, "they are _____ to each other in meaning."

15. Refusing to be _____ by unjust laws, the American colonists rose in revolt against the British government.

16. After beating off the enemy's initial assault, our brave troops delivered a series of crippling counterattacks that _____ the foe.

17. Since I am a very close friend of his, you cannot expect me to be totally _____ in judging your criticisms of him.

18. The distraught mother's _____ expression reflected her sense of anxiety over her lost child.

19. Have you ever tried to _____ a bicycle tire with one of those old-fashioned hand pumps?

20. Modern technology has provided us with the computer, a device for collecting, sorting, and _____ information quickly.

Synonyms

*Choose the word from this unit that is **the same** or **most nearly the same** in meaning as the **boldface** word or expression in the given phrase. Write the word on the line provided.*

1. will **convey** the message by e-mail   _____

2. had an **exaggerated** sense of her importance   _____

3. attended a **dull** series of lectures   _____

4. will **subdue** all foes of the realm   _____

5. ate a **wholesome** meal before the game   _____

6. was taken in by the **ruse**   _____

7. had light hair and a **pallid** complexion   _____

8. must **listen to** the captain's command   _____

9. would **muse** on the meaning of the universe   _____

10. will comfort her in her time of **anguish**   _____

11. showed our **appreciation** for their support   _____

12. had a truly **global** point of view   _____

13. was taken in by the **pretender**   _____

14. will **lengthen** the program by adding commercials   _____

15. a **festive** celebration to honor the winners   _____

Antonyms

*Choose the word from this unit that is **most nearly opposite** in meaning to the **boldface** word or expression in the given phrase. Write the word on the line provided.*

16. was **dissimilar** to the views she held   _____

17. sought to **liberate** his subjects   _____

18. was surprised by the **tasteful** furnishings in his home   _____

19. cooked with a **lavish** amount of spices   _____

20. would be a truly **biased** witness   _____

Choosing the Right Word

*Circle the **boldface** word that more satisfactorily completes each of the following sentences.*

1. Education and compassion are the only weapons by which we will (**heed, vanquish**) prejudice and superstition once and for all.

2. Is there any country in the world in which the terrible (**affliction, impostor**) of poverty has been entirely overcome?

3. When she came out on the stage, she was greeted by a (**meager, gaudy**) round of applause; before she left, she had the audience cheering.

4. Each scholarship candidate was identified by a number so that the people doing the grading would be absolutely (**impartial, pedestrian**).

5. We are so accustomed to TV that we tend to forget what a marvel it is to (**oppress, transmit**) colored images from one place to another.

6. A viewing diet made up entirely of game shows may be entertaining, but it is not particularly (**meager, nutritious**), mentally speaking.

7. Try as he might, the sideshow barker couldn't convince me that the "real live mermaid" inside the tent wasn't just a clever (**hoax, gala**).

8. After a lifetime of travel in dozens of countries all over the world, she is highly (**cosmopolitan, akin**) in her tastes and ideas.

9. The man's pathetically (**wan, elongated**) personality is matched only by the hopelessly bland and lifeless statements that issue from his mouth.

10. Is it necessary for you to go into the woods to (**meditate, inflate**) every time you have to make a routine decision?

11. Such extravaganzas as the "Night of 100 Stars" are usually designed to be (**gala, wan**) charity benefits for worthy causes.

12. The speaker had important things to say, but his way of expressing himself was so unimaginative and (**nutritious, pedestrian**) that he lost our interest.

13. By continuing to praise his extremely modest accomplishments, you are helping to (**inflate, transmit**) his already oversized ego.

14. We won the game because we kept our heads and paid no (**gratitude, heed**) to the insulting remarks made by our opponents.

15. Have you ever noticed that as the sun sinks lower in the sky, shadows become (**elongated, cosmopolitan**)?

16. I'd describe nostalgia as a feeling more (**meager, akin**) to yearning than to grief.

17. My mind and body were so (**oppressed, heeded**) by the stifling heat that afternoon that I couldn't do anything at all.

18. He claimed to be a famous multimillionaire, but when he tried to borrow bus fare, we realized he was a(n) (**pedestrian, impostor**).

19. Mere words cannot express our (**affliction, gratitude**) for your splendid services to our school.

20. Shakespeare's advice about dressing—"rich, not (**gaudy, akin**)"—still holds true in today's sophisticated world.

Vocabulary in Context

*Read the following passage, in which some of the words you have studied in this unit appear in **boldface** type. Then complete each statement given below the passage by circling the letter of the item that is **the same** or **almost the same** in meaning as the highlighted word.*

"Chess on Ice"

(Line)

You step onto the **elongated** "sheet" of ice, which is twice the size of a bowling alley, push off from a "hack," then "slide" your "stone" with a "broom" and "lay it up just past the hog line." Huh? What kind of game are you playing? Is it shuffleboard on ice? No, like more than one million people worldwide, you are curling.

(5) A subtle game, curling probably had its beginnings on a frozen lake (*loch*) somewhere in Scotland more than 400 years ago. By the 1700s curling had become Scotland's national pastime, and many curling clubs were established in that country, with numerous rules for curlers to **heed**. These rules included no wagering, swearing, or political discussions

(10) while curling, in addition to detailed instructions for sweeping the 42-pound granite stone which, today, looks like a tea kettle, across the "keen" ice. During the French and Indian War, Scottish soldiers

(15) brought curling to North America.

Today, particularly in the icy Midwest, curling clubs have sprung up, as has enthusiasm for the sport. Just ask residents of Mapleton, "the curling capital of southern

(20) Minnesota." They'll tell you how they drive for hours, in bad weather, to attend curling tournaments, called "bonspiels." In Canada, curling is nearly **akin** to ice hockey in its number of supporters.

American women's curling team at Nagano

(25) Clearly, curling has come a long way from its **meager** beginnings. In fact, in 1998 it officially became an Olympic sport. That year, in Nagano, Japan, the Canadian women's curling team **vanquished** Denmark to take the gold medal. Curling's popularity continues to grow in the United States. In fact, our nation's largest curling club, in St. Paul, Minnesota, now boasts 700

(30) members. In an age of raucous sports, with celebrity athletes and **inflated** salaries, curling remains a game of manners, a kind of chess on ice.

---

1. The meaning of **elongated** (line 1) is
a. slippery   c. shortened
b. frozen   d. extended

2. Heed (line 8) is best defined as
a. be guided by   c. ignore
b. memorize   d. create

3. Akin (line 23) most nearly means
a. unrelated   c. similar
b. plentiful   d. dissimilar

4. Meager (line 26) is best defined as
a. slight   c. ample
b. lavish   d. ancient

5. Vanquished (line 27) most nearly means
a. succumbed to   c. tormented
b. diminished   d. defeated

6. The meaning of **inflated** (line 30) is
a. flattened   c. enlarged
b. typical   d. modest

Definitions

Note carefully the spelling, pronunciation, part(s) of speech, and definition(s) of each of the following words. Then write the word in the blank space(s) in the illustrative sentence(s) following. Finally, study the lists of synonyms and antonyms given at the end of each entry.

1. authoritative
(ə thär′ ə tā tiv)

(*adj.*) official, coming from a source that calls for obedience or belief; dictatorial

A dictionary is an _____ source for the spelling, pronunciation, and definition of words in a language.

SYNONYMS: reliable, authoritarian
ANTONYMS: unofficial, unreliable

2. bankrupt
(baŋk′ rəpt)

(*adj.*) in a state of financial ruin; (*v.*) to ruin financially; (*n.*) one who has been ruined financially

The _____ company was closing its doors forever.

Another bad sales year will _____ the failing firm.

A _____ will have trouble getting credit.

SYNONYMS: (*adj.*) flat broke, insolvent
ANTONYMS: (*adj.*) financially sound, solvent

3. clamor
(klam′ ər)

(*n.*) a public outcry; any loud and continued noise; (*v.*) to call for by loud, continued outcries

The coal miners began to _____ for better working conditions in the mine.

The _____ of the trumpets was piercing.

SYNONYMS: (*n.*) uproar, din, racket; (*v.*) cry out for

4. coincide
(kō in sīd′)

(*v.*) to be in full agreement; to be the same in nature, character, or function; to happen at the same time

Our political beliefs would _____ with theirs on the issues of term limits and tax reform.

SYNONYMS: agree, concur, match

5. cynical
(sin′ ə kəl)

(*adj.*) inclined to believe the worst of people; bitterly mocking or sneering

The radio personality's _____ attitude made it difficult for the station manager to find sponsors for the talk show.

SYNONYMS: skeptical, sarcastic, contemptuous
ANTONYMS: hopeful, optimistic

6. despot
(des′ pət)

(*n.*) a ruler who oppresses his or her subjects, a tyrant

That film director is known for acting like a

_____ on the movie set.

SYNONYMS: dictator, autocrat, strongman

7. feud
(fyüd)

(*n.*) a bitter, long-term quarrel; (*v.*) to fight or quarrel with

A senseless _____ caused the division between the two clans.

What originally caused the clans to

_____ has long been forgotten.

SYNONYMS: (*n.*) dispute, vendetta
ANTONYMS: (*n.*) pact, agreement, harmony, concord

8. haggle
(hag′ əl)

(*v.*) to argue in a petty way, especially about a price

Let's not _____ over the price of admission until we finish writing the play!

SYNONYMS: bargain with, dicker with, wrangle

9. hardy
(här′ dē)

(*adj.*) able to bear up under difficult conditions or harsh treatment; brave and tough

The saguaro is a _____ variety of the cactus family.

SYNONYMS: rugged, sturdy, resolute, stalwart
ANTONYMS: frail, feeble, weak

10. harmonious
(här mō′ nē əs)

(*adj.*) able to get along together well; combining different elements that blend pleasingly; melodious

The two companies' negotiations were

_____ and resulted in a merger.

SYNONYMS: agreeable, compatible, tuneful
ANTONYMS: harsh, grating, discordant

11. hoard
(hôrd)

(*v.*) to store up, save; (*n.*) a hidden store or supply

Where did the miser keep his _____ of money?

SYNONYMS: (*v.*) amass, stockpile, cache
ANTONYMS: (*v.*) waste, throw away, squander

12. indisposed
(in dis pōzd′)

(*adj., part.*) slightly ill; disinclined to do something

My sister was _____ with a bad head cold.

SYNONYMS: (*adj.*) ailing, unwell, reluctant
ANTONYMS: (*adj.*) healthy, willing, eager

13. legacy
(leg′ ə sē)

(*n.*) an inheritance; something handed down from an ancestor or from the past

The _____ from her grandmother
made her a wealthy woman.
SYNONYMS: bequest, heritage

14. legitimate
(lə jit′ ə mət)

(*adj.*) lawful, rightful; reasonable, justifiable
There is a new committee that rules on whether complaints
are _____ .
SYNONYMS: legal, right, proper, genuine
ANTONYMS: unlawful, illegal, improper, unauthorized

15. mirth
(mərth)

(*n.*) merry fun, gaiety; laughter
The children were filled with _____ as
they exited the Fun House.
SYNONYMS: merriment, glee
ANTONYMS: gloom, sadness, sorrow

16. officiate
(ə fish′ ē āt)

(*v.*) to perform the duties of an office; to conduct a religious
ceremony; to referee
Will a judge _____ at the ceremony?
SYNONYMS: chair, preside, emcee, moderate

17. partial
(pär′ shəl)

(*adj.*) not complete; favoring one side over another; showing a
strong liking for someone or something
To say that she is _____ to sweets
would be an understatement.
SYNONYMS: incomplete, biased, prejudiced, fond of
ANTONYMS: complete, fair, just, unbiased

18. patronize
(pa′ trə nīz)

(*v.*) to give one's business to regularly as a customer; to
support, provide financial help; to treat someone as an inferior
while making a show of being kind or gracious
We like to _____ the family-owned
stores in the neighborhood.
SYNONYMS: do business with, deal with, trade with
ANTONYMS: boycott, refuse to deal with

19. rite
(rīt)

(*n.*) a ceremony; the customary form of a ceremony; any formal
custom or practice
A minister will perform the marriage

_____ .
SYNONYMS: observance, ritual, liturgy

20. sagacious
(sə gā′ shəs)

(*adj.*) shrewd; wise in a keen, practical way
History has shown that _____ leaders
exercise tolerance and fairness, along with good judgment.
SYNONYMS: smart, clever, astute
ANTONYMS: silly, foolish, ill-advised, dopey

Completing the Sentence

From the words for this unit, choose the one that best completes each of the following sentences. Write the word in the space provided.

1. Where can I get a(n) _____ estimate of how the population of the United States is likely to change in the years ahead?

2. The pioneers who settled the West were _____ people who could cope with difficulties and dangers of all kinds.

3. We must be prepared to defend the _____ of freedom that we have inherited from earlier generations of Americans.

4. Historians are still examining the deadly _____ that arose between the Hatfield and McCoy families more than 100 years ago.

5. Since your program for cleaning up the lakefront _____ with ours, why can't we work together?

6. Nothing will be accomplished unless the members of the committee work together in a(n) _____ fashion.

7. When you say that "everyone is out to take advantage of everyone else," I think you're being much too _____ .

8. The pagan religions of ancient times revolved around the performance of various _____ designed to ensure the fertility of the land.

9. Is it true that squirrels _____ nuts and other foods that they can use during the winter?

10. Although she had no previous experience as a treasurer, she showed herself to be highly _____ in the way she handled money.

11. I am making only a(n) _____ payment at the present time and will pay off the balance in installments.

12. I think your price for the tennis racket is too high, but since I'm in no mood to _____ with you, I'll take it.

13. The students were urged to _____ the local merchants who advertised in the school paper.

14. True, business has been poor, but we are covering our expenses and can assure you that there's no danger of our going _____ .

15. The fact that the baseball season is opening today is certainly not a(n) _____ excuse for being absent from school.

16. The referee who _____ at a hockey game needs the stamina to keep up with the players and the patience to put up with them.

17. I like a good laugh as much as anyone, but I realized that such a solemn ceremony was not the time for _____ .

18. My aunt called to say that she would not be able to visit us today because she was _____ with an asthma attack.

19. Our supervisor became extremely unpopular with us because he acted like a(n) _____ toward everyone in the department.

20. About five minutes before feeding time, all the babies in the nursery start to _____ for their bottles.

Synonyms

*Choose the word from this unit that is **the same** or **most nearly the same** in meaning as the **boldface** word or expression in the given phrase. Write the word on the line provided.*

1. broadcast **incomplete** details of the tragedy   _____

2. will undergo a **ritual** of initiation   _____

3. was behaving in a highly **dictatorial** manner   _____

4. would **argue** over a penny   _____

5. asked a substitute to **preside**   _____

6. was **ailing** with a headache   _____

7. proved to be the **legal** heir to the throne   _____

8. was filled with joy and **gaiety**   _____

9. would **trade with** the shops in the mall   _____

10. had taken sides in the bitter **quarrel**   _____

11. would **concur** with the judge's opinion of the case   _____

12. a **bequest** of untold value   _____

13. workers who will **cry out** for reform   _____

14. to rule with the iron hand of a **tyrant**   _____

15. made one of his usual **sarcastic** remarks   _____

Antonyms

*Choose the word from this unit that is **most nearly opposite** in meaning to the **boldface** word or expression in the given phrase. Write the word on the line provided.*

16. known to **squander** their wealth   _____

17. makes a **grating** sound   _____

18. was **foolish** in the choices she made   _____

19. would soon be a **solvent** corporation   _____

20. was a **weak** breed of cattle   _____

Choosing the Right Word

*Circle the **boldface** word that more satisfactorily completes each of the following sentences.*

1. One reason the coach is so popular is that he is firm and even tough with his players but never acts like a (**despot, bankrupt**).

2. A good sports official pays no attention to the (**clamor, mirth**) of the crowd when a decision goes against the home team.

3. Your healthy body is a (**legacy, rite**) you have received from your parents, and you should strive to protect it from harmful influences.

4. During the winter, there are always a few (**partial, hardy**) souls who take a dip in the icy waters off Atlantic Beach.

5. No matter how efficient the new chairperson may be, the meeting will not proceed (**authoritatively, harmoniously**) unless the members cooperate.

6. We will give careful attention to (**cynical, legitimate**) complaints, but we will not be influenced by silly faultfinding.

7. The jury was impressed by the fact that the testimony of two witnesses who were complete strangers (**coincided, clamored**) in every detail.

8. A party that cannot offer new ideas to deal with the pressing problems of the day must be considered politically (**legitimate, bankrupt**).

9. She may give the impression of being a simple old woman, but we have found her to be unusually (**sagacious, indisposed**) in judging people.

10. Why (**haggle, officiate**) over minor details when we are in agreement on the main issue?

11. The (**harmonious, authoritative**) tone in which she gave the order left no doubt in anyone's mind that she expected full obedience.

12. We cannot accept the idea that capital and labor must constantly (**feud, coincide**) with each other.

13. In the period ahead there may be shortages of some foodstuffs, but we will only make things worse if we resort to (**patronizing, hoarding**).

14. Isn't it (**cynical, feuding**) of you to ask other people to support a candidate in whom you yourself have no confidence?

15. I was (**hardy, indisposed**) to accept the halfhearted invitation that reached me only a day before the party.

16. If you're looking for a witty, charming personality to (**officiate, coincide**) at the awards dinner, need I say that I'm available?

17. Life cannot be all happiness; we must expect tears as well as (**legacies, mirth**).

18. I am annoyed by the (**haggling, patronizing**) way in which they keep reminding me "how a well-bred person behaves."

19. Each answer will be considered either right or wrong; no (**sagacious, partial**) credit will be given.

20. Learning to drive, graduating from high school, and entering college or the job market are all part of the (**rites, hoards**) of passage from a teenager to an adult.

Read the following passage, in which some of the words you have studied in this unit appear in **boldface** type. Then complete each statement given below the passage by circling the letter of the item that is **the same** or **almost the same** in meaning as the highlighted word.

As American as Hot Dogs

(Line)

Have you ever wondered what a picnic would be like without hot dogs? Or a baseball game? Although the origin of the hot dog is unclear (it may be related to the wiener from Vienna, Austria, or the *frankfurter wurst* from Frankfurt, Germany), this "fun food" is a **legitimate** American phenomenon. The **clamor** for hot dogs can be heard at sports stadiums and amusement parks from coast to coast. (5)

Like its origin, the name "hot dog" is also shrouded in mystery. The National Hot Dog and Sausage Council will suggest that "hot dog" may have been coined in 1906 by Harry Stevens, a concessionaire at the old Polo Grounds ballpark in New York City. According to the council, Stevens began calling the sandwich a hot dog rather than a "dachshund sausage" as it had been known at the time. (10)

Baseball fan enjoying a hot dog

Regardless of how the hot dog got its name, it soon became the favorite patriotic fare of Americans, who were soon **patronizing** hot-dog stands and gobbling up the "dogs" just as (15) fast as they could be placed in buns.

Of course, the best way to eat a hot dog depends on one's location. In fact, for years a **feud** has been raging between Chicagoans and (20) New Yorkers, as each group claims to know the best way to cook and "dress" a "frank." In the Windy City, people prefer their hot dogs boiled or steamed, mixed with pork, well seasoned, and piled high with relish, tomato, pickles, and peppers. In the Big Apple, people (25) are **partial to** all-beef hot dogs grilled and topped with mustard, onions, and sauerkraut.

No matter how Americans may "dress" their "dogs," it is clear that they love this food. In all, Americans eat 20 billion hot dogs a year, which proves just how much they "relish" this dish. (30)

---

1. The meaning of **legitimate** (line 4) is
a. rugged   c. legal
b. genuine   d. foolish

2. Clamor (line 4) is best defined as
a. function   c. glee
b. fondness   d. outcry

3. Patronizing (line 14) most nearly means
a. stockpiling   c. doing business with
b. bargaining with   d. boycotting

4. Feud (line 19) is best defined as
a. dispute   c. boycott
b. pact   d. din

5. Partial to (line 26) most nearly means
a. against   c. avoiding
b. unbiased   d. fond of

Visit us at www.sadlier-oxford.com
for interactive puzzles and games.

REVIEW UNITS 13–15

Analogies

In each of the following, circle the item that best completes the comparison.

1. harmonious is to **agree** as
a. feuding is to disagree
b. haggling is to agree
c. heeding is to disagree
d. clamoring is to agree

2. maternal is to **mother** as
a. rural is to daughter
b. paternal is to father
c. fraternal is to sister
d. global is to brother

3. legacy is to **will** as
a. definition is to dictionary
b. plot is to formula
c. character is to recipe
d. melody is to bill

4. conqueror is to **vanquish** as
a. giant is to foster
b. despot is to oppress
c. impostor is to countenance
d. celebrity is to pall

5. sagacious is to **wisdom** as
a. stodgy is to breadth
b. bankrupt is to wealth
c. hardy is to endurance
d. ignorant is to knowledge

6. reputable is to **patronize** as
a. honest is to grovel
b. shady is to boycott
c. fair is to haggle
d. untrustworthy is to countenance

7. wan is to **color** as
a. cosmopolitan is to sophistication
b. reputable is to honesty
c. bankrupt is to money
d. brave is to courage

8. infantry is to **pedestrians** as
a. artillery is to impostors
b. navy is to cynics
c. air force is to bankrupts
d. cavalry is to riders

9. rite is to **officiate** as
a. trial is to hold
b. rally is to participate
c. appointment is to keep
d. meeting is to chair

10. handicraft is to **skill** as
a. gala is to daring
b. rite is to caution
c. feud is to intelligence
d. hoax is to cunning

11. hilarious is to **mirth** as
a. pedestrian is to novelty
b. wan is to splendor
c. resentful is to gratitude
d. nutritious is to nourishment

12. sickness is to **indisposed** as
a. nervousness is to agitated
b. mirth is to afflicted
c. gratitude is to oppressed
d. boredom is to enchanted

13. hero is to **saga** as
a. judge is to romance
b. jester is to tragedy
c. detective is to mystery
d. villain is to comedy

14. meager is to **quantity** as
a. oppressed is to bulk
b. partial is to completeness
c. hardy is to stamina
d. gaudy is to brightness

15. stodgy is to **unfavorable** as
a. cosmopolitan is to favorable
b. akin is to unfavorable
c. gaudy is to favorable
d. legitimate is to unfavorable

16. miser is to **hoard** as
a. deposit is to grovel
b. impostor is to haggle
c. bankrupt is to possess
d. spendthrift is to waste

17. elongate is to **length** as
a. diminish is to width
b. coincide is to mass
c. inflate is to size
d. fluctuate is to height

18. impartial is to **prejudice** as
a. massive is to size
b. chronological is to time
c. cynical is to faith
d. authoritative is to obedience

Word Associations

In each of the following groups, circle the word that is best defined or suggested by the given phrase.

1. property left to children by parents
a. rite   b. legacy   c. gala   d. bankruptcy

2. a loud outcry from angry people
a. gratitude   b. clamor   c. affliction   d. despot

3. on a very large scale
a. chronological   b. massive   c. partial   d. sagacious

4. a festive occasion or celebration
a. affliction   b. mirth   c. hoax   d. gala

5. what a regular customer does
a. rob   b. serve   c. patronize   d. boycott

6. laughter and merriment
a. feud   b. magnitude   c. affliction   d. mirth

7. birds of a feather
a. indisposed   b. akin   c. legitimate   d. hilarious

8. a meal that supplies what the body needs
a. nutritious   b. stodgy   c. hilarious   d. harmonious

9. the look on someone's face, be it happy or sad
a. countenance   b. feud   c. impostor   d. clamor

10. typical of a mother
a. akin   b. cynical   c. maternal   d. reputable

11. carpentry, weaving, pottery, metalwork, etc.
a. pedestrians   b. handicrafts   c. impostors   d. galas

12. used to be a lot of fun, but now we're tired of it
a. heed   b. transmit   c. pall   d. foster

13. what a referee would do
a. coincide   b. officiate   c. meditate   d. hoard

14. greatness of size, like an earthquake or a conflict
a. agitation   b. magnitude   c. despot   d. handicraft

15. like a timetable
a. chronological   b. hilarious   c. gaudy   d. impartial

16. a plant that thrives even under unfavorable conditions
a. authoritative   b. massive   c. wan   d. hardy

17. what a tyrant would do to the people he ruled
a. countenance   b. patronize   c. oppress   d. revere

18. the story of the adventures of a Viking, such as Eric the Red
a. hoax   b. saga   c. rite   d. gala

19. extremely funny
a. chronological   b. impartial   c. hilarious   d. cynical

20. prices going up and down rapidly
a. fluctuate   b. ignite   c. heed   d. diminish

*Read the following passage, in which some of the words you have studied in Units 13–15 appear in **boldface** type. Then complete each statement given below the passage by circling the item that is **the same** or **almost the same** in meaning as the highlighted word.*

The World's Greatest Athlete

(Line)

Voted the greatest male athlete of the first half of the twentieth century by the Associated Press in 1950, Jim Thorpe received both **massive**
(5) praise and criticism in his lifetime. Thorpe was born in Indian Territory (now Oklahoma) in 1888. Sent to the Carlisle Indian School in Pennsylvania in 1904, Thorpe's
(10) astounding athletic ability was first discovered by Glenn S. "Pop" Warner, the legendary coach of the school. When the coach spotted Thorpe high-jumping six feet, he
(15) offered him a place on the track team, where he instantly became a star. He also became a football hero. In fact, in one of his best games, he helped the Carlisle football team
(20) **vanquish** its rival Harvard by booting four field goals. For his efforts on the football field, he was named to the All-American team.

Jim Thorpe left Carlisle in 1909 to
(25) play baseball for two seasons in the East Carolina minor league, a decision that would affect his whole life. His greatest achievement would come, however, in the 1912 Olympic
(30) Games in Stockholm, Sweden. There he would win two gold medals—in the pentathlon and the decathlon. "Sir, you are the greatest athlete in the world," said King Gustav V of
(35) Sweden, who was **officiating** at the Games. Yet as events would show, Thorpe's triumph would be only a **partial** victory.

Shortly after the Olympic games
(40) were held, a sportswriter who had seen Thorpe play baseball in the minor leagues exposed him as a professional athlete, making him ineligible for Olympic competition.
(45) The Amateur Athletic Union stripped Thorpe of his Olympic records and medals in 1913, casting a **pall** over his Olympic achievements. Thorpe joined the baseball New York
(50) Giants in that same year. The versatile Thorpe played professionally in both baseball and football. He was named the first commissioner of the new National Football League in 1920.
(55) For his achievements in football, he was inducted into the College and Pro Football Halls of Fame. In 1982, nearly 30 years after his death, the International Olympic Committee
(60) restored Thorpe's medals, thereby preserving his **legacy** as one of the world's greatest athletes.

---

1. The meaning of **massive** (line 4) is
  a. practical   c. flimsy
  b. reliable   d. great

2. Vanquish (line 20) most nearly means
  a. succumb to   c. conquer
  b. persecute   d. vandalize

3. Officiating (line 35) is best defined as
  a. voting   c. competing
  b. presiding   d. announcing

4. Partial (line 38) most nearly means
  a. elusive   c. incomplete
  b. unfair   d. instant

5. Pall (line 48) is best defined as
  a. shadow   c. fascination
  b. light   d. coffin

6. The meaning of **legacy** (line 61) is
  a. legal right   c. superstition
  b. observance   d. heritage

Choosing the Right Meaning

Read each sentence carefully. Then circle the item that best completes the statement below the sentence.

To put maximum pressure on German defenses, the Soviet Army planned a massive assault on the Eastern Front to coincide with the D-day landings in Normandy. (2)

1. In line 2 the phrase **coincide with** most nearly means

a. occur at the same time as   c. support
b. fully agree with   d. draw attention from

British comedies of the late nineteenth century are often peopled with cosmopolitan types who speak in witty, glittering epigrams. (2)

2. The best definition for the word **cosmopolitan** in line 1 is

a. global   b. stock   c. sophisticated   d. international

Warned that the least agitation might cause the mixture to explode, lab technicians handled the container with extreme caution. (2)

3. In line 1 the word **agitation** most nearly means

a. shaking   b. confusion   c. excitement   d. uneasiness

It is true that his is a hard-luck story; but when will he learn that it is difficult to feel sorry for someone who grovels in self-pity? (2)

4. The word **grovels** in line 2 is best defined as

a. crouches   b. cringes   c. cowers   d. wallows

Evidence presented at the trial showed that far from being a "crime of opportunity," the burglary had been meditated weeks before. (2)

5. The word **meditated** in line 2 is used to mean

a. reflected upon   c. discussed   b. rehearsed   d. planned

Antonyms

*In each of the following groups, circle the word or expression that is most nearly the **opposite** of the word in **boldface** type.*

1. reputable
a. well-known
b. wealthy
c. local
d. shady

2. partial
a. complete
b. scholarly
c. written
d. unfair

3. heed
a. obey
b. ignore
c. report
d. send

4. ignite
a. extinguish
b. borrow
c. offer
d. light

5. enchanted
a. pleased
b. ignored
c. surprised
d. disgusted

6. feud
a. quarrel
b. harmony
c. job
d. study

7. foster
a. hold back
b. encourage
c. pay for
d. expect

8. diminish
a. equal
b. increase
c. confirm
d. lower

9. affliction
a. experience
b. blessing
c. hardship
d. surprise

10. indisposed
a. ill
b. unqualified
c. interested
d. healthy

11. gratitude
a. joy
b. heed
c. thanklessness
d. fear

12. cynical
a. optimistic
b. bitter
c. stupid
d. intelligent

13. revered
a. invented
b. supported
c. honored
d. despised

14. oppressed
a. mistreated
b. reported
c. pampered
d. observed

15. elongate
a. shorten
b. clean up
c. clutter
d. decorate

16. sagacious
a. brief
b. silly
c. wise
d. witty

Word Families

A. On the line provided, write the word you have learned in Units 13–15 that is related to each of the following nouns.
EXAMPLE: gaudiness—**gaudy**

1. hilarity, hilariousness _____

2. reverence, reverend _____

3. impartiality _____

4. meditation, meditator, meditativeness _____

5. sagaciousness, sagacity _____

6. massiveness, mass _____

7. oppression, oppressor, oppressiveness _____

8. patronage, patron, patronization _____

9. reputability, reputation, repute _____

10. cynicism, cynic _____

11. nutrition, nutritionist, nutritiousness _____

12. fluctuation _____

13. officiation, office, official _____

14. ignition, igniter (ignitor) _____

15. transmission (transmittance), transmitter, transmittal _____

16. coincidence _____

B. On the line provided, write the word you have learned in Units 13–15 that is related to each of the following verbs.
EXAMPLE: agitate—**agitation**

17. authorize, author _____

18. harmonize _____

19. legitimize, legitimatize _____

20. afflict _____

Two-Word Completions

Circle the pair of words that best complete the meaning of each of the following passages.

1. "If we are to win this election," the senator said, "we must put aside our private
_____ and present a truly united front. Those who
_____ this advice will be helping our cause. Those who ignore it
can only hurt us."

a. afflictions . . . diminish   c. handicrafts . . . countenance
b. legacies . . . revere   d. feuds . . . heed

2. The tragic news of our friend's death in an automobile accident cast a(n)
_____ of gloom over our little gathering that evening and turned
our _____ to tears.

a. affliction . . . rite   c. saga . . . countenance
b. clamor . . . agitation   d. pall . . . mirth

3. The referees who _____ at hockey games are like judges
presiding over trials. For that reason, they and their assistants must be as
_____ as possible. If they show any favoritism in their calls, they'll
hear about it from the fans.

a. officiate . . . impartial   c. clamor . . . cosmopolitan
b. agitate . . . authoritative   d. haggle . . . partial

4. "I'm more than happy to shop at any establishment that is owned by a
_____ businessperson," Mom declared. "But I simply refuse to
_____ a store that is run by people who are out to cheat me."

a. despotic . . . bankrupt   c. cosmopolitan . . . foster
b. reputable . . . patronize   d. legitimate . . . transmit

5. "You certainly don't have to _____ your money like some miser
would," I observed, "but if you continue to throw it around quite so freely, you'll soon
be _____ ."

a. transmit . . . stodgy   c. revere . . . pedestrian
b. hoard . . . bankrupt   d. foster . . . indisposed

6. "I hate to _____ over minor details," the fussy little prince remarked
to the court magician. "But as long as you're pulling things out of a hat, couldn't you
come up with something nourishing? I'm hungry, and bouquets of fake flowers aren't
particularly _____ ."

a. haggle . . . nutritious   c. grovel . . . pedestrian
b. meditate . . . massive   d. clamor . . . gaudy

Building with Classical Roots

rupt—to break

This root appears in **bankrupt** (page 164). Literally, the word means "bank broken," that is, "unable to pay one's debts." It also means "one who is unable to pay his or her debts" or "to ruin financially and thus make unable to pay debts." Some other words based on the same root are listed below.

abrupt	disruptive	incorruptible	irruption
corrupt	erupt	interrupt	rupture

From the list of words above, choose the one that corresponds to each of the brief definitions below. Write the word in the blank space in the illustrative sentence below the definition.

1. to break in upon; to stop, halt

All day long she has to _____ her work in order to answer the telephone.

2. sudden, short, blunt; very steep

The car made a(n) _____ stop at the crosswalk to avoid hitting the pedestrian.

3. causing disorder or turmoil (*"to break apart"*)

His late arrival had a _____ influence on the meeting.

4. to burst forth (*"to break out"*)

Lava _____ from the exploding volcano as the population fled.

5. a breaking or bursting in; a violent invasion

The _____ of the Goths into Roman territory led to the collapse of the Roman Empire.

6. a breaking; to break

The engineers worked frantically to repair the _____ in the wall of the dam.

7. rotten, wicked, dishonest; to make evil; to bribe

The _____ dictatorship was replaced by a democratic republic.

8. not open to immoral behavior, honest; unbribable

He remained a(n) _____ public official despite the many attempts of the crime boss to bribe him.

From the list of words on page 177, choose the one that best completes each of the following sentences. Write the word in the blank space provided.

1. I was very much hurt when she made such a(n) _____ reply to my question.

2. Her unwillingness to listen to my side of the story caused a serious _____ in our friendship.

3. The principal warned that the parents of _____ students would be sent for.

4. When cynics remark that "everyone has a price," they are expressing their belief that no one is truly _____ .

5. The gamblers tried to _____ the athletes by offering them large sums of money to throw the game.

6. The police feared violence would _____ if the opposing groups of demonstrators were allowed to get near each other.

7. The bulkhead sprang a leak, causing a(n) _____ of seawater into the ship's hold.

8. I know I shouldn't have _____ him in the middle of a sentence, but that sentence seemed as though it would never end!

*Circle the **boldface** word that more satisfactorily completes each of the following sentences.*

1. The scandal revealed that the social service agency was riddled with (**incorruptible, corrupt**) bureaucrats.

2. Talking in the library can have a(n) (**abrupt, disruptive**) effect on those who are attempting to read or study.

3. The doctors would need to perform surgery in order to determine whether her appendix had (**interrupted, ruptured**).

4. As a(n) (**corrupt, incorruptible**) mayor of a large city, she will long be remembered for her honesty.

5. History has shown that riots sometimes (**abrupt, erupt**) during a long, hot summer in the city.

6. The valve broke off in her hand and a(n) (**irruption, rupture**) of steam filled the room.

7. The property consists of mostly flat land that makes an (**abrupt, incorruptible**) rise toward the back.

8. Her little sister has an annoying habit of trying to (**interrupt, erupt**) her when she is on the telephone.

Read the following sentences, paying special attention to the words and phrases underlined. From the words in the box below, find better choices for these underlined words and phrases. Then use these choices to rewrite the sentences.

WORD BANK

affliction	diminish	maternal	partial	rite
authoritative	elongate	nutritious	patronize	sagacious
chronological	inflate	officiate	reputable	stodgy
clamor	legacy	oppress	revere	vanquish

The Lure of Carbonated Beverages

1. Why did thirsty people around the world begin to <u>call out with loud outcries</u> for bubbly beverages, kicking off what has grown into a multibillion dollar industry?

_____

_____

2. The earliest known carbonated water came from natural springs. The Greeks and Romans <u>greatly honored</u> such waters, which they believed contained healing powers.

_____

_____

3. Americans first <u>overthrew</u> their thirst with bottled spring water containing "wild spirit gas" (or carbon monoxide) in 1689.

_____

_____

4. In 1767, Joseph Priestley's experiments led to the first drinkable glass of artificially carbonated water. Today's enormous variety of fizzy beverages is his enduring <u>thing handed down</u>.

_____

_____

5. The first carbonated waters were plain, like club soda. It was viewed as a highly <u>well thought of</u> practice to drink such waters to lose weight, ease digestion, and gain other health benefits.

_____

_____

6. By the late 19th century, customers began to <u>regularly give business to</u> "soda fountains" to get "sweetwaters"—fizzy water mixed with syrups and flavorings.

_____

_____

7. Carbonated soft drinks are not <u>valuable as food</u>, but they are in great demand, and show no sign of losing broad popularity.

_____

_____

Analogies

In each of the following, circle the item that best completes the comparison.

1. farce is to **hilarious** as
a. overture is to literate
b. anecdote is to interminable
c. paradox is to quaint
d. tragedy is to heartrending

2. impostor is to **counterfeit** as
a. notable is to prominent
b. fledgling is to proficient
c. braggart is to timid
d. parasite is to sullen

3. quibble is to **haggle** as
a. foster is to stifle
b. entreat is to implore
c. grovel is to flounder
d. entice is to oppress

4. vindictive is to **vengeance** as
a. unscathed is to recompense
b. bewildered is to clarification
c. hospitable is to seclusion
d. cynical is to gratitude

5. blindness is to **affliction** as
a. homicide is to ordeal
b. embezzlement is to catastrophe
c. pneumonia is to malady
d. perjury is to misdemeanor

6. diminish is to **inflate** as
a. seethe is to capsize
b. enchant is to pamper
c. detest is to revere
d. consolidate is to abound

7. scurry is to **feet** as
a. mull is to legs
b. snare is to eyes
c. meditate is to ears
d. bellow is to lungs

8. legacy is to **beneficiary** as
a. oration is to speaker
b. gift is to recipient
c. turmoil is to firebrand
d. flight is to fugitive

9. inflammable is to **ignite** as
a. graphic is to picture
b. unique is to prove
c. reluctant is to plan
d. insubordinate is to produce

10. lamb is to **docile** as
a. cow is to sagacious
b. horse is to fickle
c. mule is to wayward
d. sheep is to regal

Choosing the Right Meaning

Read each sentence carefully. Then circle the item that best completes the statement below the sentence.

My favorite painting in the exhibition was an Italian still life showing a pitcher, a fruit knife, and a bowl of mellow figs. (2)

1. The best definition for the word **mellow** in line 2 is
a. gentle   b. pleasant   c. ripe   d. rich

Can you name the friar who officiates at the secret wedding of the doomed lovers Romeo and Juliet? (2)

2. The phrase **officiates at** in line 1 is used to mean
a. referees   b. conducts   c. moderates   d. chairs

Although A. E. Glug tried many verse forms, he was partial to narrative poetry and indeed achieved his greatest success with the epic poem *The Clodyssey* (1906). (2)

3. The phrase **was partial to** in line 1 is used to mean

a. mastered

b. favored

c. was biased against

d. was trained in

Once exclusive to American cities such as New York and Chicago, skyscrapers have in recent years come to dominate many a European metropolis as well. (2)

4. In line 2 the word **dominate** most nearly means

a. control   b. eclipse   c. tower over   d. master

With the slogan "No taxation without representation!" American colonists protested the authoritative levies imposed by the British crown. (2)

5. In line 2 the word **authoritative** most nearly means

a. tyrannical   b.reliable   c. obedient   d. official

Two-Word Completions   *Circle the pair of words that best complete the meaning of each of the following sentences.*

1. As the police officers who had been called to the scene of the accident were _____ eyewitnesses to the incident, a large crowd of curious _____ began to collect nearby.

a. lubricating . . . buffoons

b. procuring . . . dupes

c. patronizing . . . pedestrians

d. interrogating . . . bystanders

2. I did everything I could to _____ them from pursuing a course of action that I firmly believed would end in disaster, but all my efforts were, unfortunately, _____ .

a. dissuade . . . futile

b. transmit . . . meager

c. mortify . . . spirited

d. swerve . . . disputatious

3. Though I admire the intrepid daredevils who _____ life and limb diving off towering cliffs into the sea, hundreds of feet below, I am much too _____ to try something like that myself.

a. hoard . . . hardy

b. hazard . . . timid

c. heed . . . stodgy

d. mar . . . lethargic

4. As I _____ idly through the curious book, my eye happened to light upon some interesting old photographs of haying and plowing and other scenes of life in _____ America at the end of the 19th century.

a. fluctuated . . . sodden

b. browsed . . . rural

c. tampered . . . gaudy

d. prescribed . . . radiant

5. During the 14th century, the bubonic _____, or "Black Death," suddenly swept across Europe, killing three quarters of the population and seriously _____, or even paralyzing, the social and economic life of the continent.

a. goad . . . dominating

b. luster . . . inflicting

c. plague . . . disrupting

d. hearth . . . renovating

Enriching Your Vocabulary

Read the passage below. Then complete the exercise at the bottom of the page.

The Language of Science

Scientific advances have not only contributed vast amounts of knowledge and data, but have also enriched our language with thousands of words. Many terms may originally have been coined to describe precise scientific concepts or phenomena. Over time and with repeated usage, science words can take on informal, nonscientific meanings that expand our ability to communicate.

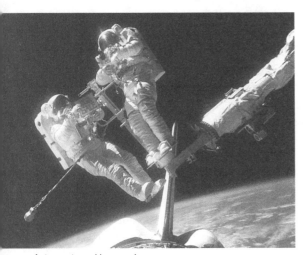

Astronauts making repairs

Modern astronomy forever changed in 1957, when *Sputnik,* the world's first earth-made satellite, was sent into orbit. This landmark achievement led to even young school children learning what it meant for a satellite to circle a larger planet. Soon people began to speak of satellite nations and satellite offices.

In biology, a *parasite* (Unit 10) is an organism that lives off another organism, taking its food from its host—usually at the host's expense. From its explicit scientific meaning, *parasite* has come to describe a person who lives off others without a fair return—a hanger-on, sponge, or deadbeat, to use popular slang. In physics, *radiant* (Unit 5) energy is sent out as rays of light or heat. But the bright, joyful smile of a blissful person can also be described as radiant, although no beams of light or heat are visible.

In Column A below are 6 more scientific words. With or without a dictionary, match each word with its meanings in Column B.

Column A

_____ **1.** hybrid

_____ **2.** magnetic

_____ **3.** galaxy

_____ **4.** eclipse

_____ **5.** inertia

_____ **6.** gravity

Column B

a. the tendency for an object at rest to remain at rest, or for a moving object to keep moving; resistance to change

b. a large independent system of stars and other heavenly bodies; a gathering of distinguished people

c. the natural force that tends to cause all objects to move toward the center of the earth; importance or seriousness

d. the partial or total blocking of the light of one heavenly body by another; a decline in importance or use

e. being able to attract iron; having the power to attract

f. the offspring of two distinct plants or animals of different varieties; anything of mixed origin or unlike parts

Selecting Word Meanings

*In each of the following groups, circle the word or expression that is **most nearly the same** in meaning as the word in **boldface** type in the given phrase.*

1. without any **incentive**
   a. money   b. right   c. inducement   d. selfishness

2. something that we **detest**
   a. know   b. hate   c. welcome   d. understand

3. **entreat** them to leave
   a. command   b. beg   c. require   d. expect

4. made a **fruitless** effort
   a. strenuous   b. futile   c. planned   d. successful

5. a **foretaste** of things to come
   a. return   b. result   c. anticipation   d. cause

6. received **innumerable** warnings
   a. countless   b. threatening c. official   d. detailed

7. made a **cynical** comment
   a. poetic   b. long-winded c. necessary   d. skeptical

8. **gruesome** details
   a. delicious   b. novel   c. horrifying   d. unexpected

9. made **lavish** preparations
   a. hasty   b. careful   c. extravagant   d. stingy

10. **tamper** with the evidence
    a. begin   b. interfere   c. agree   d. argue

11. carry on a **feud**
    a. machine   b. quarrel   c. movement   d. alliance

12. a rather **animated** discussion
    a. scholarly   b. dull   c. useless   d. lively

13. committed **homicide**
    a. embezzlement b. theft   c. murder   d. lying

14. left **ajar**
    a. alone   b. partly open c. untouched   d. sealed

15. an **impartial** decision
    a. unbiased   b. incomplete   c. unhurried   d. effective

16. an **anonymous** donor
    a. innocent   b. eager   c. unnamed   d. angry

17. was **available** only on Fridays
    a. obtainable b. necessary   c. needed   d. qualified

18. **bewilder** one's teammates
    a. help   b. confuse   c. teach   d. please

19. capsize the vessel
a. seize   b. overturn   c. purchase   d. repair

20. a **cosmopolitan** point of view
a. mechanical   b. sophisticated   c. false   d. important

21. the **downtrodden** workers
a. well-paid   b. happy   c. skillful   d. oppressed

22. a grueling **ordeal**
a. race   b. test   c. setback   d. interview

23. guilty of **perjury**
a. kidnapping   b. stealing   c. killing   d. lying

24. where fish **abound**
a. leap   b. produce young   c. are protected   d. are plentiful

25. foster a new policy
a. plan   b. object to   c. encourage   d. reexamine

Antonyms   *In each of the following groups, circle the **two** words or expressions that are **most nearly opposite** in meaning.*

26. a. swerve   b. veto   c. maul   d. ratify

27. a. reputable   b. domestic   c. shady   d. humdrum

28. a. heed   b. decrease   c. officiate   d. accelerate

29. a. hostile   b. hardy   c. hilarious   d. heartrending

30. a. vital   b. leisurely   c. grueling   d. miscellaneous

31. a. remnant   b. bystander   c. regime   d. participant

32. a. graphic   b. injured   c. unscathed   d. pending

33. a. boycott   b. patronize   c. hurtle   d. grovel

34. a. quaint   b. puny   c. gigantic   d. orthodox

35. a. inflammable   b. cheerful   c. substantial   d. despondent

36. a. indifference   b. melancholy   c. narrative   d. enthusiasm

37. a. persist   b. reinforce   c. seethe   d. undermine

38. a. insinuate   b. entice   c. renovate   d. dissuade

39. a. enchant   b. presume   c. trickle   d. pall

40. a. spotless   b. ultimate   c. disputatious   d. grimy

Supplying Words in Context

In each of the following sentences, write in the blank space the most appropriate word chosen from the given list.

Group A

stifle	botch	potential	nub
dominate	meager	fledgling	impostor
nomadic	mull	malignant	flagrant
uncertainty	downright	inflict	interrogate

41. When I was just a(n) _____ in my very first pro season, one of the veteran players took me under his wing.

42. Though the situation in that part of the world is calm now, it is a(n) _____ powder keg that may go off at any moment.

43. This mistake is so _____ that it cannot be overlooked, even though the manager's son was responsible for it.

44. Although I realize you have many interesting stories to tell, I do wish you wouldn't always _____ the conversation.

45. He decided to give up trying to become a professional writer when he realized that his talents were really very _____.

46. With a great effort, I managed to _____ my anger and replied as courteously as I could.

47. Inexperienced as we were, we knew we would _____ the preparation of the meal, so we decided to go out to eat.

48. Instead of giving me all those unimportant details, let's get right to the _____ of the matter.

49. I know I would have to _____ over the events of the evening before I could determine if I had acted inappropriately.

50. It was _____ rude of her to ignore my kind offer of help.

Group B

adjacent	interminable	recompense	cache
implore	dilapidated	malady	elongate
transmit	iota	morbid	pamper
utmost	snare	preview	casual

51. Luckily, the communications officer was able to _____ an SOS signal just before the ship's radio stopped working.

52. The wait outside the operating room seemed _____ to the parents of the injured child.

53. In a tearful voice, the guilty man's wife _____ the court to treat her husband leniently.

54. The smile of joy she gave me when she received the award was ample _____ for all the time and effort I had spent in helping her.

55. If you had a(n) _____ of consideration for us, you would turn down the volume on the television set.

56. Even though he lives in a house _____ to the school, he is often late for his first class.

57. The trick was to _____ him in his own web of lies and deceit.

58. Religious intolerance is a social _____ that simply cannot be countenanced in a democracy such as ours.

59. The deserted cabin was so _____ that it looked as though any strong breeze would cause it to collapse.

60. When the younger players went in for the last few minutes of the game, we had a(n) _____ of what the team would be like next year.

Words Connected with Moods

*The words in Column A may be applied to various moods that are typical of many people. In the space before each word, write the **letter** of the item in Column B that identifies it.*

Column A	Column B
_____ **61.** docile	a. sad, depressed
_____ **62.** fickle	b. filled with resentment or anger over something
_____ **63.** wayward	c. changing rapidly, especially in one's affections
_____ **64.** vigilant	d. not caring one way or the other
_____ **65.** peevish	e. extremely cruel
_____ **66.** spirited	f. irritable, cross, easily annoyed
_____ **67.** indignant	g. full of life and vigor
_____ **68.** melancholy	h. willing to forgive almost anything
_____ **69.** lethargic	i. on the lookout, alert
_____ **70.** indifferent	j. easily controlled and taught
	k. disobedient, insisting on having one's own way
	l. unnaturally sleepy or slow moving

Words That Describe Behavior

Some words that describe the way people behave are listed below. Write the appropriate word on the line next to each of the following descriptions.

dupe	parasite	insubordinate	lax
firebrand	prudent	poised	dynamic
fallible	inimitable	tactful	scrimp
regal	reluctant	proficient	vindictive

71. She shows great drive, originality, and ability to get things done. _____

72. He uses care and good judgment in handling his affairs. _____

73. She is sensitive to the feelings of other people and careful not to hurt them. _____

74. He dances in a way that no one else can equal or even try to match. _____

75. His speech arouses the fury of his audiences. _____

76. She is so trusting that she is easily deceived and used by others. _____

77. He expects to live off other people. _____

78. She is motivated by revenge. _____

79. Hours of practice have made her a skillful pianist. _____

80. Like everyone else, she makes mistakes from time to time. _____

Word Associations

*In each of the following, circle the word or expression that best completes the meaning of the sentence or answers the question, with particular reference to the meaning of the word in **boldface** type.*

81. Which of the following would be most likely to create **havoc**?
a. a summer breeze
b. a game of volleyball
c. a school assembly
d. a tornado

82. An example of a **grim** event is
a. a graduation
b. a fatal accident
c. a family reunion
d. a holiday

83. A person who **quibbles** during an argument is
a. winning the argument
b. splitting hairs
c. being courteous
d. getting angry

84. Memories that have been **eroded**
a. are still bright and clear
b. have been worn away by time
c. are painful
d. are set down in writing

85. You would probably find it **mortifying** to
a. snack between meals
b. earn enough money to buy your own clothes
c. win a dance contest
d. do poorly on this Final Mastery Test

86. If there is **mutual** admiration between two people,
a. the admiration is not genuine
b. they admire each other
c. the admiration is one-sided
d. the admiration won't last

87. Which of the following suggests a person who is **frustrated**?
a. "It's a great idea!"
b. "Foiled again!"
c. "I won!"
d. "I'll do it!"

88. A customer gives a storekeeper a $1 bill that is seen to be **counterfeit**. The storekeeper will probably
a. accept it with thanks
b. offer $2 for it
c. refuse to accept it
d. donate the bill to charity

89. Which of the following is likely to be **sodden**?
a. a desert
b. toast
c. a rain-soaked field
d. a dust storm

90. A **stalemate** lacks
a. a solution
b. a sense of humor
c. freshness
d. opponents

91. You would be most likely to **brood** over
a. an event of no importance
b. tomorrow's lunch
c. an exciting sports victory
d. failing an important examination

92. Which of the following would *not* be likely to **canvass** an area?
a. an interviewer
b. a homebody
c. a pollster
d. a door-to-door salesperson

93. A **braggart** would be most likely to
a. grin and bear it
b. stick to his or her guns
c. fly off the handle
d. toot his or her own horn

94. Which of the following would *not* be found in **rural** areas?
a. skyscrapers
b. water
c. cows
d. people

95. Which nickname would most likely be given to a **stodgy** person?
a. "Trickster"
b. "Doc"
c. "Stuffed Shirt"
d. "Egghead"

96. You would be most likely to **browse**
a. in a library
b. on the tennis court
c. when you are asleep
d. during a test

97. A person facing the **hazards** of life is
    a. making money
    b. taking risks
    c. winning victories
    d. playing golf

98. Which of the following is *not* **transparent**?
    a. a pane of glass
    b. a feeble excuse
    c. air
    d. a wooden door

99. A person who receives a **legacy** has gained something as a result of
    a. inheriting it
    b. hard work
    c. dishonesty
    d. gambling

100. Which of the following cannot be **quenched**?
    a. fire
    b. ambition
    c. a flood
    d. thirst

INDEX

The following tabulation lists all the basic words taught in the various units of this book, as well as those introduced in the *Vocabulary of Vocabulary, Working with Analogies, Building with Classical Roots,* and *Enriching Your Vocabulary* sections. Words taught in the units are printed in **boldface** type. The number following each entry indicates the page on which the word is first introduced. Exercise and review materials in which the word also appears are not cited.

abnormal, 91
abound, 131
abrupt, 177
accelerate, 98
adequate, 124
adjacent, 21
affliction, 157
agitation, 150
ajar, 124
akin, 157
alight, 21
allegory, 83
alliance, 51
amiss, 84
analogy, 13
anecdote, 58
animated, 35
anonymous, 65
antonym, 8
authoritative, 164
autobiography, 111
autograph, 111
available, 28

bankrupt, 164
barren, 21
bellow, 117
beneficiary, 117
bewilder, 51
biography, 111
blurt, 150
botch, 117
braggart, 131
brawl, 84
brood, 35
browse, 65
buffoon, 51
bystander, 98

cache, 131
canvass, 98
capsize, 91
casual, 98
catastrophe, 91
cater, 28
cavalcade, 149
chorus, 116
chronological, 150
circumscribe, 78
clamor, 164
clarification, 131

clutter, 117
coincide, 164
connotation, 7
connote, 144
consolidate, 58
context clue, 9
contrast clue, 9
controversial, 51
corsair, 149
corrupt, 177
cosmopolitan, 157
countenance, 150
counterfeit, 58
culminate, 35
customary, 28
cynical, 164

decrease, 91
denotation, 7
denote, 144
dependent, 48
despondent, 131
despot, 165
detest, 84
dialogue, 124
dilapidated, 117
diminish, 150
dishearten, 51
dismantle, 117
dispensary, 48
dispense, 48
disputatious, 91
disrupt, 21
disruptive, 177
dissuade, 28
docile, 58
domestic, 84
dominate, 58
downright, 35
downtrodden, 98
drone, 35
dupe, 65
dynamic, 65
dynasty, 21

eclipse, 182
eject, 91
elongate, 157
embezzle, 131
emblem, 124
enchant, 150

entice, 98
entreat, 58
entrepreneur, 28
eradicate, 65
erode, 99
erupt, 177
espionage, 149
expendable, 48
expenditure, 48
extravaganza, 149

fable, 83
fallible, 59
farce, 118
feud, 165
fickle, 59
figurative usage, 7
firebrand, 28
flagrant, 84
flaw, 84
fledgling, 85
flounder, 99
flourish, 92
fluctuate, 151
fluster, 85
foremost, 85
foretaste, 21
foster, 151
fruitless, 51
frustrate, 65
fugitive, 59
futile, 118

gala, 157
galaxy, 182
gaudy, 157
geography, 111
germinate, 22
gigantic, 124
goad, 35
graphic, 99
graphite, 111
graphology, 111
gratitude, 158
gravity, 182
grim, 66
grimy, 59
grovel, 151
grueling, 118
gruesome, 99

haggle, 165
handicraft, 151
hardy, 165
harmonious, 165
havoc, 124
hazard, 29
hearth, 124
heartrending, 131
heed, 158
hilarious, 151
hoard, 165
hoax, 158
homicide, 29
hospitable, 118
hostile, 52
humdrum, 22
hurtle, 22
hybrid, 182
hygiene, 116

ignite, 151
impartial, 158
implore, 125
impostor, 158
incentive, 92
incorruptible, 177
indescribable, 78
indifference, 29
indignant, 29
indispensable, 29
indisposed, 165
indulge, 36
inertia, 182
infamous, 125
inference clue, 10
inferno, 149
inflammable, 52
inflate, 158
inflict, 52
ingredient, 36
inimitable, 66
innumerable, 125
inscription, 78
insinuate, 22
insubordinate, 92
interminable, 22
interrogate, 22
interrupt, 177
iota, 59
irruption, 177

lair, 118
lavish, 118
lax, 125
legacy, 165
legend, 83
legible, 92
legitimate, 166
leisurely, 132
lethargic, 132
literal usage, 7
literate, 36
loom, 36
lubricate, 29
luster, 36

maestro, 149
magnetic, 182
magnitude, 151
makeshift, 66
malady, 132
malignant, 52
manifesto, 149
mar, 125
marginal, 66
massive, 152
maternal, 152
maul, 59
meager, 158
meditate, 159
melancholy, 99
mellow, 132
memoir, 83
mirth, 166
miscellaneous, 36
misdemeanor, 125
momentum, 85
monopoly, 116
morbid, 118
mortify, 52
mosaic, 116
mull, 125
mutual, 29

narrative, 126
nomadic, 132
notable, 85
notary, 144
notation, 144
noteworthy, 144
notify, 144
notion, 144
notoriety, 144
notorious, 119
nub, 92
nurture, 85
nutritious, 159

officiate, 166
onslaught, 92
oppress, 159
oration, 36

ordain, 92
ordeal, 99
orthodox, 52
outstrip, 93
overture, 126

pact, 126
pall, 152
pamper, 119
parable, 83
paradox, 85
parasite, 119
parch, 99
partial, 166
patronize, 166
pedestrian, 159
peevish, 37
pelt, 30
pending, 66
pension, 48
perjury, 86
perpendicular, 48
persist, 100
pervade, 93
pictograph, 111
piecemeal, 132
plague, 30
poised, 30
postscript, 78
potential, 59
prefix, 11
prescribe, 66
presume, 86
preview, 66
prior, 86
procure, 52
proficient, 86
prominent, 67
proscribe, 78
prudent, 93
puny, 100

quaint, 67
quench, 93
quest, 133
quibble, 100

radiant, 60
random, 133
rant, 133
ratify, 100
recompense, 22
regal, 100
regime, 30
reinforce, 133
reluctant, 67
remnant, 93
renovate, 23
reputable, 152
restatement clue, 10
résumé, 23

retard, 30
revere, 152
rite, 166
root, 12
rupture, 177
rural, 60

saga, 152
sagacious, 166
salvo, 86
scrimp, 67
script, 78
scurry, 52
seclusion, 133
seethe, 37
seismograph, 111
shirk, 119
simultaneous, 93
singe, 37
snare, 67
sodden, 53
sphere, 116
spirited, 53
stalemate, 126
status, 133
stifle, 100
stodgy, 152
strategy, 116
subscribe, 78
substantial, 60
suffix, 11
sullen, 23
surplus, 119
suspense, 48
svelte, 149
swerve, 93
synonym, 8

tactful, 60
tall tale, 83
tamper, 60
timidity, 119
titanic, 116
tragedy, 116
transcribe, 78
transmit, 159
transparent, 30
trickle, 23
trivial, 23
truce, 23
turmoil, 133
tyrant, 116

ultimate, 60
uncertainty, 60
unique, 37
unscathed, 30
upright, 37
utmost, 67

vanquish, 159

vengeance, 67
verify, 37
veto, 119
vicious, 23
vigilant, 86
vignette, 83
vindictive, 126
virtual, 53
vista, 149
vital, 100
void, 53

wan, 159
wayward, 53
wilt, 126
wince, 53
wrath, 86

yarn, 83
yearn, 37